Masters of Modern Manners

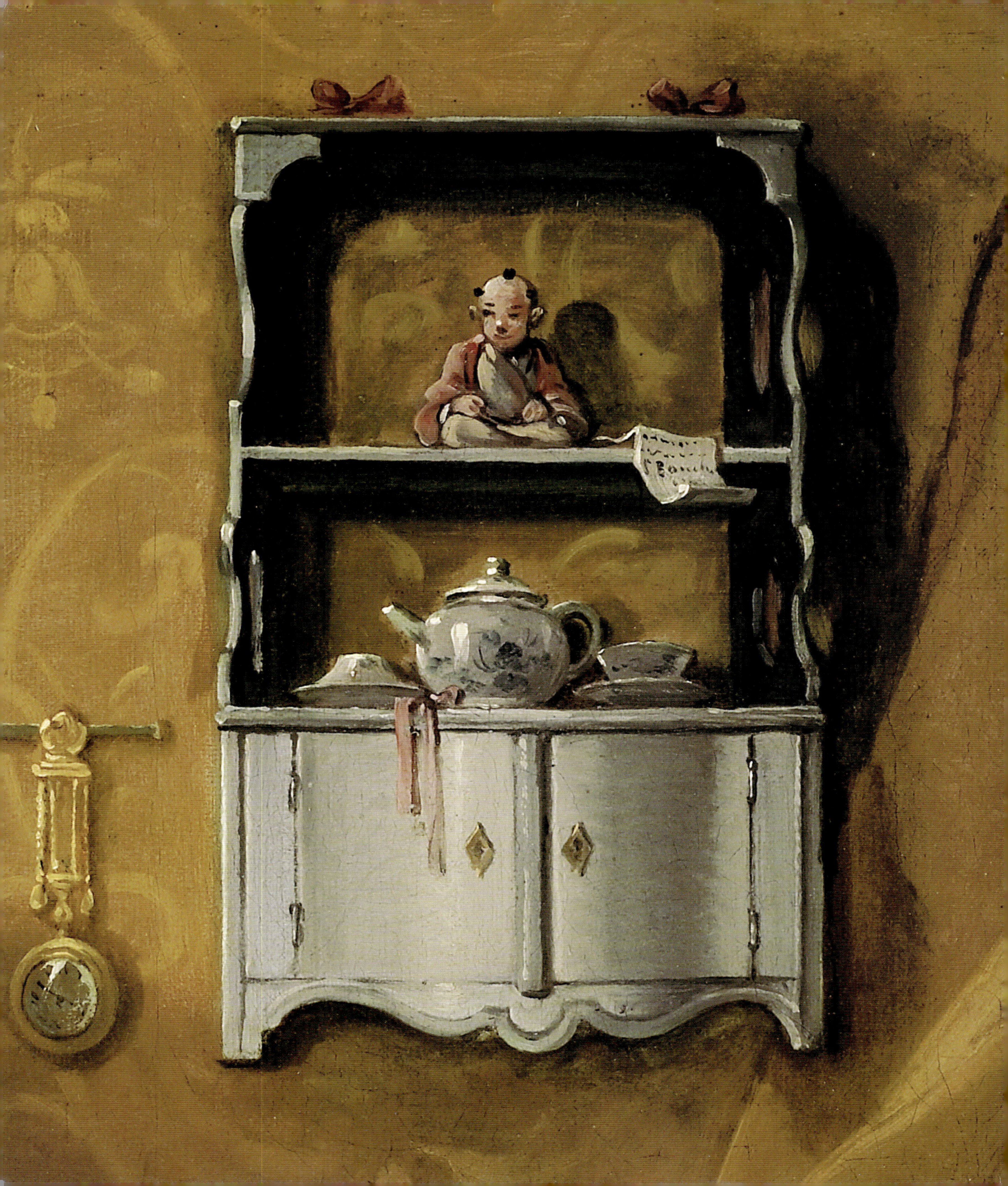

BOUCHER & CHARDIN
Masters of Modern Manners

EDITED BY ANNE DULAU

With contributions by
CHRISTOPH MARTIN VOGTHERR
ANN EATWELL

The Hunterian, University of Glasgow

in association with

Paul Holberton publishing, London

First published 2008 to accompany the exhibition *Boucher & Chardin:
Masters of Modern Manners* at the Wallace Collection, London,
12 June – 7 September 2008 and the Hunterian Art Gallery,
University of Glasgow, 24 September – 13 December 2008

ISBN 978 1 903470 75 6 (paperback)

British Library Cataloguing in Publication Data
A catalogue record for this book is available from the British Library

Produced by Paul Holberton publishing,
89 Borough High Street, London SE1 1NL
www.paul-holberton.net

Designed by Roger Davies
rogerdaviesdesign@btinternet.com

Printed by e·GRAPHIC in Verona, Italy

Front cover: Jean Siméon Chardin, *Lady taking Tea*, 1735, cat. 1
and François Boucher, *Woman on a Daybed*, 1743, cat. 2
Back cover: Nicolas Lancret, *The Four Times of the Day: Morning*, 1739, cat. 6

Frontispiece: Detail of François Boucher, *Woman on a Daybed*, 1743
Page 8: Detail of Jean Siméon Chardin, *Lady taking Tea*, 1735

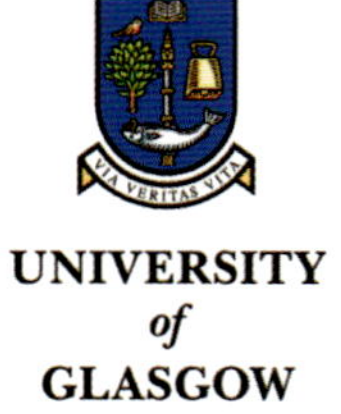

UNIVERSITY
of
GLASGOW

CONTENTS

<h1>ACKNOWLEDGEMENTS</h1>

LENDERS

This exhibition would not have been possible without the support of the following organizations and individuals:

The Frick Collection, New York

Nationalmuseum, Stockholm

Museo Thyssen-Bornemisza, Madrid

National Gallery, London

Day & Faber, London

National Gallery of Scotland, Edinburgh

National Gallery of Ireland, Dublin

Burrell Collection, Glasgow Museums

British Museum, London

Glasgow University, Department of Special Collections

Rothschild Family Trust: Waddesdon Manor

The Wellcome Library, London

Private collectors who wish to remain anonymous

RESEARCH

Many have helped research along the way and we are extremely grateful to the following for their assistance: Lynda McLeod (Christie's Archives, Librarian); David Beasley (London Goldsmiths' Company, Librarian); Errol Manners; Alastair Laing; Aileen Ribeiro; Matthew Storey (National Gallery, Librarian); Pippa Shirley (Waddesdon Manor, Head of Collections); Professor Nick Pearce and Alison Yarrington (University of Glasgow, History of Art Department); Charlotte Hartigan; Alex Werner; Nick Humphrey, Christopher Maxwell, Sarah Medlam, Helen Persson, Roxanne Peters, Carolyn Sargentson and Hilary Young (Victoria and Albert Museum); staff at the Wallace Collection, particularly Stephen Duffy, Rebecca Wallis, Andrea Gilbert, Nell Carrington and Eleanor Tollfree; and colleagues at the Hunterian Museum and Art Gallery, especially Mungo Campbell, Peter Black, Sally-Anne Coupar and John Faithfull.

Generous help in reading drafts was received from Peter Black, Mungo Campbell, Martin Hopkinson, Alastair Laing, Errol Manners, Pamela Robertson, Pippa Shirley, Jeremy Warren and Hilary Young. Thank you. And particular thanks to Diana Simpson, who edited Anne Dulau's contributions.

SUPPORT

We are extremely grateful to the Paul Mellon Centre for Studies in British Art for their generous support. Anne Dulau received a grant towards the cost of research on Boucher and Chardin paintings in eighteenth-century Britain, carried out in London and elsewhere. The support of Brian Allen, Mary Peskett Smith and everyone at the Mellon Centre in Bedford Square is very much appreciated. Particular thanks to Stella Mason for supporting the grant application.

This publication was made possible by a grant from the Gordon Fraser Charitable Trust.

It is an enormous pleasure for our museums to host this splendid exhibition, which marks the first collaboration between our institutions. Both the Hunterian Museum and Art Gallery and the Wallace Collection have their origins in the enthusiasm for collecting which is such a prominent feature of eighteenth-century culture. That our happy collaboration on this venture should bring Dr William Hunter's great Chardins to a museum housing the most important collection of eighteenth-century French art in Britain is entirely appropriate. Indeed the Hunterian's founder counted among his friends and patients Isabella, Countess of Hertford, grandmother of that 3rd Marquess of Hertford whose collecting instincts played such a significant role in assembling the Wallace Collection's extraordinary array of French art.

We should also acknowledge that the initial idea for the pairing of Boucher and Chardin emerged from the wonderful collaboration between Glasgow University and the Frick Collection, New York, occasioned by the commemoration of James McNeill Whistler's centenary in 2003.

The Hunterian Museum and Art Gallery, University of Glasgow, and the Wallace Collection are delighted that this small but exquisite exhibition, centred on an outstanding group of pictures by Boucher and Chardin, has brought us together in this, our first collaboration. We would like to acknowledge the generosity of those who have contributed financial support to this project, thank warmly those on our staffs who have made it possible, and also give particular thanks to the lenders and the contributors to the catalogue.

Sir Muir Russell
PRINCIPAL, UNIVERSITY OF GLASGOW

Dr Rosalind Savill
DIRECTOR, THE WALLACE COLLECTION

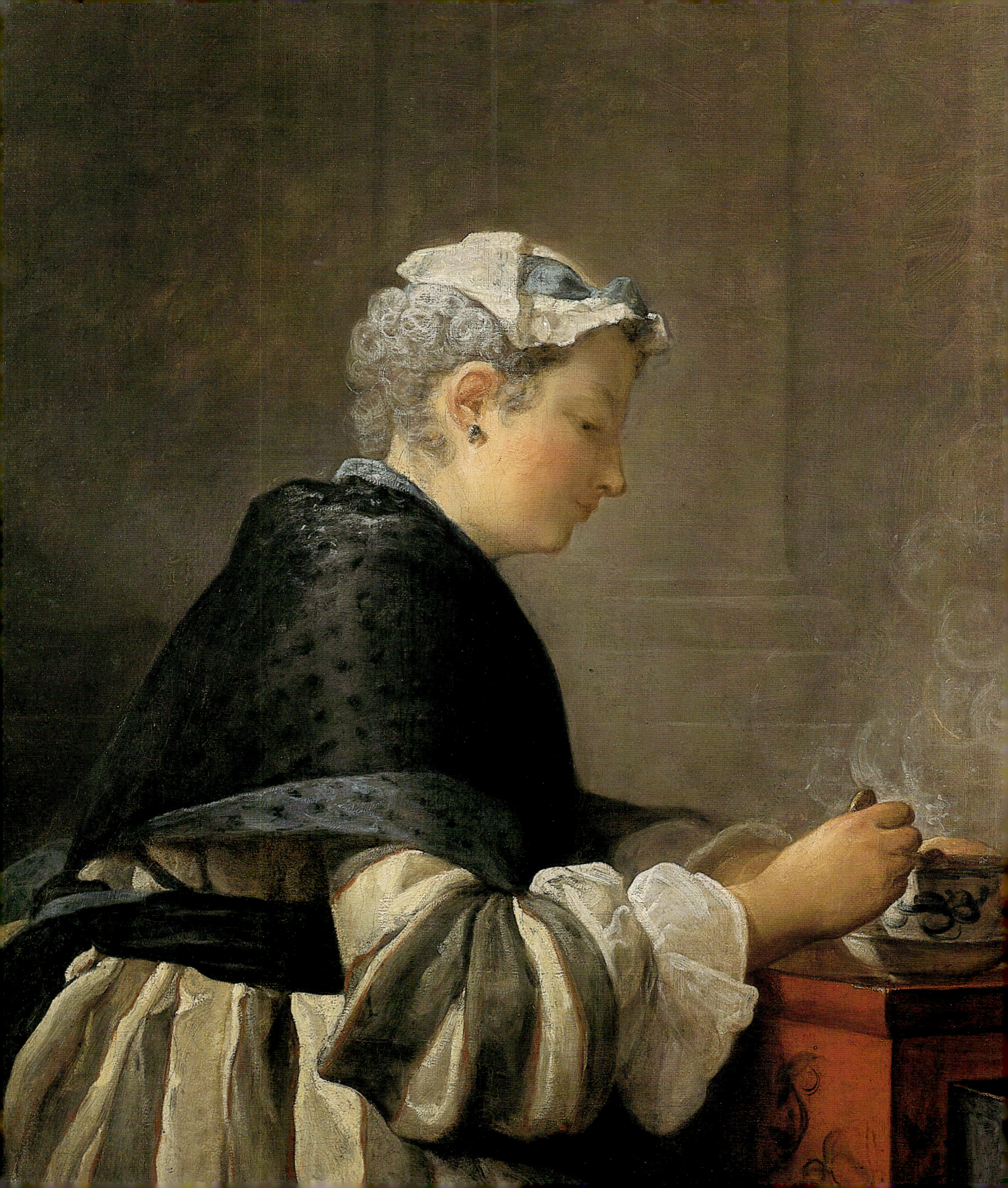

In Focus: *Lady taking Tea* and *Woman on a Daybed*

ANNE DULAU

Boucher and Chardin represent two very different trends of French eighteenth-century art, yet the two paintings at the heart of the exhibition this catalogue accompanies share a number of fascinating similarities: one evocative, delicate and muted, the other colourful, vibrant and descriptive, both belong to a small group of enchanting works painted between 1733 and 1750 about women engaged in routine activities at home. Critics and connoisseurs did not take particular note of Chardin's *Lady taking Tea* (cat. 1; fig. 1) and Boucher's *Woman on a Daybed* (cat. 2; fig. 2) at the time, but surviving contemporary comments on Boucher and Chardin's depictions of women in modern interiors show that they saw in them reflections of their own world. Twentieth-century scholars, on rediscovering these half genre/half portrait works, pounced on the idea that they were looking at the first Mme Chardin and Mme Boucher themselves.

To gain a better understanding of these two disparate but equally representative images of the time, we should first establish whether there is truth in the identification of *Lady taking Tea* and *Woman on a Daybed* as the artists' wives and secondly consider whether the interiors represented really offer a glimpse into the personal, domestic lives of these painters. We will also want to examine their interest in the fashion for drinking tea and in the Orient whence it came. Let us summarize briefly what contemporary sources tell us about Boucher and Chardin, their spouses, and the artists' employment of models.

Destined to become two of the great masters of eighteenth-century French art, these artists were born four years apart in Paris, Boucher in 1703 at rue de la Verrerie near the Louvre and Chardin in 1699 at rue de Seine in Saint-Germain-des-Prés. Boucher's father was a master painter and Chardin's a master cabinetmaker. Chardin was accepted at the French Royal Academy aged twenty-nine as a specialist in still life and Boucher at thirty-one as a history painter. In the 1730s both achieved fame and

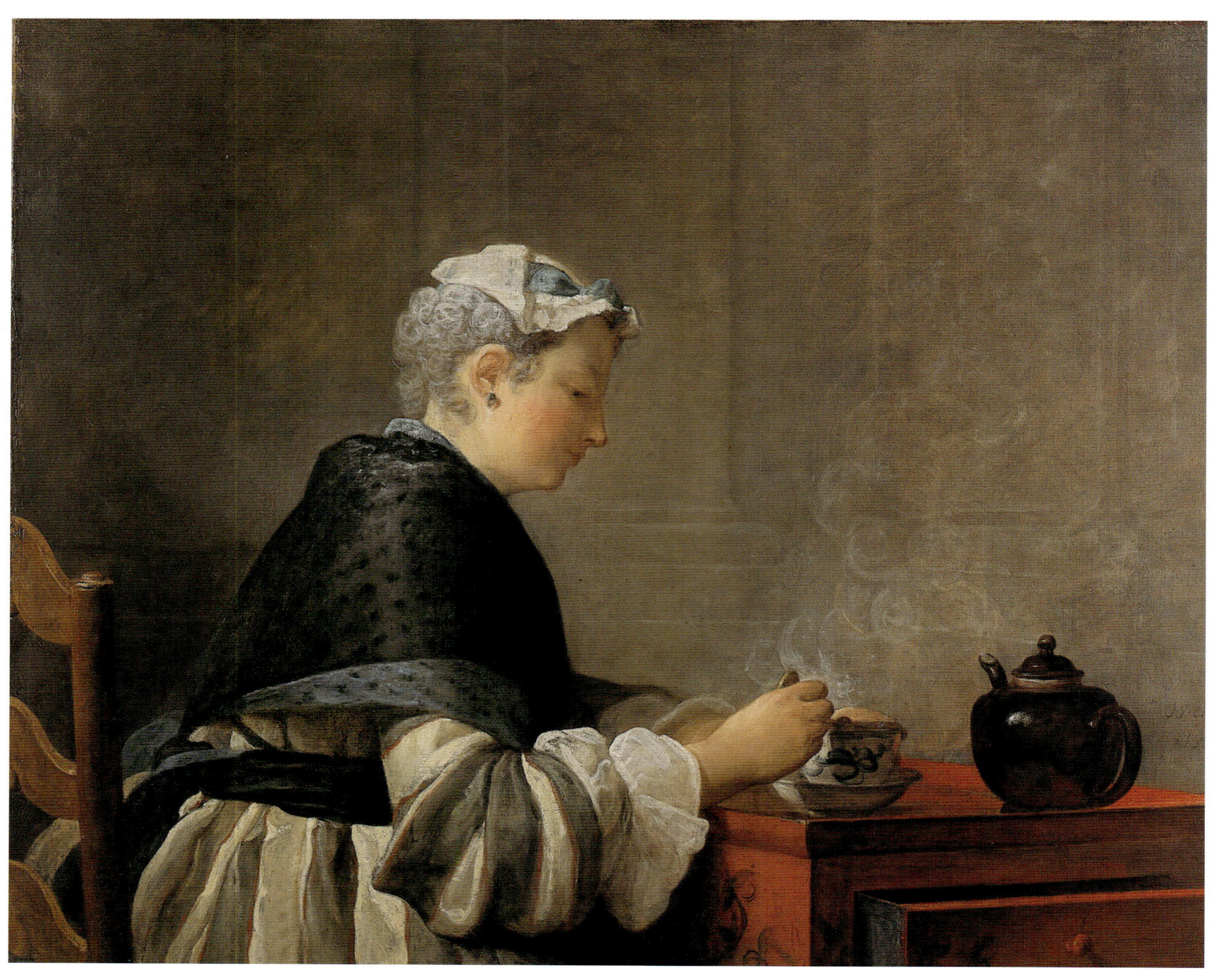

Fig. 1
Jean-Siméon Chardin
Lady taking Tea, 1735
Oil on canvas, 80 × 101 cm
Hunterian Museum and Art Gallery, Glasgow
inv. no. GLAHA 43512

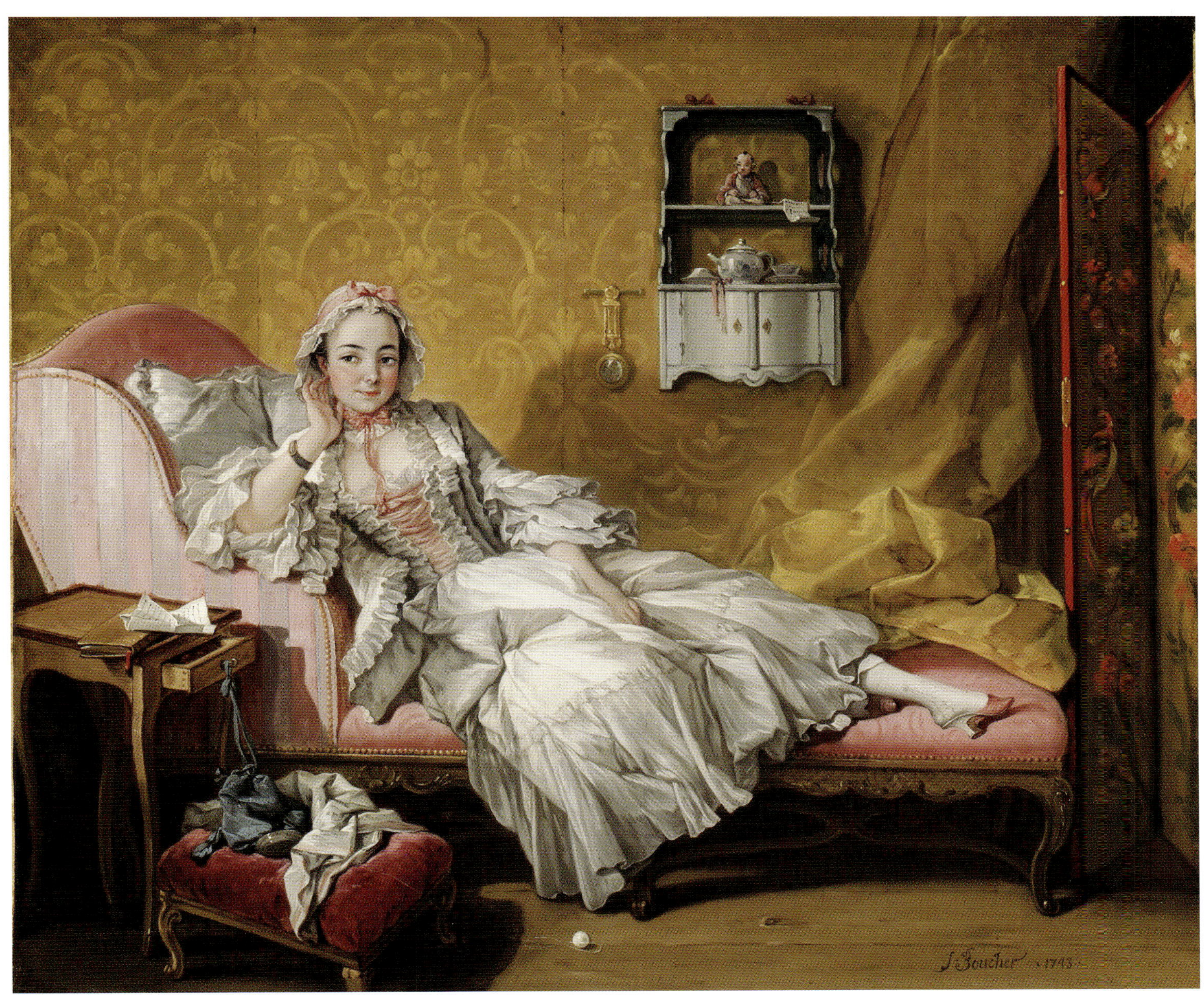

Fig. 2
François Boucher
Woman on a Daybed, 1743
Oil on canvas, 57.2 × 68.3 cm
The Frick Collection, New York
inv. no. 1937.1.139

success with innovative genre paintings that did not quite match the rules set out by the French establishment.

The painters married within two years of each other. The author of the *Essai sur la vie de M. Chardin* (1780) tells us that Chardin married at the age of thirty-two. Having been invited to a small bourgeois dance, he was introduced to a young woman whom he found charming and attractive. They became engaged, but the marriage was postponed for several years at the insistence of the girl's parents, who felt that the young man's position should be more secure. By the time they finally married, the family of Marguerite Saintard, Chardin's affianced bride, had suffered financial misfortune and could not provide her with as generous a dowry as originally planned.[1] She nonetheless brought furniture and a thousand *livres* in cash.[2]

Another source describes Marguerite as "of charming aspect, but delicate, sickly and valetudinarian", later reporting that "the poor woman died from a disease of the lungs four years after her marriage".[3] That Chardin waited nine years before marrying again indicates he must have been very much in love.

What of Boucher's wife? More public a figure than Marguerite Saintard, she appears regularly in contemporary writings and sources refer to several portraits of her, such as one by Maurice Quentin de La Tour presented at the 1737 Salon (now lost).[4] The Goncourt brothers were the first to gather this material: "Somewhat weary of a bachelor life, Boucher planned to take a wife, and on 21 April 1733", they tell us, "he married Marie-Jeanne Buseau, an extremely pretty girl of seventeen, whom he had chosen for her appearance …".[5] They added that the artist was not faithful to his wife nor she to him. This image of a libertine couple dominated writing on Boucher until in recent times Alastair Laing and George Brunel returned to contemporary sources.[6]

Alastair Laing quoted, for example, Christian IV of Zweibrücken, who, seeing his protégé Christian von Mannlich struck by Mme Boucher's enduring beauty at the age of forty, told him: "You should have seen her twenty years ago, my dear Mannlich: she was then not just the most beautiful woman in Paris, but in the whole of France … but she was as virtuous as she was beautiful, and she made herself generally loved and esteemed".[7] With this and other contemporary evidence Laing and Brunel drew a convincing portrait of a devoted couple. The daughter of Jean-Baptiste Buseau, "*bourgeois de Paris*", so from a similar background to the first Mme Chardin's, Marie-Jeanne brought a considerable dowry of six thousand *livres*.

Nothing in the early history of the two paintings connects them definitely with either wife, but in 1743 the woman depicted by Boucher would have been of an age with the twenty-seven-year-old Marie-Jeanne and similarly

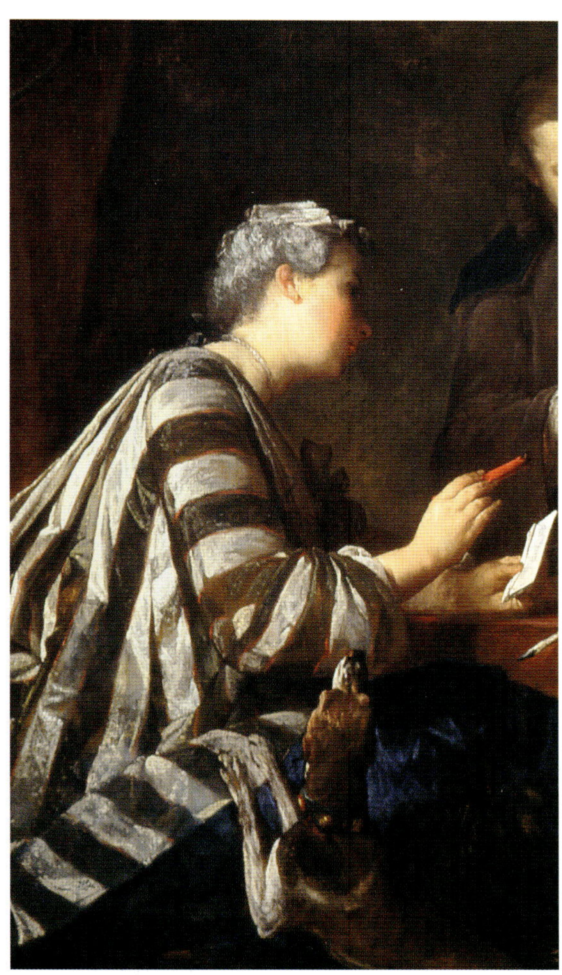

Fig. 3 (detail)
Jean-Siméon Chardin
Woman sealing a Letter, 1733
Oil on canvas, 146 × 147 cm
Schloss Charlottenburg, Berlin, Stiftung
Preußische Schösser und Gärten Berlin-
Brandenburg
inv. no. GK I 4507

Marguerite Saintard with the woman daydreaming in *Lady taking Tea*.[8] Does this uxorial connection of *Lady taking Tea* and *Woman on a Daybed* emanate from what contemporary sources tell us of Boucher and Chardin and their use of models?

Pierre-Jean Mariette, Charles-Nicolas Cochin and those who knew Chardin well stress his need to have the subject before him from first outline to last finishing touch. Writing about the artist's early years, Cochin mentions that Chardin's first genre painting was a shopsign of a lively Paris scene painted for a surgeon friend of his father's.[9] When the sign appeared in a sale of 1783, it was bought by the painter's nephew, who "believed that he recognized in this picture the portraits of the principal members of his family, whom his uncle had taken as models".[10]

Chardin's only other known early genre scene, *La Partie de billard* (*c.* 1720–25), was inspired by his father and brother's profession of cabinet-making (*fournisseur ordinaire du garde-meuble royal et des Menus-Plaisirs* from 1701), specializing in billiard tables, and caused the Goncourt brothers to comment that "the people he paints resemble his own family".[11]

Two years after his marriage to Marguerite Saintard, Chardin painted *Woman sealing a Letter* (1733; fig. 3). His next depiction of a fashionable woman in a modern interior was *Lady taking Tea*, dated 1735. Pierre Rosenberg notes that art historians have often commented on the resemblance between the model for this work and that for *Woman sealing a Letter* and, as each wears the same dress, have inferred that the model for both is the first Mme Chardin. He strengthens this supposition by pointing out the brown teapot and the cabaret table – which will later be discussed in detail – noted in the posthumous inventory of her possessions in 1737.

Woman sealing a Letter was among Chardin's first representations of the human figure following his youthful shopsign, filled with familial faces. It seems credible that both in this early attempt at depicting a woman and again two years later, when he returned to a similar subject-matter, Chardin should have turned for inspiration to his wife – she was after all before him every day. However, there is no specific evidence to support this theory. What is more, her face has much in common with the typical, homogeneous face found in the work of Chardin's contemporaries.

Jean-François de Troy, the acknowledged predecessor of Chardin and Boucher in these *sujets gallants et agréables* of fashionable women in contemporary interiors, tended to give stereotyped faces to his protagonists. The echoes of de Troy's faces in Chardin's work clearly show that, even if he were to have used his first wife as a model, he significantly modified the features of the women in his paintings to fit the favoured mould (figs. 4 and 5).

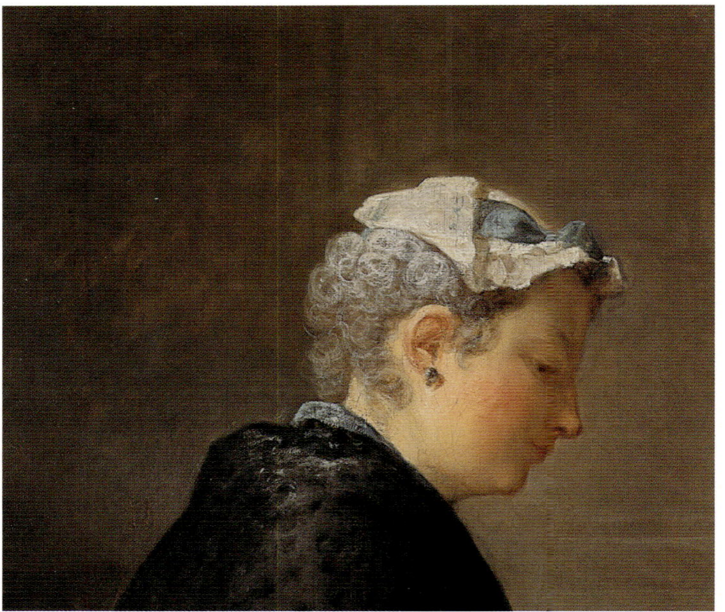

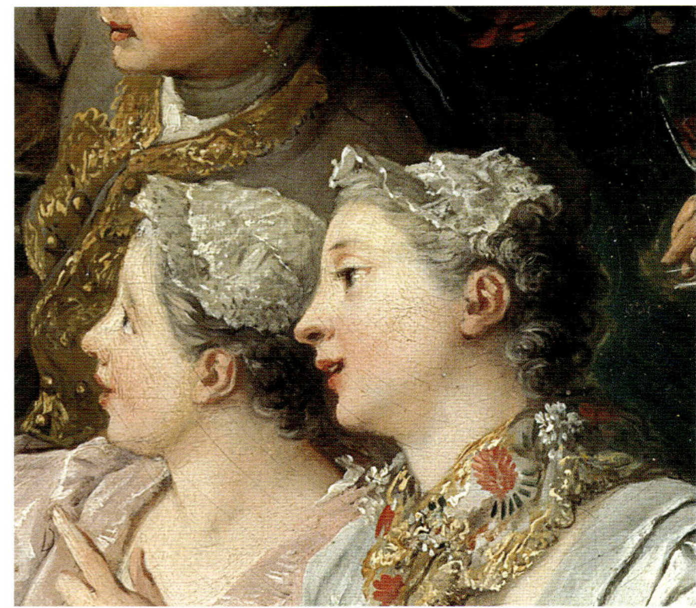

Fig. 4 (detail) Chardin
Lady taking Tea

Fig. 5 (detail)
Jean-François de Troy
The Hunt Luncheon (*Le Repas de Chasse*), 1737
Oil on canvas, 241 × 170 cm
Musée du Louvre, Paris
inv. no. RF1990.18

Information on Boucher and his use of models is more copious. Several contemporary accounts comment both on the beauty of Marie-Jeanne Buseau and on her suitability as an inspiration and model for her husband. In 1739, four years before *Woman on a Daybed*, the critic and essayist Bachaumont wrote to Boucher: "Happy Apelles, who has a living Psyche at home, of whom you can make a Venus whenever it pleases you …".[12]

Colin Bailey has recently remarked that "Such authentic testimony may have encouraged Boucher's earliest historians to view Mme Boucher as her husband's principal muse and model …. While it would have been unthinkable for the bourgeois wife of an Academician to model for such compositions, it seems, rather surprisingly, that Boucher also refrained from reproducing his wife's features." He concludes that *Woman on a Daybed* cannot be Mme Boucher and should be interpreted as a "genre scene of coquettish subject, commensurate with those 'fashionable paintings at which he excels' much in demand at the beginning of that decade".[13] The Goncourts, describing a now lost portrait of Mme Boucher by François La Tour exhibited at the 1737 Salon, talk of a fair-haired woman with infinitely sweet dark eyes and the most mischievous smile.[14] A later portrait by Roslin, dated 1761 (fig. 6), confirms this description, and, though dark-eyed, the *Woman on a Daybed* cannot be described as fair-haired. It is fair to conclude that their youth, their renown as beauties and the love their husbands bore them qualified Mmes Boucher and Chardin as muses. But they were no more than that.

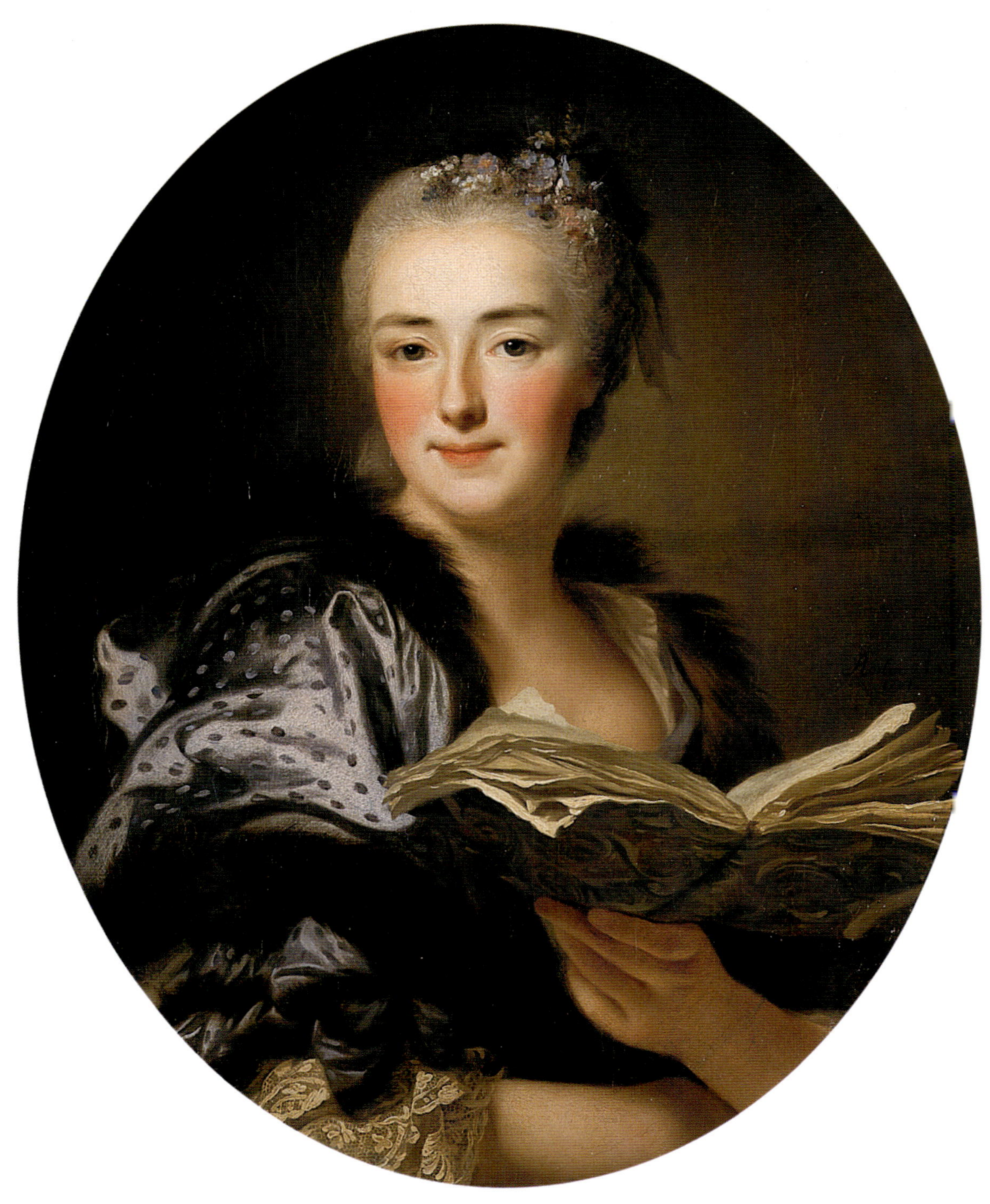

Fig. 6 Alexander Roslin
Marie-Jeanne Buseau, Mme Boucher, 1761
Oil on canvas, 63 × 51 cm
Neues Schloß, Bayreuth
inv. no. BayNS.G 132

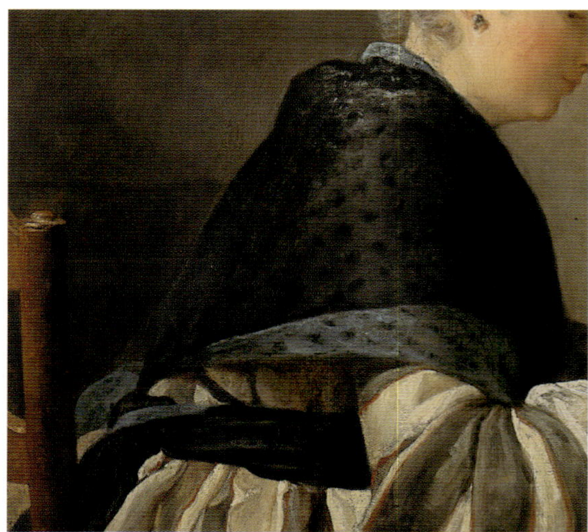

Fig. 7 (detail)
Chardin, *Lady taking Tea*

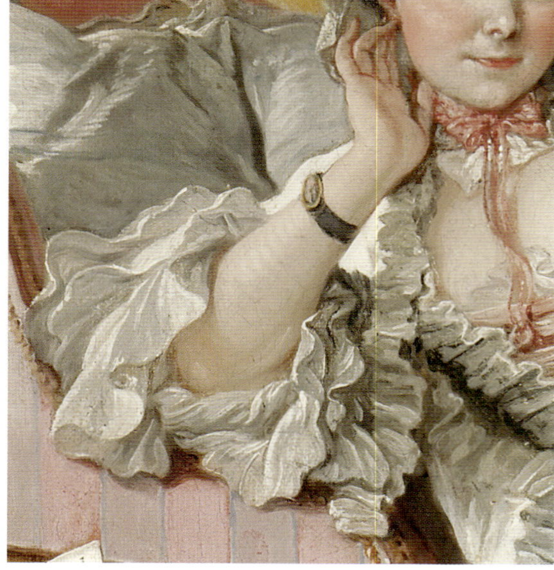

Fig. 8 (detail)
Boucher, *Woman on a Daybed*

If the women portrayed by Boucher and Chardin illustrate their personal interpretations of the current stereotypes, what of their dress and accessories and the interiors they inhabit? How much do they tell us about the artists' world, and what can we learn from them?

Chardin's woman taking tea and woman sealing a letter wear an identical gown of grey blue with white stripes edged in red, identifiable as a taffeta or silk *robe volante*, a style in fashion from the 1720s onwards.[15] An interesting note found by the Goncourt brothers states that her costume resembled that of Marie Thérèse Geoffrin (1699–1777), the celebrated hostess of one of Paris's finest salons.[16] Another consideration speaks of the costliness of the dress – its reappearance in several works painted by Chardin after his first wife's death, for it was the early modern practice to recycle expensive clothes as cherished possessions, to be presented to relatives, friends and faithful servants. Chardin's model also wears a shawl or indoor shoulder-mantle of black lace on sumptuous blue silk (fig. 7). Such garments, needed to protect the bare skin and cover the *décolletage*, represent the highest Parisian fashion of the 1730s and 1740s – particularly when fashioned of black lace.

The *Woman on a Daybed*, painted eight years after *Lady taking Tea*, wears a white taffeta gown known as a sacque dress or *robe à la française* which reappears with minor variations and different colours in all Boucher's contemporary depictions of women in fashionable interiors. Such a dress has come to epitomize the wonderful playfulness of Rococo in female contemporary fashion.[17] Note, for example, the flounced sleeves cut very short inside the bend of the arm but long over the elbow (fig. 8), with the aim of pinpointing her elegance, drawing attention to the smooth, soft hands of the wearer and to the gracefulness with which she could handle such a volume of sleeve above fragile objects such as dainty teacups.

Boucher's sitter illustrates well another principal feature of such garments, their restriction. In costumes fitted with laced stays, boned about the ribs to give the rigid form with elevated bosom so fashionable at the time, women could not bend at the waist and could not attempt to recline without a quantity of pillow to maintain them in position.

Since society required that a married woman cover her hair, caps and other such ornaments were an essential part of any hairstyle in the eighteenth century. The small, neat close-curled hair of the woman taking tea, called *tête de mouton* (because of its resemblance to a lamb's fleece; fig. 9), could not be achieved without the offices of a personal maid or male hairdresser (*friseur*). By 1740 the style had been adopted by all Parisian women with means. Both Chardin's and Boucher's women wear a fashionable linen head-dress with ribbons that match their outfits, and little jewellery. The

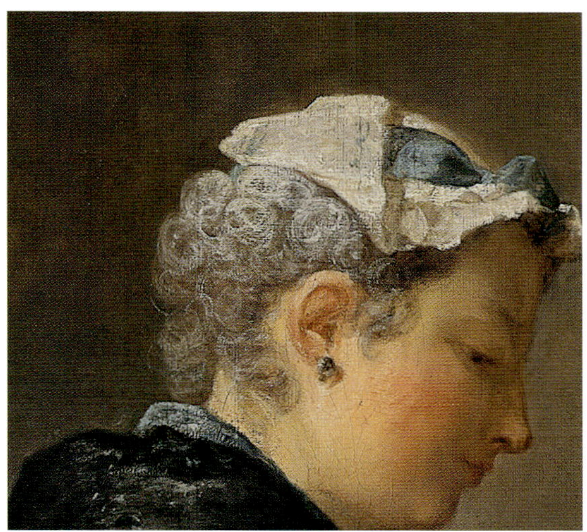

Fig. 9 (detail)
Chardin, *Lady taking Tea*

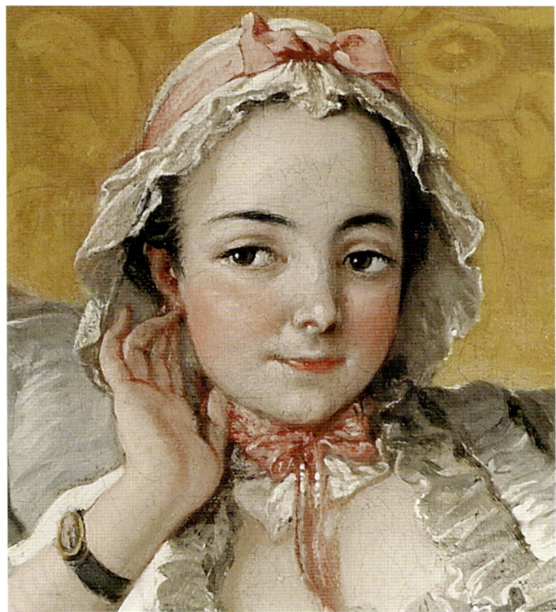

Fig. 10 (detail)
Boucher, *Woman on a Daybed*

dormeuse (fig. 9) of *Woman on a Daybed*, a more covering style inspired by nightcaps, was considered the most *chic* of all indoors caps in the 1740s.

The woman taking tea wears an earring, perhaps one of the "*boucles d'oreilles … de petits diamans dans leur chaton d'argent*" (earrings of small diamonds in their silver setting) listed among Mme Chardin's jewellery in the 1737 inventory that has been mentioned. The diamond may be brilliant-cut, the product of technical advances in cutting and the greater availability, thanks to the recent discovery of mines in Brazil, of fine-quality stones: in the early eighteenth century such jewels were starting to make their way into Europe and their bright glitter was in vogue among wealthy fashionable circles. The bauble worn by the woman on a daybed is a bracelet displaying the likeness of a loved one. Bracelets of this type, popular in the mid eighteenth century, appear both in portraits such as de Troy's 1734 *Lady showing a Bracelet Miniature to her Suitor* (private collection) and in numerous representations of contemporary women, including Boucher's own 1734 painting of *Morning: Lady at her Toilette* (lost, but known through an etching by Gilles Edme Petit) and his later portrait of *Mme de Pompadour at her Toilet* (Fogg Art Museum, Cambridge) of 1758. In all three the bracelets adorned with miniatures refer to a loved one, as would that of *Woman on a Daybed*.

It is evident that the women portrayed both in Boucher's and in Chardin's paintings would have fitted well within fashionable Parisian circles. In their depictions of such modish women Boucher and Chardin would surely not have hesitated to homogenize their dress as they had their faces, making them conform to a look easily identifiable as fashionable. The similarities end there however for while Boucher always presented his sitters to their best feminine advantage, in *Lady taking Tea* the dress, graceful neck and elegant wrist displayed to such advantage in *Woman sealing a Letter* have been subordinated to the artist's principal aim of capturing the contemplative nature of a moment of rest as the lady, cosily wrapped in a shawl, warms her hands on a bowl of steaming tea.

INTERIORS

From the late nineteenth century on it has often been suggested that the two paintings show us the artists' own world. How true can this be? To answer this it will be useful first to summarize what is known of their homes.

Thanks to the survival of several important archival documents we have a fair idea of what Chardin's lodgings and furnishings were like in 1735.[18] In typical eighteenth-century fashion for a man of his background – a rising artist from a comfortable family of Parisian craftsmen married to a *bourgeoise* – Chardin, his wife and their two young children shared a three-

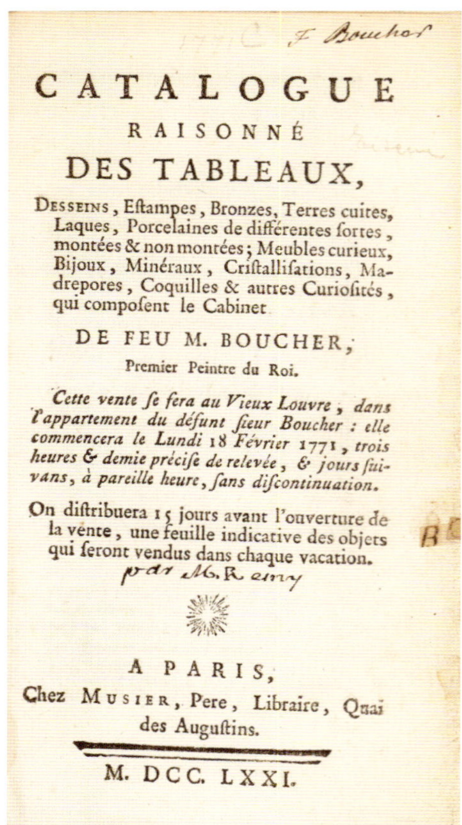

Fig. 11

P. Remy, *Catalogue Raisonné des Tableaux, Desseins, Estampes, Bronzes, Terres cuites, Laques, Porcelaines de différentes sortes, montées et non montées; Meubles curieux, Bijoux, Minéraux, Cristallisations, Madrépores, Coquilles & autres Curiosités qui composent le Cabinet DE FEU M. BOUCHER, Premier Peintre du Roi*, title page, Paris, 1771

The Wallace Collection, London

storey house with other members of his family.[19] Their accommodation consisted of two handsome rooms on the first floor, a small bedroom on the second and two bedrooms on the third.

Green satin from Bruges and three mirrors lined the walls of the first-floor "*cabinet*", where family, friends and potential patrons were received. The master bedroom was hung with Aubusson tapestry and a large mirror above the fireplace. Both rooms were home to the painter's most precious possessions, whether two fashionable rosewood corner-cupboards with rose marble tops, a clock following the latest *rocaille* trend by the well-known Parisian clockmaker Fiacre Clément, or a tea service with modish tea table. The third floor was home to the kitchen and a sparsely furnished studio with a screen, a few cane seats and an oak table covered with a large Turkish carpet, which probably provided the setting for *Woman sealing a Letter* of 1733.[20]

Writers on Chardin such as George Wildenstein, Pierre Rosenberg and Marie-Laure de Rochebrune have noted that these articles can often be identified in Chardin's oeuvre,[21] confirming what the Goncourts wrote with such eloquence in the nineteenth century: "He confines himself to the representation of the scenes that touch him in his familiar environment. He introduces into his pictures his wash-basin, his mastiff puppy, the objects and creatures to which he is accustomed in his home. In the same way he paints the people whom he sees around him, the faces to which daily habit has accustomed him …. The genius of the painter was the genius of the home."[22]

What of Boucher's domestic arrangements for 1743? He had just moved from rue Saint-Thomas du Louvre (now destroyed, it was in the courtyard of the modern day Louvre) to rue de Grenelle Saint-Honoré in the first *arrondissement* (today named rue Jean-Jacques Rousseau). There is neither inventory nor contract of marriage to allow us a glimpse into Boucher's familiar surroundings. Alastair Laing comments, "For a painter who achieved such eminence, we have extraordinarily little evidence of Boucher's non-artistic life and character".

The only document likely to help establish whether Boucher had in his possession the objects he depicts is the sale catalogue of his collection by the Parisian art dealer Pierre Remy, published in 1771 (fig. 11).[23] At over two hundred pages long it reads like a treasure trove of the exotic, rare and precious, attesting to a real connoisseur's knowledge of the decorative arts of the Far East.

Lady taking Tea is furnished with no more than a cabaret table and a wooden chair (fig. 12) of a type regularly found in paintings of the time, being simply of turned wood with a straw seat in a style dating from the later years of the seventeenth century and still popular more than three

Fig. 12 (detail) Chardin, *Lady taking Tea*

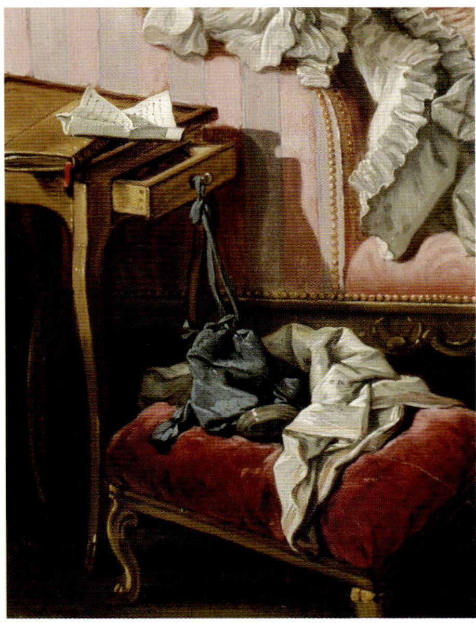

Fig. 13 (detail)
Boucher, *Woman on a Daybed*

hundred years later. Sturdy, practical and easy to carry, it would have been found in most French households of the time, from Versailles to a maid's modest lodgings. Note, for example, the chairs used by the court in *The Hunt Luncheon* (*Le Repas de Chasse*, Musée du Louvre, Paris) by de Troy, dated 1737. The chair described by Chardin could be one of the three *"chaises de bois de frêne fond de paille"* (ashwood chairs with straw seats) listed among the contents of his studio in 1737, and the simple yet fashionable cabaret table has long been identified with the *"table en cabaret à pieds de biche de bois verni"* (varnished wood cabaret table with curled back ends [literally, hoof feet]) in his wife's bedroom.

By contrast Boucher's painting is filled with an abundance of detail (fig. 13). The opulent gold brown brocade or damask wall covering is of a type frequently found in Boucher's paintings of the time, such as *Woman fastening her Garter* of 1742 (cat. 4, fig. 15). It is typical of the period, as are the voluminous folds of the same material on the right, hung above the door to help minimize draughts. The daybed that dominates the room probably dates from the second decade of the eighteenth century: backed in Louis XIV style with a wooden support carved in the Régence manner, it has been updated with modish, elegant upholstery in pink and grey white.[24] Simple pieces, typical of the reigning Louis XV style, such as a foot-stool, walnut writing-table and a small wall-cupboard holding porcelain, complete the furnishing. In Boucher's hands the middle-class interior has been deftly glamorized with a few beautiful objects and fabrics.

THE FAR EAST

If a sense of the very latest fashion pervades *Woman on a Daybed* and *Lady taking Tea* that is due not least to the objects they depict reflecting the taste for Chinese and Japanese porcelain, lacquerwork and screens, which was particularly strong among court circles and the artists' patrons.[25] By the late 1730s Parisian merchants such as Edme François Gersaint, originally a dealer in paintings, were selling exotic objects imported from China. Copies of Japanese and Chinese ware were also proliferating, the Saint-Cloud factory having now brilliantly succeeded in imitating the blue and white porcelain so admired by Europeans since the late seventeenth century, and another porcelain factory having been set up at Chantilly by Louis Henri de Bourbon, prince de Condé. The brothers Etienne-Simon and Guillaume Martin were producing lacquer (known as *vernis martin*) superior in quality, according to Voltaire, to the same made in China.[26] Artists such as Gabriel Huquier were producing ornament books and series of prints inspired by Chinese design which would swell the growing production of European goods with a Far Eastern flavour.

Fig. 14 (detail)
Boucher, *Woman on a Daybed*

Chardin occasionally dressed his scenes with porcelain but Boucher, a highly active painter of *chinoiserie*, was partly responsible for the 'China mania' that reached an apogee in France in the 1740s.[27] Having started to collect Oriental objects in the mid 1730s, in 1740 Boucher designed the calling card for Gersaint's shop, *A la Pagode*, and subsequently produced many Chinese designs for Huquier and other publishers.[28] By the time he painted *Woman on a Daybed* he was designing Chinese subjects for the Beauvais tapestry factory and sets and costumes for Charles Simon Favart's parody of the ballet *Les Indes Galantes*, *L'Ambigu de la Folie* or *Le Ballet des Dindons* (The dance of the turkeys).

In *Woman on a Daybed* Boucher's references to the Far East comprise a small pale-blue lacquered wall-cupboard, a pagoda (or figure of Putai, the god of good luck), a delicate teapot with matching cups and saucers (see frontispiece) and an Oriental screen (fig. 14). Although it is impossible to ascertain whether these were the objects listed in the 1771 catalogue of the artist's possessions, they correspond in type and style to the items it lists. For example, either lot 943, "*Un paravent de quatre feuilles de papier de la Chine, à figures et paysages, monté en bois rougi*" (a screen with four leaves of paper from China, with figures and landscape, mounted with reddened wood), or lot 946, "*Neuf écrans chinois*" (nine Chinese screens), could be the screen in *Woman on a Daybed*. The catalogue also includes over sixty pagodas, thirty teapots and countless teacups and saucers.

Chardin's painting bows to the popularity of the Far East with a cabaret table in *vernis martin*, a brown teapot and a blue and white cup and saucer, all almost certainly in the artist's possession. His wife's 1737 inventory describes "*quatre soucoupes, quatre tasses et un pot à sucre de faïence bleue et blanche, une tayère de terre de Flandre*" and a "*table en cabaret à pieds de biche de bois verni*" (four saucers, fours cups and a sugar bowl of blue and white earthenware, a teapot in Flanders earthenware and a cabaret table with curled back ends in varnished wood) in the bedroom and another "*quatre soucoupes, quatre tasses … le tout tant verre que porcelaine*" in the reception room (four saucers, four cups … either glass or porcelain).[29]

Whilst Boucher's hanging cupboard and Chardin's cabaret table could be found all over fashionable middle-class Paris, a detailed look at the other objects depicted reveals two trends in the Oriental mania of the time – on the one hand valuable collectors' pieces imported from the Far East (like *Woman on a Daybed*'s magnificent Oriental screen, teapot and cups and saucers, which are probably Xangxi period [1662–1722] porcelain; fig. 17) and on the other European-produced interpretations of decorative objects such as the pagoda. *Lady taking Tea*'s brown teapot and blue and white cup and saucer (fig. 16) are not as easily identified.[30] The

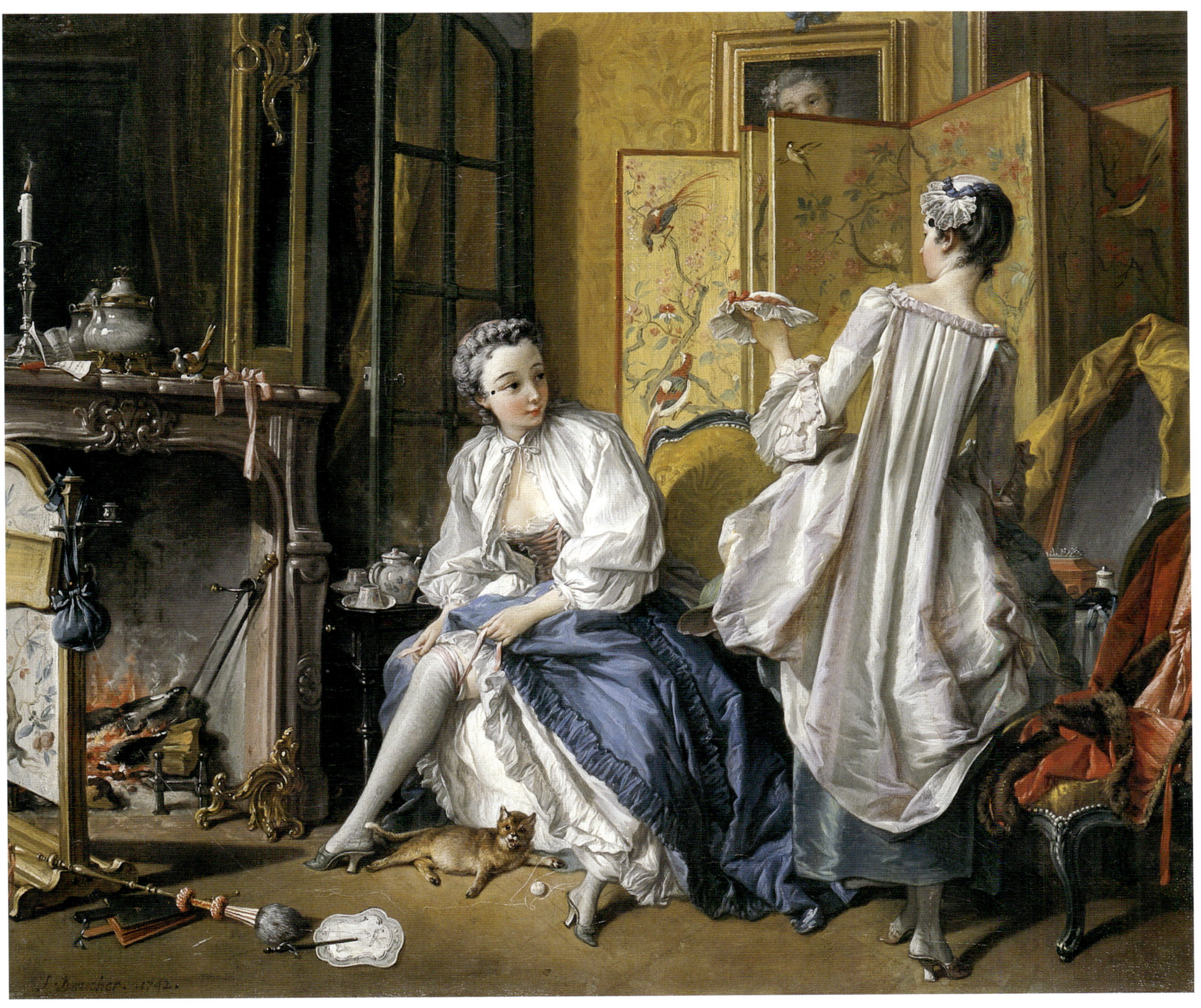

Fig. 15 François Boucher
Woman fastening her Garter, 1742
Canvas, 52.5 × 66.5 cm
Museo Thyssen-Bornemisza, Madrid
inv. no. 58

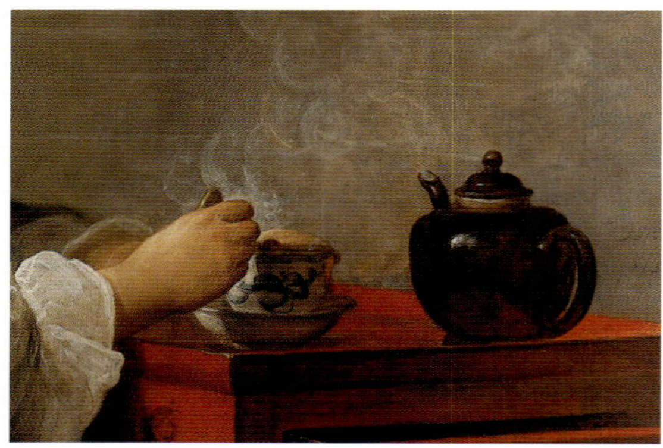

Fig. 16 (detail)
Chardin, *Lady taking Tea*

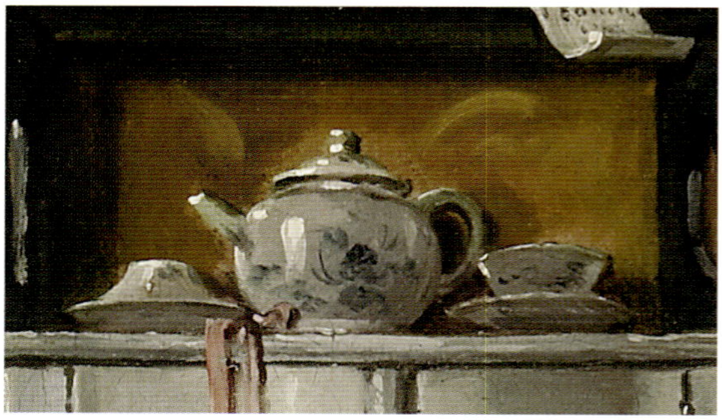

Fig. 17 (detail)
Boucher, *Woman on a Daybed*

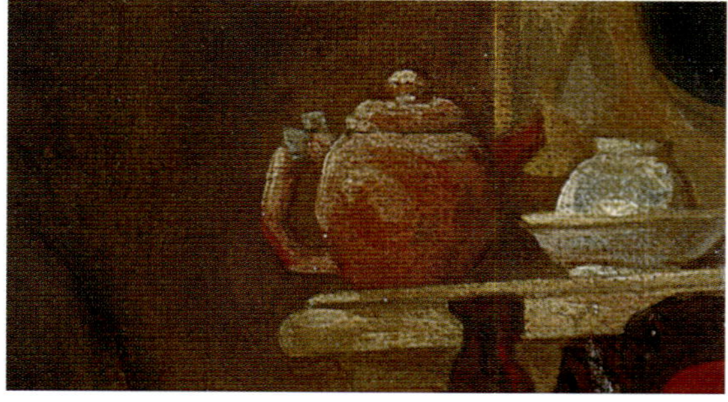

Fig. 18 (detail)
Jean-Siméon Chardin
The Diligent Mother, 1740
Oil on canvas
Stockholm, Nationalmuseum
inv. no. NM 784

probably European origin of Chardin's wife's tea set points to the fact that European manufactories looked to the most popular Oriental ware when making practical objects destined for everyday use. Both also point to the growing demand for European imitations of the Oriental objects collected by connoisseurs like Boucher as well as more affordable and practical adaptations. Interestingly, Chardin's tea service is more akin to those depicted by his English colleagues in their group portraits of London middle-class tea parties than to those shown by contemporary French painters.[31]

TAKING TEA

Although both *Woman on a Daybed* and *Lady taking Tea* refer to tea drinking, it does not seem to have been common in the Paris of the 1730s and early 1740s. It appears only occasionally in contemporary French literature; Marivaux's novel *Le Paysan parvenu*, published in the same year as *Lady taking Tea*, was among the few publications to mention any devotee of the beverage.[32] Tea was consumed mainly in salon and court society or privately at the morning *toilette*. Why then did Boucher and Chardin include teapots and teacups in several of their depictions of contemporary life? In Boucher's case the explanation is relatively simple. In the late 1730s and early 1740s the obsession with Oriental objects had reached a peak in France. The painter seems to have been unable to conceive of a fashionable interior without accessories such as china.[33] Furthermore, by the early 1740s drinking tea itself had become an essential element of the pictorial vocabulary of China and its inhabitants he had developed.[34] Other French contemporary painters besides Boucher illustrated the vogue for Oriental porcelain, too.[35] However, none focused on the act of drinking tea as Chardin did. Even in his portrait of the well known tea-drinker Mme Crozat, dated 1740 (Musée Fabre, Montpellier), Jacques Louis Aved only hinted at her taste for tea with a teapot and cup on the mantelpiece behind her.

To understand Chardin's interest in tea and its accessories one must go back to 1731, the year Chardin married Marguerite Saintard. The brown teapot is first mentioned among the contents of her dowry. It takes centre stage in *Lady taking Tea*, signed and dated by Chardin two months before his wife's death of a long and painful lung disease. Could Chardin's interest in tea and in a woman lost in thought while warming her hand on a tea bowl have been inspired by his wife's daily intake of tea for medicinal reasons? After 1735 Mme Chardin's brown teapot and blue and white cup are no longer prominent, though they remain in the background of Chardin's work. There is, for example, a similar pot and cup displayed in the traditional way on the mantelpiece in *The Diligent Mother* (Nationalmuseum, Stockholm; detail, fig. 18) of 1740 and a solitary teapot in *The Attentive Nurse*

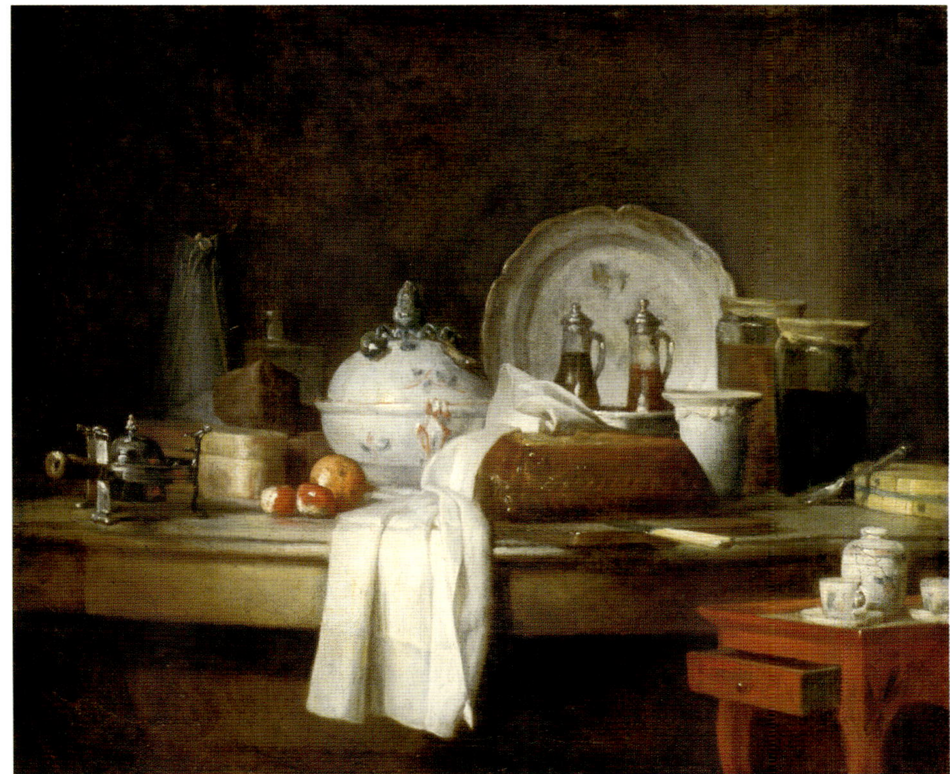

Fig. 19
Jean-Siméon Chardin
The Pantry Table
(*La Table d'Office*), 1763?
Oil on canvas, 38 × 46 cm
Musée du Louvre, Paris
inv. no. M.I. 1040

(National Gallery, Washington) of 1748, but they are treated in the same sketchy manner as the fireplace itself. Perhaps Chardin's familiarity with tea drinking died with his wife. Interestingly, still lifes such as *The Pantry Table* (fig. 19; detail, fig. 20), painted after his second marriage in 1744, include a sophisticated set of dainty Chinese porcelain teacups and saucers, more like the type collectors admired and Boucher lovingly depicted in paintings such as *Woman on a Daybed*.[36]

CONCLUSION

The analysis of the paintings in their context clearly shows that, although there is some truth in the association of *Woman on a Daybed* and *Lady taking Tea* with the artists' own wives and interiors, Boucher and Chardin did not reproduce faithfully what they saw. Instead, they created images referring to what potential patrons would recognize as fashionable Parisian women, of the type ubiquitous in contemporary art and literature. Similarly, although they used elements from their own interiors as studio props to create appropriate stages for their models, they removed all personal connections from them. The study of surviving inventories tells us that Chardin's wife's enthusiasm for drinking tea must have inspired the theme of *Lady taking Tea* and highlights Boucher's activities as a collector of Oriental objects.

23

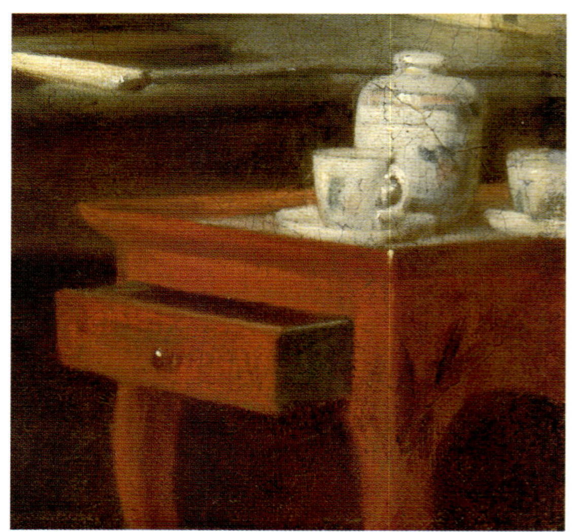

Fig. 20 (detail)
Jean-Siméon Chardin
The Pantry Table

Both paintings display the attention to detail and sophistication characteristic of eighteenth-century French fashion and decorative arts. In Chardin's picture the abstract swirls in the tea bowl refer to the type of decoration found on blue and white Chinese porcelain and complements the lines lightly etched on the surface of the *cabaret* table, and the red line edging the blue-grey stripes of the lady's dress is echoed in the same table's red *vernis martin*. In Boucher's painting the colour scheme of the daybed complements the model's pink and white outfit and the curving shapes of her ankle and slipper echo those of the side table and stool.

The similarities end there. This analysis confirms that Boucher and Chardin emphasized different aspects of eighteenth-century French life. Boucher, with his eye for fashion and decoration and his love of Oriental decorative arts, shared his century's devotion to the cultivated art of gracious living. In paintings such as *Woman on a Daybed* everything contributes to create the illusion of a world "arranged and refined to create a highly sophisticated type of visual seduction, designed to please both the senses and the intellect".[37] More psychologically minded, Chardin was interested in capturing a moment, retaining only such essentials as created the mood. Seeking to please the eye in a very different manner, he too magisterially orchestrated colours and forms to convey on to canvas his harmonized illusion of a world.

1 Cochin 1780, in Michel 1994, p. 268: "*Vers ce temps-là, M. Chardin ayant par hasard été conduit dans un petit bal d'honnête bourgeoisie, y fit la connaissance d'une demoiselle fort estimable à qui il s'attacha. Ils ne tardèrent pas à être accordé ; mais comme l'état de M. Chardin n'était pas encore bien consolidé, le mariage fut remis à un autre temps, et par diverses circonstances a été retardé de plusieurs années. Dans cet intervalle, les affaires du père de la demoiselle s'étant dérangées, il se trouva qu'au lieu d'une fortune honnête, qu'elle avait été fondée à espérer, elle n'avait plus rien. M. Chardin se piqua de constance, et l'épousa malgré ce revers.*"

2 Brunel 1986, p. 28. The average dowry of artists' wives in the eighteenth century was roughly 1000 to 2000 *livres*.

3 *The Nècrologue*, quoted by Edmond and Jules de Goncourt in Goncourt 1948. For the latest information on Marguerite Saintard, see Bruyant 2000.

4 For an up-to-date appraisal of portraits of Mme Boucher, see Bailey 2005.

5 Goncourt 1948, p. 63.

6 Brunel 1986; Alastair Laing in New York, Detroit, Paris 1986–87.

7 Laing in New York, Detroit, Paris 1986–87, p. 65.

8 *Lady taking Tea* was exhibited at the Salon of 1739, where it went unnoticed by critics. *Woman on a Daybed* does not seem to have been exhibited during the artist's lifetime. They are both first noted by critics in the late nineteenth and early twentieth centuries.

9 Michel 1994, pp. 267–69.

10 The engraver, printseller and picture-dealer Philippe Le Bas was a good friend of Chardin. This information was inserted in a manuscript note of the sale

catalogue, according to Goncourt 1948, pp. 110–12.

11 *Ibid.*, p. 145; for further information on this early genre scene, now lost, see Jacques Wilhelm, '*La partie de billard est-elle une œuvre de jeunesse de Chardin?*', *Bulletin du Musée Carnavalet*, vol. 22, June 1969, pp. 7–13.

12 Quoted in Cailleux 1966, p. iii: '*Heureux Apelle, qui avez une Psyché vivante chez vous, de laquelle vous pouvez faire une Vénus quand il vous plaira …*'.

13 Bailey 2005, p. 228.

14 Goncourt 1948, p. 96.

15 For further information on *robes volantes*, see p. 86.

16 Goncourt 1948, p. 119. The note was made by the expert Paillet on a sketch for *Woman sealing a Letter* at the Houdebot sale 5 April 1809.

17 Ribeiro 2002, p. 136.

18 The main archival documents are Chardin's second marriage contract with Marguerite Saintard of 26 January 1731 and the estate inventory of Marguerite Saintard of 18 November 1737, published by Pascal and Gaucheron 1931. Relevant studies of these documents include M. Herbet, 'Les maisons de Chardin', *Bulletin de la Société Historique du Ve arrondissement*, 1899, pp. 143–44; Wildenstein 1959, pp. 98–106; Pierre Rosenberg, 'Objects from Chardin's Household', in Paris, Cleveland and Boston 1979, pp. 67–71; Marie Laure de Rochebrune, 'Ceramics and Glass in Chardin's Paintings', in Paris, Düsseldorf, London and New York, 1999–2000, pp. 37–54; and Bruyant 2000, pp. 85–104.

19 The whole household consisted of his mother (his father had died in 1731); his brother and his wife and their children; his own wife and their two young children.

20 Marie-Laure de Rochebrune, 'Zu einigen Gegenstäim Gemälde «Die Briefsieglerin» von Jean-Siméon Chardin', in Berlin 2003–04.

21 See note 18 for the relevant studies.

22 Goncourt 1948, p.127.

23 Remy 1771: *Catalogue Raisonné des Tableaux, Desseins, Estampes, Bronzes, Terres cuites, Laques, Porcelaines de différentes sortes, montées et non montées; Meubles curieux, Bijoux, Minéraux, Cristallisations, Madrépores, Coquilles & autres Curiosités qui composent le Cabinet de FEU M. BOUCHER, Premier Peintre du Roi.*

24 Pierre Verlet, *French Furniture and Interior Decoration of the 18th Century*, Barrie & Rockliff, London, 1967, p. 146.

25 For further information see Ann Eatwell's essay and Perrin Stein, 'Les Chinoiseries de Boucher et leurs sources: l'art de l'appropriation', in Paris 2007, pp. 88–89.

26 '*… et ces cabinets où Martin a surpassé l'art de Chine*', 'Epître connue sous le nom des Vous et des Tu', in *Poëmes, épîtres et autres poésies. Par M. de Voltaire*, Paris, 1779, p. 225.

27 For Chardin and Oriental ceramics, see Marie-Laure de Rochebrune, 'Ceramics and Glass in Chardin's Paintings', in Paris, Düsseldorf, London and New York 1999–2000, pp. 37–54.

28 As note 25.

29 Pascal and Gaucheron 1931, p. 67.

30 See cat. 12, 13 and 14 for further information on the likely origin of Chardin's teapot and tea bowl.

31 See, for example, *An English Family at Tea*, dated *c.* 1725, by Joseph van Aken, Tate Britain, London.

32 Pierre Carlet de Chamblain de Marivaux, *Le Paysan Parvenu: or, the fortunate peasant. Being memoirs of the life of Mr. – translated from the French of M. de Marivaux*, London, 1735.

33 The 1736 drawing of an amorous courtesan (Waddesdon Manor) for illustrations of La Fontaine's *Fables* has a tea bowl and cup on its fireplace. Within his *tableaux de mode*, *Le Déjeuner* of 1739 includes a teapot on a wall shelf; *La Toilette* of 1742 a teapot with steam and two teacups.

34 See, for example, prints such as Boucher's calling card for Gersaint engraved by Caylus, *A la Pagode* (Bibliothèque Nationale de France, Paris); the 1740 set representing the four elements, engraved by Aveline; overdoors entitled *Le Thé à la Chinoise* such as the one now in the collection of the Count of Chichester.

35 The Musée des Arts Décoratifs in Paris has two well-known still lifes from the 1720s and 1730s showing Oriental porcelains as well as a red lacquered tea table. They are by Desportes and an anonymous French artist.

36 For further information see Marie Laure de Rochebrune in Paris, Düsseldorf, London and New York 1999–2000.

37 Hedley 2004, p. 68.

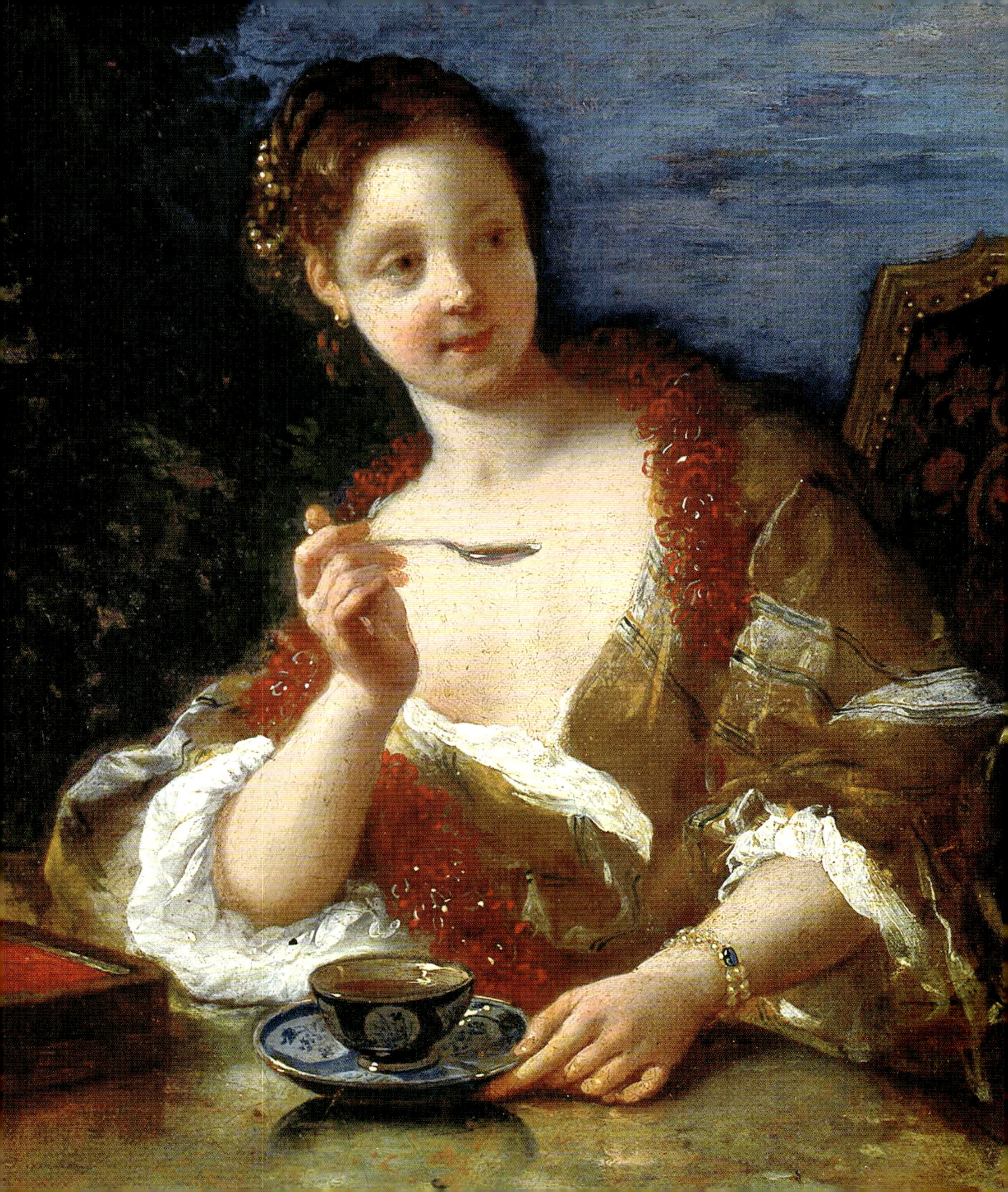

New Beginnings in French Genre Painting
de Troy, Chardin, Boucher

CHRISTOPH MARTIN VOGTHERR

Fig. 21 (detail)
Jean-François de Troy
Woman taking Coffee
Oil on canvas, 34 × 25 cm
Staatliche Museen zu Berlin,
Gemäldegalerie
inv. no. 469

In the early eighteenth century painting in France was profoundly re-defined by Antoine Watteau. For the first time genre painting reached the forefront of French art, becoming both an important, innovative force and economically a highly successful venture. In the following decades many of the most important French painters – Nicolas Lancret, Jean-François de Troy, Jean-Siméon Chardin, François Boucher, Jean-Honoré Fragonard, Jean-Baptiste Greuze – excelled as genre painters and created an impressive sequence of masterworks. Only the rise of Neoclassicism and the success of Jacques-Louis David changed these parameters again.[1] While the central importance of genre painting for French eighteenth-century art is today undisputed, contemporaries had mixed feelings about the phenomenon. Nor were they able to talk easily about genre painting, as a precise terminology was not to be introduced until the nineteenth century. This problem highlights the gap which existed between a contemporary normative view of French painting, focusing on history painting – very often motivated by wishful thinking – and the actual taste of collectors, artists and the art market for lower genres .

The remarkable success of genre painting had its origin in the work of Watteau in the years after 1710.[2] Following the artist's untimely death in 1721, however, it took French genre painting more than a decade to re-adjust, until a group of mainly younger artists successfully developed new and very personal approaches. In the period between 1730 and 1745 a whole new range of genre paintings was created by some of the best painters of their day. This crucial moment is epitomized by the masterworks in the exhibition this catalogue accompanies. As a group they reveal immediately how hard it is to compose a history of French genre painting of this period. While strong Parisian institutions politically controlled and officially defined French painting, as a whole it was stylistically heterogeneous. The powerful idea of a supposedly logical development of the school was mainly created by French writers (and eagerly followed abroad), but it was based more on the desire to create a positive self-image than on reality. Genre painting in particular was created primarily by a sequence of strong artistic personalities who were not always related in obvious ways. The following essay will focus on Jean-Siméon Chardin, probably the most important figure in French genre painting around the middle of the century, who was an artist as exceptional and as stylistically isolated as Antoine Watteau.[3]

In 1735 Chardin painted his masterwork as a genre painter – the picture of a woman taking tea (fig. 1, p. 10). Over the last decades this work has attracted considerable critical attention.[4] To an attentive observer it soon becomes apparent that the painting's apparent simplicity is misleading and conceals an utmost complexity and maturity. A young woman in a wide, striped gown is sitting at a bright red lacquer table. She is leaning slightly forwards to stir a hot drink in a blue and white cup on the table in front of her. The steam, which rises from the cup, fills most of the upper right of the painting. The woman has poured tea from a shiny, dark brown teapot which is visible further to the right on the table. The composition of the painting circumscribes her personal space inside a triangle formed by her back, her head and the teacup on the lacquer table. She is shown in half-figure and close up. Everything that might impose a distance between her and us is omitted, but the woman herself seems to be completely unaware of being observed and does not look at us. The back of her simple wooden chair to the left frames the intimate scene. Classical pilasters are just visible in the grey background. We should probably interpret them as part of a *boiserie* – a carved, wooden wall decoration – painted in a greyish colour, which subtly changes its shade from a dark hue on the left to a brighter grey on the right. Its tone is further brightened by the steam rising from the teacup. Chardin chose a surprisingly grand background for a simple domestic scene.

The composition of the painting is rigid and concentrated. The background wall runs parallel to the picture plane and the figure of the woman is shown in exact profile. Only the furniture eases this strict framework. The chair and table are positioned obliquely, a small drawer at the front of the table is half pulled open, and the spout of the teapot points inwards to the left. Chardin subtly balances the rigidity of the composition's general outline with the seemingly careless position of chair, table and tea utensils. In fact, these objects are hardly depicted and combined in a spatially convincing way, but their position is instead determined by pictorial needs. The seemingly distorted foreshortening of the teapot has troubled many observers, but helps to keep the painting focused. The decorative patterns on the table and the cup are simplified to an extreme degree.[5] Chardin subjects all details to the figure and the restrained action of the pensive woman.

Equally subtle is the painting's colour scheme, which is based on the foil of the grey background. The woman is dressed in a wide gown with blue-grey and white stripes divided by fine red lines. Her white bonnet is held by a blue ribbon, while the shawl in blue and black around her shoulder is tied behind her back. All colours reappear in the painting and form a dense composition: the blue and white of her dress are reflected in the blue and white teacup, the black of her shawl reappears in the teapot and in the swirling ornaments on the sides of the table. The fine red stripes in her dress prepare us for the strongest colour accent in the entire painting, the shining red lacquer table. Its colour reflects on the steam above and gives it a sufficiently reddish note to enliven the grey background colour. The warm, red skin-colour of the woman's face is heightened by reflections from the red table. These interlocking colours create a subtle and exciting visual balance. In spite of its monumentality the scene achieves a great sense of immediacy.

Chardin's seemingly effortless and simple pictorial solution was the result of at least three years of a breathtakingly rapid and brilliant development.[6] He had started as a still-life painter with only occasional, and less than successful, ventures into genre painting. Around 1733 he redirected his career into figure painting.[7] The Glasgow painting is only his fourth dated genre painting: after the *Woman drawing Water at a Cistern* (*La Fontaine*) of 1733 in Stockholm, the *Woman sealing a Letter* of 1733 in Schloss Charlottenburg, Berlin (fig. 22), and the *Portrait of Joseph Aved* (*Le Soufleur*) of 1734 in the Louvre.[8]

In his obituary of Chardin of 1780, the engraver Charles-Nicolas Cochin described the painter's move into genre (incorrectly dating it to 1737): "Until 1737, Chardin had never tried figure paintings. It is quite extraordinary that he decided to try. M. Aved, a portrait painter, was his close friend. He often took Chardin's advice and was content to do so. But one day, when Chardin gave him a hard time with his thoughts, M. Aved answered with force: 'You seem to imagine that this is as easy to paint as pastries [*langues fourrées*] and sausages'. M. Chardin was extremely hurt by this response, but he held back and did not answer right away. But the next day he began a figure painting: it was the one showing a woman drawing water from a cistern."[9] Pierre-Jean Mariette relates a similar story in his *Abecedario* (a manuscript collection of artists' biographies), though with some significant differences. While he does not date the incident, he adds the information that Chardin at that time was working on a *devant de cheminée* (a screen covering the open fireplace in summer), probably the painting now in the Art Institute of Chicago.[10] More importantly, he cites the head of a young man who makes soap bubbles ("*une teste de jeune homme qui fait des bulles de savon*") as his first figurative painting and lets some time pass between the conversation in Aved's studio and Chardin's first genre painting.[11] The *Soap Bubbles* exists in three versions (in New York, Los Angeles and Washington; fig. 23), but none of them seems to be Chardin's original composition.

In fact the earliest figure painting by Chardin is arguably his *Woman sealing a Letter* of 1733 in Berlin (fig. 22).[12] Together with the painting in Stockholm, it bears the earliest date of any of the painter's figure paintings and reveals an artist still inexperienced in the rendering of the human figure. Its large format, its signature and its dating suggest the immense importance of the canvas for the newly status-conscious artist. *Woman sealing a Letter* leaves no doubt about the difficulties caused by the new genre and size for the painter. The woman in the painting sits somewhat obliquely (and in an impossible position) on her armchair. She is about to seal a letter which a servant on the right waits to deliver to an unknown recipient. A large drapery frames the composition on the left. Significant pentimenti bear witness to Chardin's struggle to come to terms with the ambitious composition.

Two years later, Chardin attempted in his painting in Glasgow a corrected and perfected version of the *Woman sealing a Letter*. He again shows a young woman sitting at a table facing right. She is wearing the same dress and otherwise closely resembles the woman of the painting in Berlin. The canvas in Glasgow frames the composition more closely: the young woman is seen only down to her waist, and the servant and dog are omitted. Her position is convincing, the space clear and simple. By drastically reducing the accessories Chardin has created a sense of concentration. Single luxury items are visible in both paintings: the carpet in Berlin is an equivalent of the lacquer table in Glasgow (in fact a similar table now covered by the carpet was originally meant to be visible on the painting in Berlin, before Chardin painted it over), but in Glasgow the accessories are controlled by a remarkable discipline of pictorial composition.

Chardin's *Lady taking Tea* has no close relation in French painting of its period. The painter took advantage of his situation as a beginner in figurative painting, and genre painting was in itself less dominated by tradition. He was also able to achieve a highly original solution because he arranged his few well-chosen objects as a still-life painter would, according to almost abstract principles. Chardin's unique pictorial solutions may well be closely tied to the fact that he was the only major genre painter who started out painting still lives.

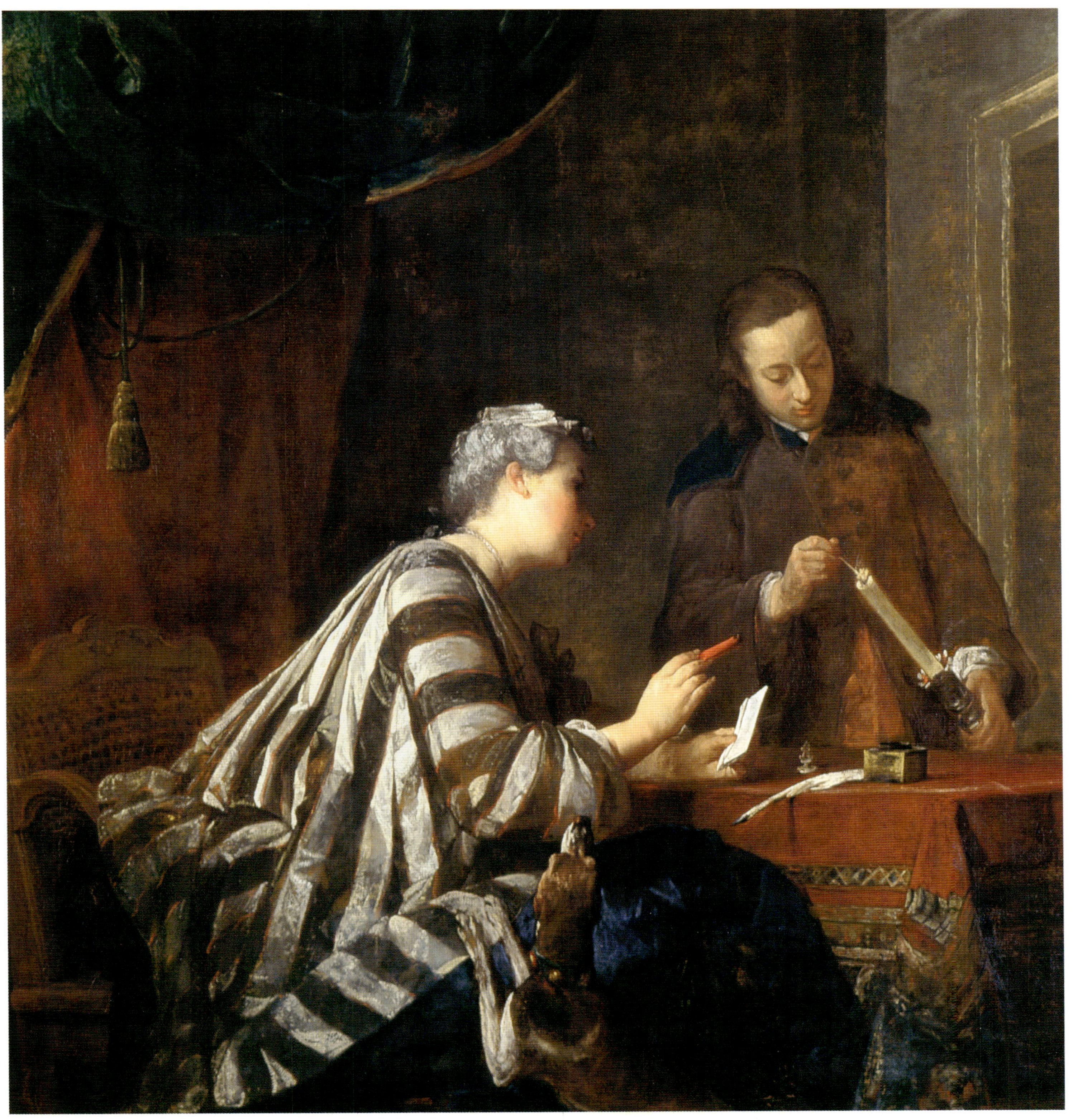

Fig. 22
Jean-Siméon Chardin, *Woman sealing a Letter*, oil on canvas, 146 × 147 cm
Schloss Charlottenburg, Berlin, Stiftung Preußische Schlösser und Gärten Berlin-Brandenburg, inv. no. GK I 4507

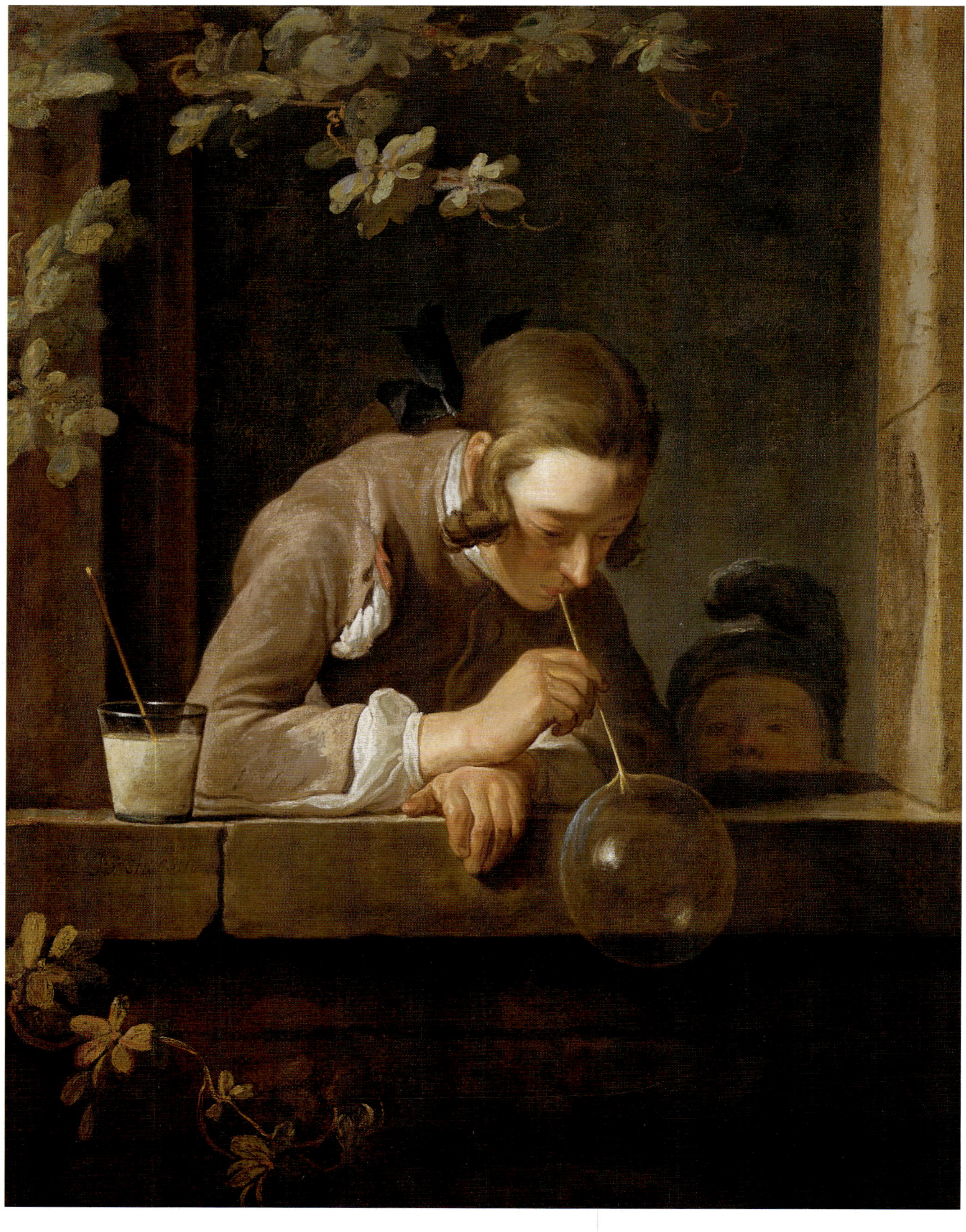

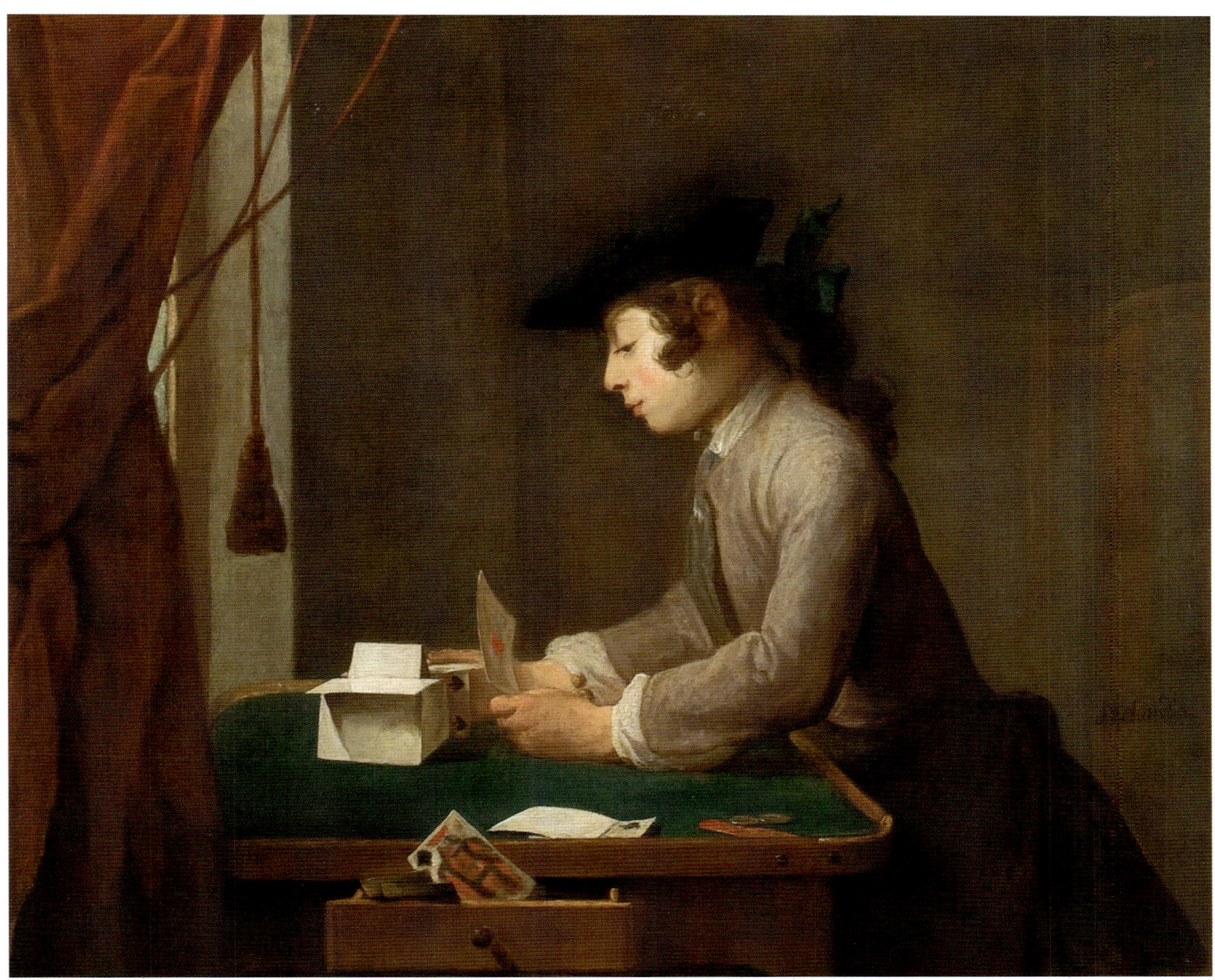

Chardin's early development as a genre painter can be further illustrated by the probable pendant to the *Lady taking Tea,* the *House of Cards* in the Rothschild collection at Waddesdon Manor (cat. 26, fig. 24).[14] The painting depicts a boy building a house of cards on a table next to a window. Together these paintings illustrate the economy of means quickly evolving in Chardin's early figurative painting. The elements which two years earlier had been combined in the *Woman sealing a Letter* were now explored in two separate compositions. One painting uses the grand interior, the other drapery which, in his later works, Chardin would stop using. But both show their subjects completely absorbed in their occupations, an effect not yet fully achieved in the Berlin painting.

The pictorial material of the Berlin *Woman sealing a Letter* turns out to have been the starting point for several developments in Chardin's work, for the full-length genre scenes which he began painting between 1738 and

1740 also seem to be rooted in its more narrative, many-figured composition. His *Scullery Maid* (*L'Ecureuse*, cat. 27, fig. 25) in Glasgow is a prime example of these concentrated single-figure interiors, which became a speciality of Chardin's. These paintings follow a pattern which transforms his half-lengths into full-lengths, but at the same time translates their monumentality to a different, small format.

While Chardin's work of the 1730s constitutes one of the summits of French genre painting, it remains an extraordinary exception in the development of French art of the period. It still seems hard today to link Chardin with more general contemporary development. François Boucher's *Woman on a Daybed* (fig. 3, p. 11),[15] the other outstanding masterpiece of the exhibition, was painted eight years after Chardin's *Lady taking Tea*. A comparison between the two works may help to define both the exceptional characters of Chardin's work and the power of a contemporary masterwork closer to the artistic mainstream.

Like Chardin's, Boucher's painting is set in an interior, but the relationship between the young woman and her environment is quite different. Boucher depicts her full-length, resting on a daybed in a semi-upright position. Her gaze is slightly averted towards the window. She might be observing something through it or reacting to a person invisible to us. While Chardin only gives us a vague hint of the surrounding space, Boucher's interior is a defining characteristic of the unknown woman and an equal element of the painting's subject-matter. Luxurious objects engulf her: her daybed is covered in pink silk, a screen in Chinese style is visible on the right, a small lacquer cupboard on the back wall displays a Chinese pagoda and a blue and white tea set, and a *châtelaine* (ornamental chain) hangs next to it. Only the small table and the footstool are made of simple materials, but they are embellished by a picturesque arrangement of everyday objects. A ball of thread lies on the floor. Even if the woman remains the main feature of the painting, one's eyes are continuously tempted to wander off. The bright white of her dress keeps pulling our attention back in, but leads the eye to her lap rather than to her face. Her white and pink dress blends with the cover of the daybed, fusing her visually with the furniture and reducing her to one of the many precious objects in the interior. While Chardin suggests pensive concentration, Boucher displays decorative disorder and luxurious *ennui*. Chardin's objects serve a compositional purpose; Boucher's objects are the purpose of the painting.

Boucher was in Italy between 1728 and 1731. He had painted his first genre scenes before he left for Rome, where he fell under the spell of Bloemaert's drawings, which he copied there. He had also, before his trip to Italy, engraved Watteau's drawings for Jean de Jullienne and so was well

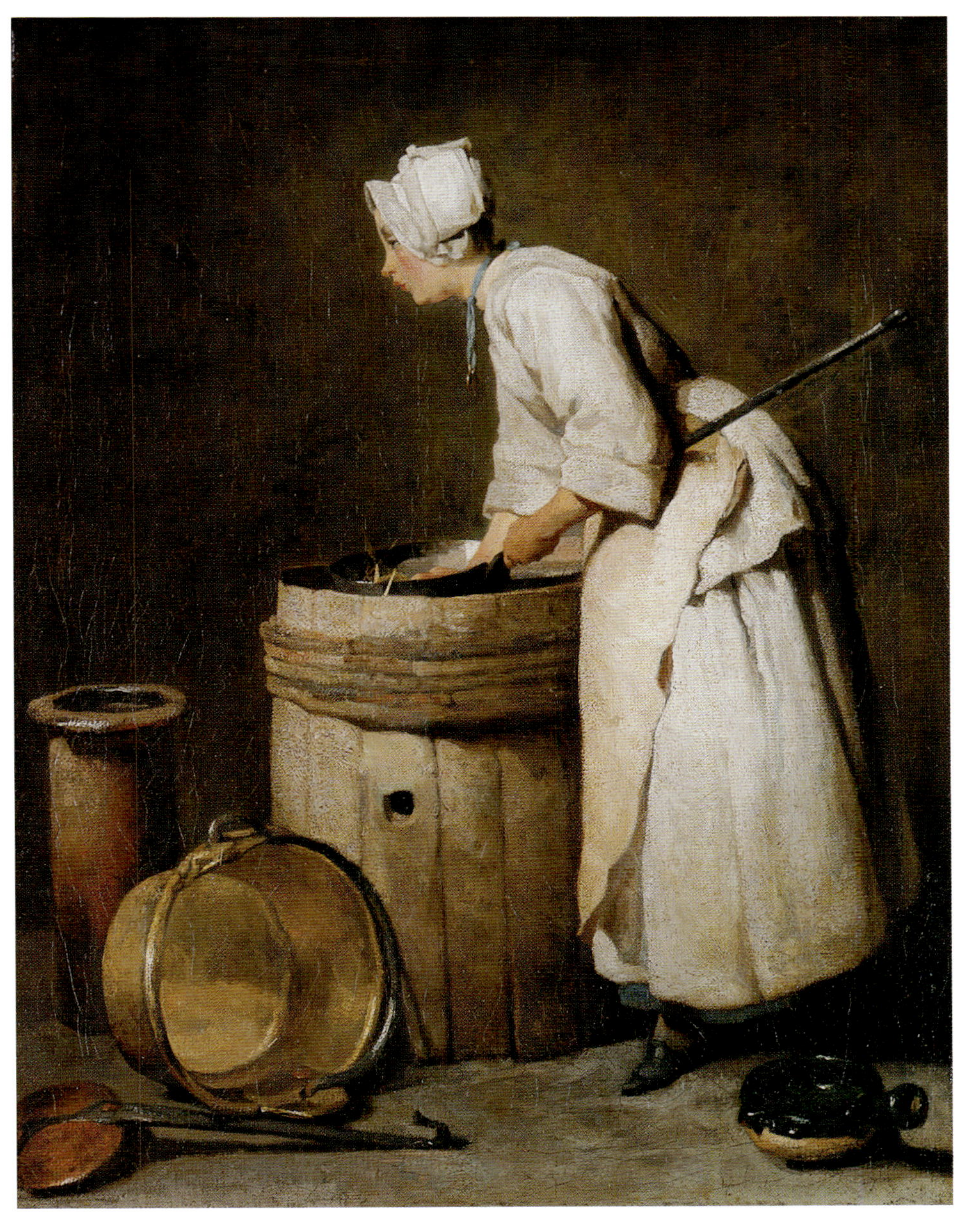

Fig. 25
Jean-Siméon Chardin
The Scullery Maid
Oil on canvas, 45.7 × 36.9 cm
Hunterian Museum and Art Gallery, Glasgow
inv. no. GLAHA 43511

acquainted with French genre painting. The real start of his career as a genre painter is hard to date. His genre scenes may equally well postdate his return to Paris in 1731. Genre in a Dutch style remained a short episode in his œuvre,[16] as opposed to pastoral genre scenes, which became one of his most successful specialties and one that he practised for most of his career. These hardly aim at describing or evoking the real world, and the artist's few genre paintings in the exhibition are major exceptions to this rule.

The strong sense of immediacy created by both Chardin and Boucher following their own different strategies led early on to the identification of

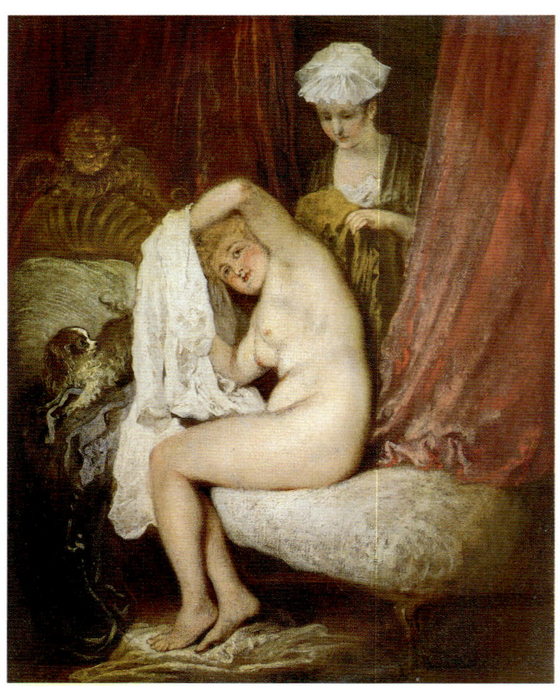

Fig. 26
Antoine Watteau
A Woman at her Toilet
Oil on canvas, 45.2 × 37.9 cm
The Wallace Collection, London
inv. no. P439

the women depicted with the artists' wives (see Anne Dulau's essay). These identifications (or projections) tell us primarily about the success of both painters in creating a scene that is entirely convincing in its private character and immediacy. Chardin brings us close to the woman in the painting and abolishes all devices which might separate us from her. We are on one level with her, close to her, sharing in a very intimate moment of thoughtful absorption. Boucher gives us the feeling of having slipped into the personal space of a woman in a state of usually unobserved disarray, which is carefully staged but entirely conceals the artificiality of its arrangement.

What was the situation in art when these two exceptional works were created? The introduction of genre into the mainstream of French painting was a consequence of the success of Antoine Watteau. However, no more than a few of his paintings show interiors, and they are always the setting for openly erotic scenes: *A Woman at her Toilet* (fig. 26) is a telling example.[17] It was rather Nicolas Lancret, from the painter's immediate circle, who fundamentally modernized and redefined genre painting. While Watteau's art was immensely successful, it was Lancret who made it the basis for a fashionable description of contemporary life, in a way which then had consequences for the further development of French painting. Lancret's contribution was an interest in contemporary reality, which he constantly injected into the dream world of Watteau's *fêtes galantes*, and the development of new ranges of subjects – games and interior scenes – which had not been central to Watteau's concerns. Lancret's *Morning* (*Le Matin*; cat. 6, fig. 27) shows that interior scenes had become important subjects in the immediate Watteau circle, but apparently not under Watteau's direct influence. Lancret took over Watteau's overtly erotic depiction of women in an intimate interior, and transformed it into a representation of contemporary life. If we look for possible models for Chardin's and Boucher's paintings, however, we have to turn elsewhere. Two of Lancret's contemporaries, Charles-Antoine Coypel and Jean-François de Troy, excelled in genre scenes in the early 1730s and seem to anticipate more of what we see in Chardin's and Boucher's works.

Charles-Antoine Coypel staged scenes with an evident anecdotal dimension. His *Young Widow in front of a Mirror* of 1730 (fig. 28) might serve as a good example.[18] Coypel, who for a long time hesitated between becoming a painter or a playwright, created what is obviously a moment in a narrative. The young widow looks at herself in a mirror to assess her beauty. She is about to forget her grief and now poses to titillate the male observer. With Chardin some years later, the same scene – a woman at a table, concentrating on a simple occupation – becomes credible, simple and sincere.

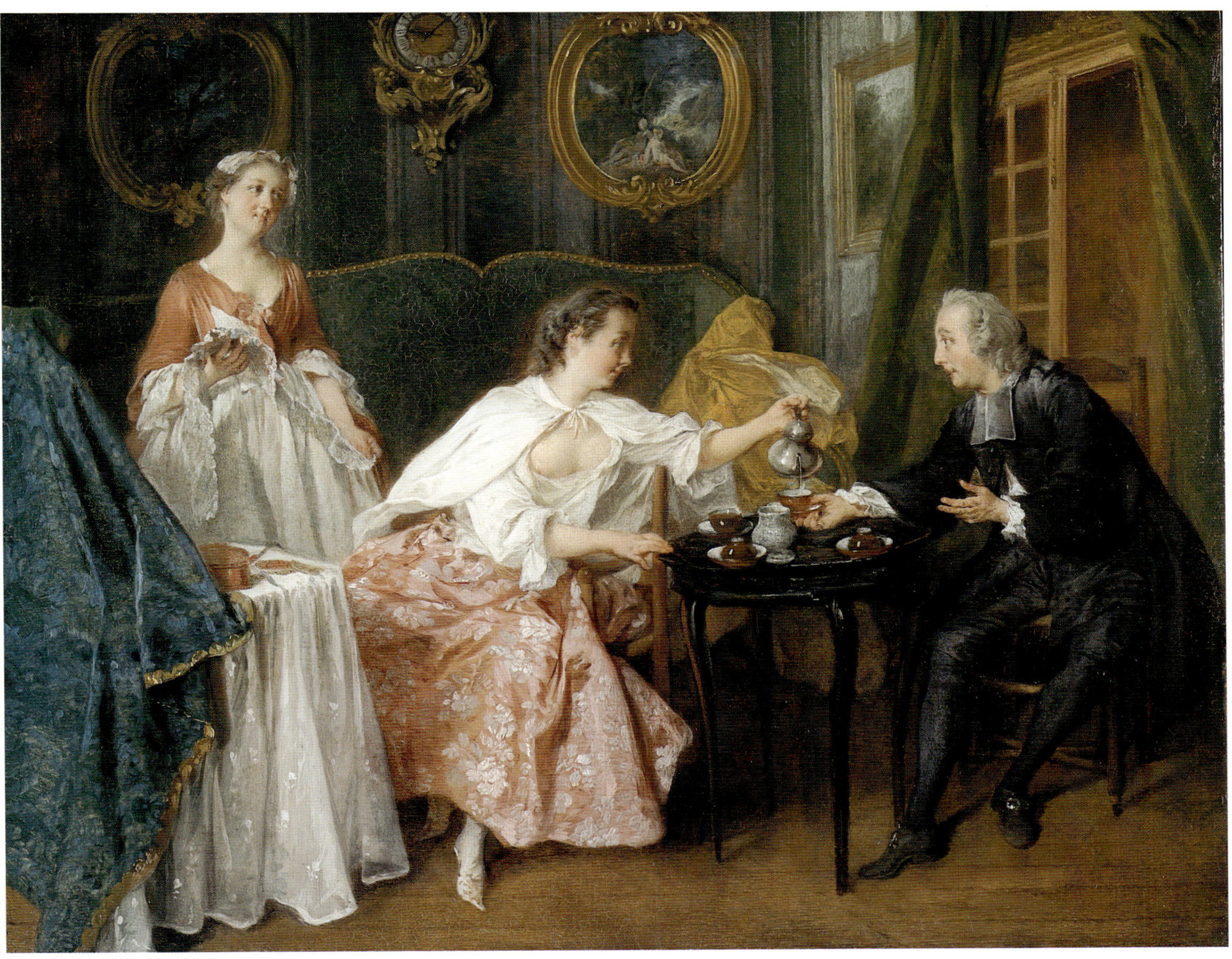

Fig. 27
Nicolas Lancret
The Four Times of Day:
Morning (Le Matin), before 1739
Oil on copper, 28.6 × 36.5 cm
National Gallery, London
inv. no. 5867

The action is not performed for us, but seems to be a product of the very life of the person depicted. Boucher's *Woman on a Daybed* on the other hand is very conscious of being observed. She guards her own space and a considerable distance from the spectator. In fact she rather plays with us, allowing us into her room and keeping us at arm's length. Thus Coypel's importance lies in introducing a depicted female space, a distinctly contemporary interior and the fiction of an unobserved daily routine or situation, which Chardin and Boucher developed into opposite directions.

Another painter of Coypel's generation is even closer in spirit and also considerably predates Boucher's interest in a more intimate female

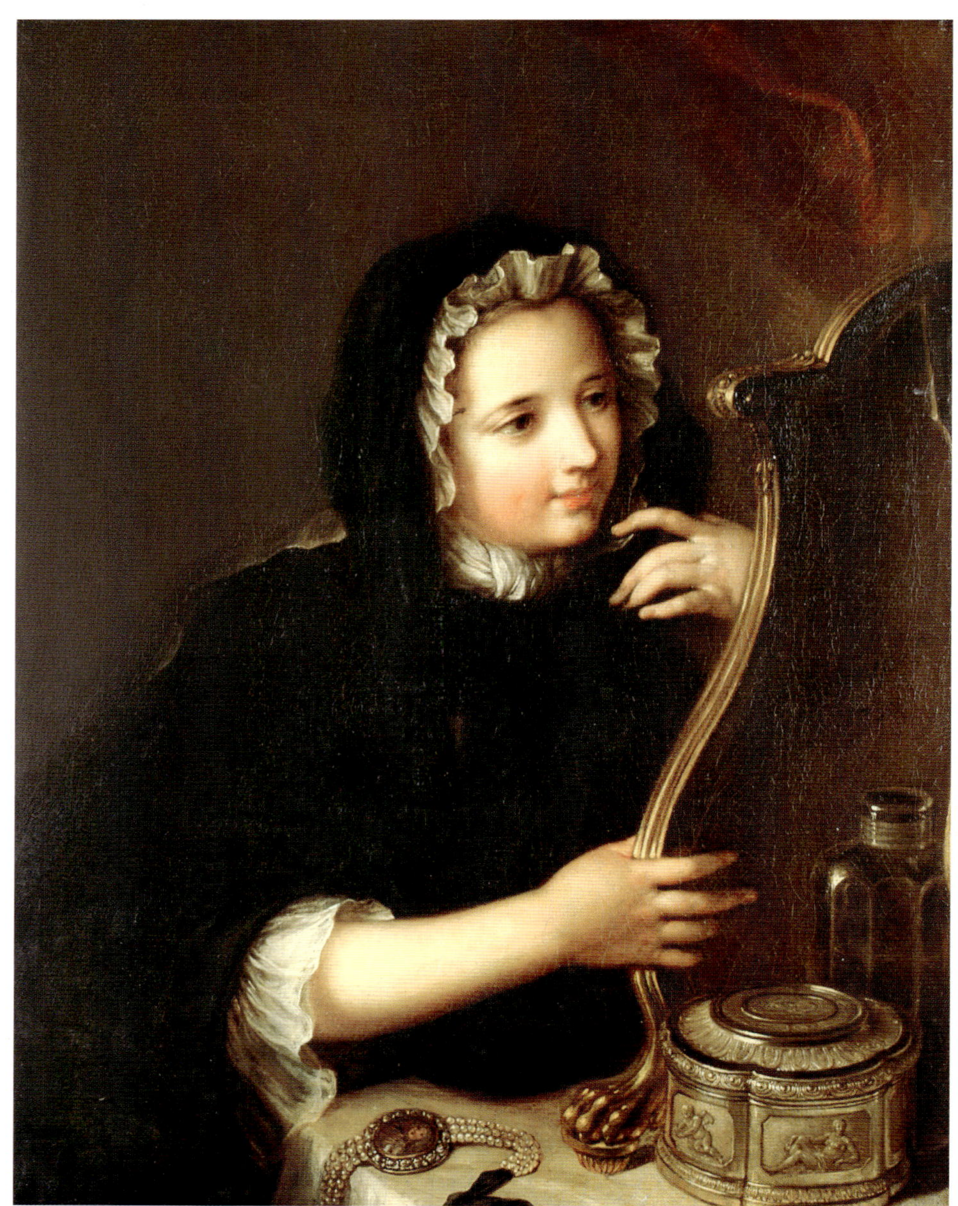

Fig. 28
Charles-Antoine Coypel
Young Widow in front of a Mirror
Oil on canvas, 75 × 63 cm
Schloss Sanssouci, Potsdam
Stiftung Preußische Schlösser und Gärten
Berlin-Brandenburg
inv. no. GK I 5636

facing page
Fig. 29
Jean-François de Troy
Woman taking Coffee
Oil on canvas, 34 × 25 cm
Staatliche Museen zu Berlin,
Gemäldegalerie
inv. no. 469

interior. Jean-François de Troy became widely known for his *tableaux de mode*, genre scenes set in contemporary fashionable interiors (sometimes also in gardens) showing the everyday routines of a wealthy upper class without seriously suggesting a narrative context. De Troy produced a dense series of them between 1724 and 1737, a year before he left Paris to become the new director of the French Academy in Rome.[19] One pair of pendants preceded this sequence, *Woman taking Coffee* in Berlin (fig. 29), dated 1723, and its recently rediscovered pendant, *Woman reading*.[20] The two paintings were in the collection of Jean de Jullienne, the man who had encouraged

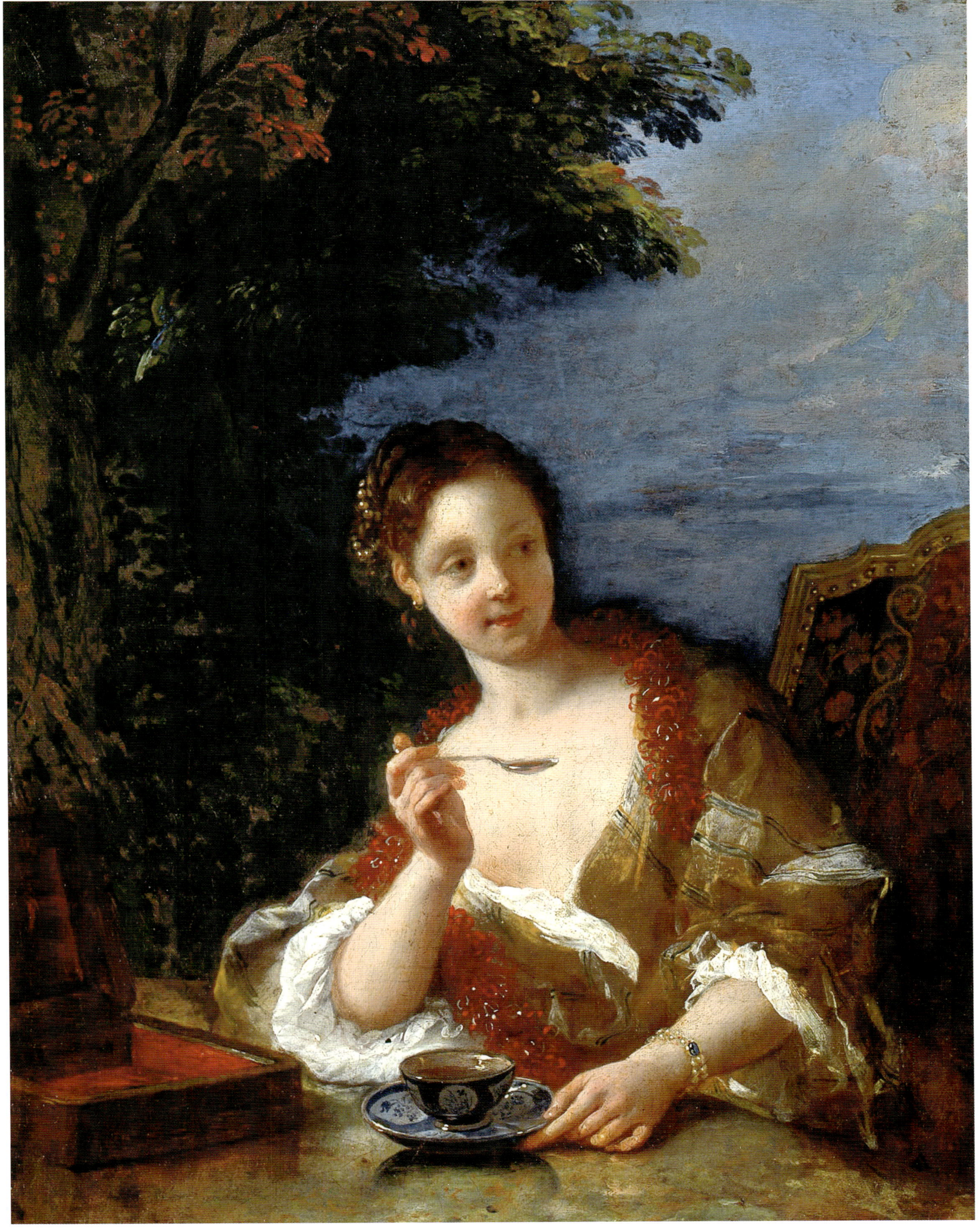

and then profited from the commercial success of Watteau among leading Parisian collectors.

In de Troy's small painting a woman is shown in half-length sitting outside at a table taking coffee. The empty case for the coffee service is visible on the left – a motif which Watteau had used three years earlier in his *Enseigne* (Shopsign) for the dealer Gersaint. With the spoon in her right hand she tastes the coffee in the large blue and white cup. Invitingly she looks at us and has us take part in her enjoyment – about to open a conversation. Her attire is fashionable. A striped yellow dress and a red stole form a brilliant colour contrast. The picture is halfway between an outdoor *fête galante* and a Dutch interior scene, revealing its transitional character, still heavily under the influence of Watteau. De Troy's painting shares its subject with Chardin's painting in Glasgow – a woman at a table, enjoying her hot drink from a cup of blue and white China. The focus on the woman and on the small daily routine is similar, although Chardin gives it a dignity unknown to de Troy, who revels in the attraction of a fashionable pastime. Boucher meanwhile might have taken his depiction of luxurious female leisure from de Troy's paintings, though this was an aspect considerably toned down by Chardin in his earlier painting.

Why did both Chardin and Boucher become interested in genre scenes and why, although their results were so different, did they refer to similar models? Instead of turning to Watteau himself, by then already a little out of date, Chardin had a close look at a younger generation of genre painters using the new fashion for genre initiated by Watteau. All of them were history painters who used genre painting as another field in which to generate custom. It seems that Chardin picked them as role models for his own ascent from still life to figure painting. His experience as a still life painter enabled him to find unique compositional solutions immediately.

Boucher had begun his career etching Watteau's drawings for Jullienne's *Figures de différents caractères de Paysage, et d'Etudes dessinées d'après nature par Antoine Watteau* of 1726 and 1728, a task which had required him to study Watteau's drawings closely for several years. Like Lancret, he aimed to translate Watteau's inventions into a more contemporary language and to avoid the ambiguity that one often finds in Watteau's subject-matter. For this project he looked towards more recent successful models, which provided a formula for up-to-date fashionable indoor scenes. Boucher's training and ambition as a history painter probably motivated these choices. We can easily trace the line from the feminine interior of Boucher's *Woman on a Daybed* back to Lancret and de Troy (who, according to some accounts, had been his teacher). Lancret's *Morning* (*Le Matin*) creates a similar female space, though in a more obviously narrative context. De Troy's so-called

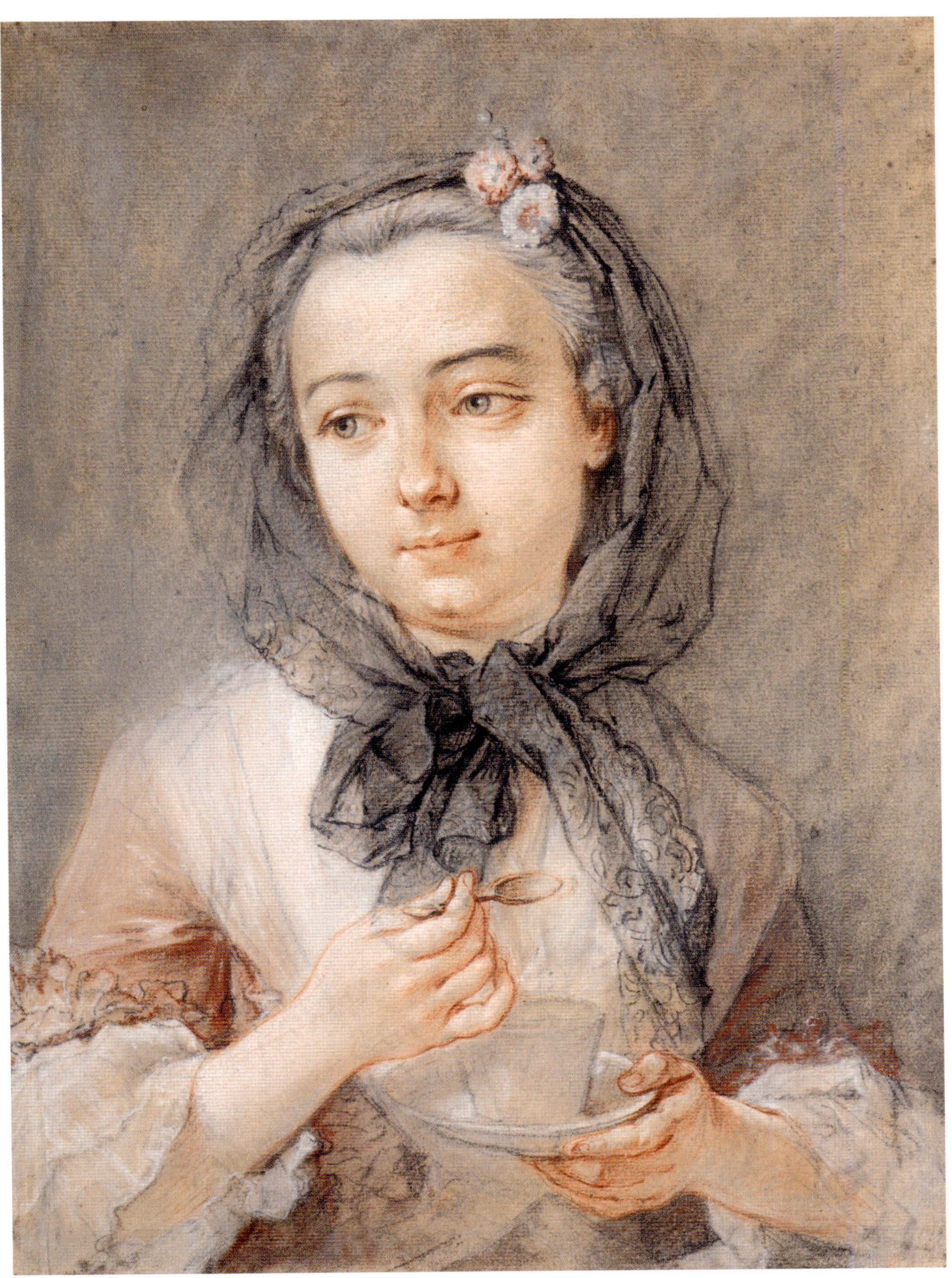

Fig. 30
François Boucher
Charlotta Sparre
Red, black and white chalk on buff paper,
34.3 × 26.5 cm
Day & Faber, London

Reading of Molière (private collection) of 1731 shows a lavish female interior used for an intimate gathering of men and women. Boucher's portrait drawing of Charlotta Sparre of 1740–41 (cat. 7, fig. 30) can serve as an example of the way he also, shortly before he painted his *Woman on a Daybed*, adapted de Troy's formula of *Woman taking Coffee* to a portrait with a strong genre element.[21] The same model could be used both for a portrait and for a genre scene which may or may not be a portrait.

All the paintings discussed so far were created within a theoretical framework which was ill adapted to these kinds of painting, indeed did not allot any prescribed space to genre painting.[22] The system had been formulated with most authority by André Félibien in 1667 and was not officially questioned until much later. History painting was regarded as the summit of the hierarchy, and portrait, landscape, still-life and animal painting were lesser genres or classes of art, but easy to define and describe. What was harder to grasp in theoretical terms was what remained. Terminology often oscillated between "the genres" and "genre". Even writers using the term "genre" usually did not use it in the way we would understand it today, but rather as a catch-all for any class of painting below history painting or for all paintings that could not easily be classified. This academic question was likely to cause problems, because, at least officially, French painting was a highly regulated and structured collective venture.

Since the nineteenth century, the term 'genre painting' has been used more narrowly to indicate scenes of everyday life with anonymous characters. During the lifetimes of Boucher and Chardin, however, it was not easy to describe such a group of works, or even to see them as a well-defined group. As is often the case in art history, the word followed the phenomenon, one which had already long existed without being properly recognized in terminology. Such a theoretical difficulty might seem less than relevant today, but it confronted all genre painters with a serious obstacle to their finding a space in the academic hierarchy. Genre painters could not easily claim the status they wanted and which they might regard as equivalent to their abilities and their public success. While Coypel, de Troy and Boucher defended their positions by primarily staying within history painting, Chardin used genre to climb up the ladder. He had started as a still-life painter who apparently had never received a full training as a history painter, and became successful as a genre painter. These questions had no impact on the critical and economic success of the painters discussed here but it affected their official commissions and position and, more importantly, their ambition.

This problem of terminology is obvious when one looks at the painters who were received in the Paris Academy with works which we would today consider genre paintings.[23] Watteau became a member in 1717 with his *Pélerinage à l'île de Cythère* (Pilgrimage to the Isle of Cythera) as a history painter, as Christian Michel has recently proved.[24] The title of his painting was crossed out in the minutes of the academy and replaced by "*Une feste galante*". Lancret's two reception pieces were simply called "*festes galantes*" in 1719. The sequence continued with François Octavien's *Foire de Bezons* (Fair in Bezons) in 1725. Watteau's more immediate followers were all received as "painters of *fêtes galantes*". This term was descriptive, but did not correspond to a defined academic category. Such terminological problems contrast strangely with the evident flowering of genre painting at the same period.

It is possible to look at this question from a different angle. For it was not by chance that so many of the important French paintings of that age were genre paintings. The theoretical vagueness concerning genre created considerable freedom. While within official prescriptions, genre could become a field for experiment and discussion. This framework, or lack of it, encouraged experimentation with subject-matter and with the borderline between public and private, as seems so striking in Chardin's and Boucher's paintings. It also enabled painters to take a fresh and uninhibited look at related Dutch painting.

Although there were very few precise theoretical statements on genre painting, plenty of examples of it by famous painters existed in Paris. What we today consider genre painting had already begun in the sixteenth century and attained its classic and most influential form in Dutch painting of the seventeenth century. Hundreds of important Dutch and Flemish genre paintings had reached Paris by the 1730s and were eagerly studied by French painters.[25] Flemish and Dutch genre paintings provided the background for all French works of the period. French genre painters were in effect trying to translate an older Dutch phenomenon into a contemporary French idiom. They shared their interest in Dutch genre scenes with contemporary collectors. The creation of de Troy's, Lancret's, Chardin's and Boucher's masterworks coincided with a surge in the collecting of Flemish and Dutch painting in Paris. It first became fully apparent in the immediate environment of Antoine Watteau, in which the comtesse de Verrue became one of the first major collectors of Dutch genre scenes in Paris. This phenomenon soon caused complaints about the neglect of Italian painting and was also blamed for a lack of commissions to French painters. It seemed a logical step for contemporary painters to emulate this successful model and to continue the Dutch tradition in France.

Gerard ter Borch's *Woman reading a Letter* might serve as a good (but random) example for this relationship (fig. 31).[26] It is easy to discover the source for Chardin's early genre scenes in paintings like ter Borch's. Chardin's *Woman sealing a Letter* takes up ter Borch's scheme directly – the position of the figure, the motif of the letter, the personal interior, accessories like the table and the carpet. Chardin at that point was trying to add grandeur to the scene, which was alien to ter Borch, but his starting point is clear. Both show the same interest in a personal and domestic routine, show similar spaces and evoke a settled middle-class life.

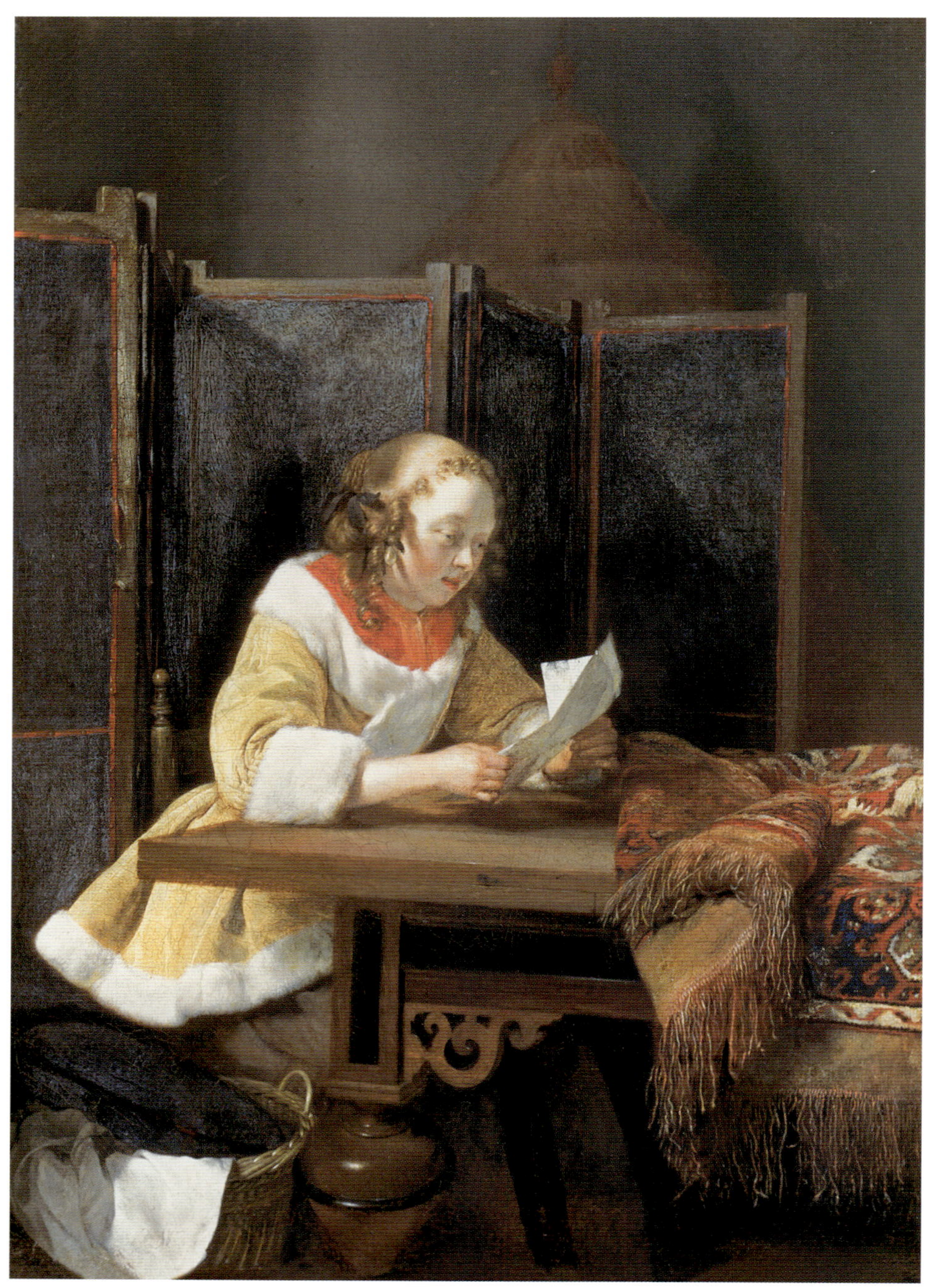

Fig. 31
Gerard ter Borch
Woman reading a Letter
Oil on canvas, 44.2 × 32.2 cm
The Wallace Collection, London
inv. no. P236

The same is true for de Troy. His *Woman reading a Letter* averts her face
from us, but she is shown in a situation similar to ter Borch's main character. Both painters revelled in the richness of surfaces. Like Chardin, de
Troy translated Dutch models into a contemporary French environment,
but he continued the Dutch tendency for meticulously painted surfaces and
for small formats. He also applied the idea of pairing similar subjects. Ter

Borch's *Woman reading a Letter* was in 1757 combined with the painting of a young woman writing.

The parallel between Boucher's *Woman on a Daybed* and Dutch paintings might be less obvious. But it is known that Boucher started out with a strong interest in Dutch art. During his stay in Rome he extensively copied drawings by Abraham Bloemaert, a remarkable choice of model for a young artist making his first steps on classical ground.[27] In his early work Dutch motifs constitute a major thread. Paintings like *La Belle Cuisinière* (*The Beautiful Kitchen-maid*; fig. 32) of 1733–34 (the moment when Chardin turned to genre) are a direct translation of a Dutch genre scene into a modern French context. Boucher also continued the emblematic aspects of Dutch art.[28] A profound transformation had meanwhile taken place in his oeuvre and his Dutch models had been seamlessly translated into a contemporary French idiom. In *Woman on a Daybed* the Dutch inspiration can still be felt – the importance of the interior and of the daily routine, the seemingly unobserved scene, its immediacy, its narrative and picturesque elements.

French genre painting after the death of Antoine Watteau constituted an impressive laboratory of artistic creativity. It produced highly personal solutions by some of the greatest artists of their day. In most cases genre painting was a more or less subsidiary element of their production. Only Nicolas Lancret and – after 1733 – Jean-Siméon Chardin could qualify as primarily genre painters. Chardin learned from Watteau systematically to avoid an obvious narrative, but created scenes instead which seem to lack any action because of the profound absorption they express. This strategy created a fascination and mystery which have given his painting an enduring attraction. It was Chardin who uncovered the domestic scene as the ideal mirror of contemporary longings, projections and morals – and as a stage for middle-class psychology. He remained a strangely isolated figure but the consequences of his work go far beyond the limits of the eighteenth century. A little later, Greuze continued this stance and created genre painting with a moral message more overt than Chardin's. Greuze radically but unsuccessfully challenged the dividing line between history painting and genre.

These brilliant works of art and highly personal approaches were all rooted in the tradition of Dutch genre painting. French painters were often asked to confront these models directly. We know of numerous cases in which artists were commissioned to paint pendants to existing Dutch works.[29] Quite often they also 'improved' existing seventeenth-century works. A rare example of this once common practice survives in the Wallace Collection (fig. 33).[30] Here we can see a dynamic in both directions. While

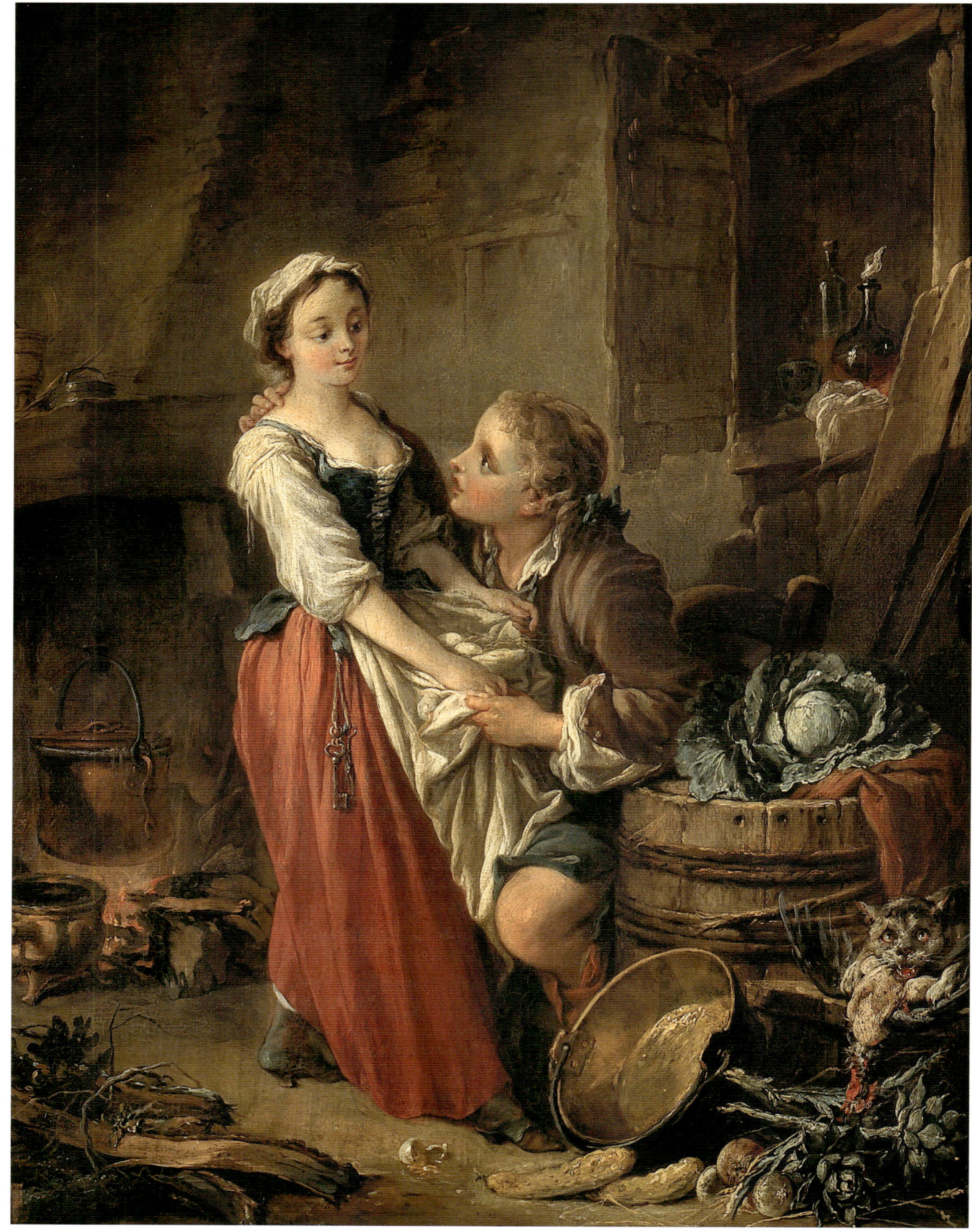

Fig. 32
François Boucher,
*The Beautiful
Kitchen-maid*
(*La Belle Cuisinière*)
Oil on panel,
55.5 × 43.2 cm
Musée Cognacq-
Jay, Paris
inv. no. 13

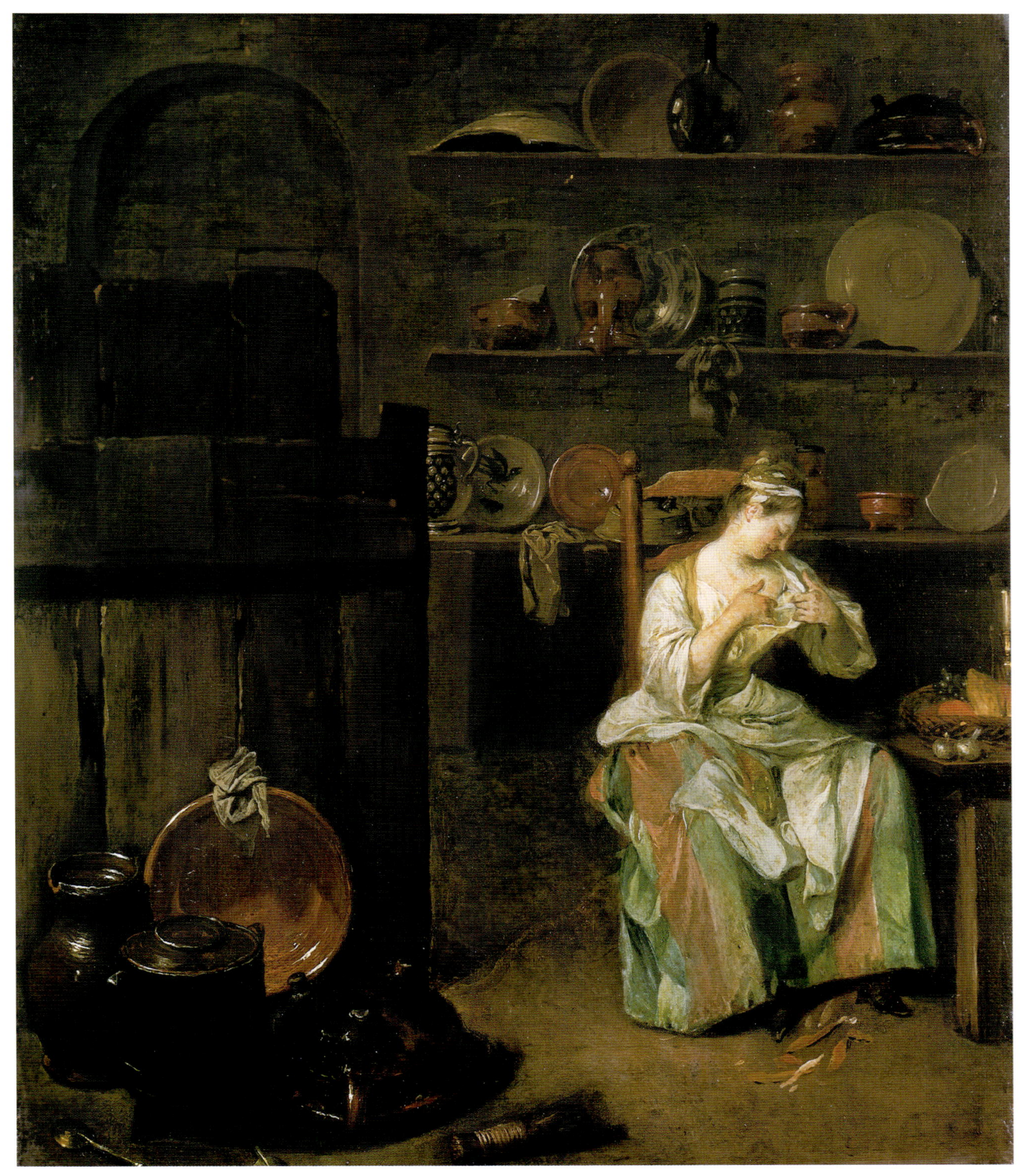

Fig. 33 Nicolas Lancret and a Dutch painter of the 17th century
A Woman in a Kitchen
Oil on oak panel, 29.7 × 25.5 cm
The Wallace Collection, London
inv. no. P378

Dutch works were promoted and presented as models and inspiration for French painters, they also occasionally needed embellishment and modernization. It remains an open question whether the new interest in genre painting in France was first initiated by artists or by a new class of collectors. Even if we cannot be sure how it started, we do know that it fundamentally changed the course of French painting in the eighteenth century.

1 Recent accounts of French genre painting include: Conisbee 1981, pp. 143–70; Ottawa, Washington and Berlin 2003–04, in particular Colin Bailey's introduction, 'Surveying Genre in Eighteenth-Century French Painting', pp. 2–39; and, most recently, Conisbee (ed.) 2007.

2 On Watteau and the *fêtes galantes* see most recently Valenciennes 2004.

3 On Chardin see Paris, Cleveland and Boston 1979; Paris, Düsseldorf, London and New York 1999–2000; Karlsruhe 1999. The best introduction to his work is still Conisbee 1986.

4 Carritt 1974; Kemp 1976; Kemp 1978, pp. 22–23; Michael Baxandall, *Patterns of Intention. On the Historical Explanation of Pictures*, New Haven and London 1985, pp. 74–104; Paris, Düsseldorf, London and New York, 1999–2000, pp. 216–17. Chardin's painting is dated by an inscription on its verso.

5 Rosenberg's assumption (Paris, Düsseldorf, London and New York, 1999–2000, pp. 216–17) that this can be explained by Chardin's lack of experience seems unlikely. As a still-life painter he should have been able to master these parts of the painting much more easily than the faultlessly rendered figure of the woman. Michael Baxandall's interpretation of the work as a conscious pictorial *mise-en-scène* seems more convincing (Baxandall 1985, pp. 74–104).

6 As discussed further in the text, the evidence for Chardin's beginnings as a genre painter is confusing. Cochin and Mariette mention different works as Chardin's first figure painting. The *Soap Bubbles* (*Les Bouteilles de savon*) of Mariette's account exists in three versions, but none of them is early. The *Woman sealing a Letter* in Berlin and *Woman drawing Water at a Cistern* (*La Fontaine*) in Stockholm are Chardin's earliest dated genre paintings, which seems to support Cochin's account. At the same time, *Woman sealing a Letter* in Berlin shows a particularly large number of important *pentimenti*, and, from an art historical perspective, seems more likely than the Stockholm painting to be Chardin's first figure painting: it is the most logical starting-point for the artist's further development. On Chardin's beginnings as a genre painter see most recently Christoph Martin Vogtherr, 'Jean-Siméon Chardins "Briefsieglerin". Ein Schlüsselwerk der französischen Genremalerei im 18. Jahrhundert', in Berlin 2003–04, pp. 9–43.

7 Marianne Roland Michel, '"Die Seele und die Augen" – "Die Ausführung und die Idee". Chardin und die Gattungen der Malerei', in Karlsruhe 1999, pp. 13–22.

8 On the painting in Stockholm see Paris, Cleveland and Boston 1979, pp. 195–98, and, most recently, Roger de Robelin, 'Chardin and Tessin. Still Life with Leeks and Casserole – a new acquisition with an unknown history', *Art Bulletin of Nationalmuseum Stockholm*, vol. 13, 2006, pp. 75–84. On the Aved portrait see Paris, Cleveland, Boston 1999, pp. 210–13; Paris, Düsseldorf, London and New York 1999–2000, pp. 212–13. On the Berlin painting see the preceding footnote.

9 Cochin 1780, pp. 417–41, 436–37: "*Jusque vers 1737, il [Chardin] n'avoit point tenté de tableaux de figures. Le fait qui le détermina à en essayer est assez singulier. M. Aved, peintre de portraits, étoit fort son ami. Il prenoit souvent des avis de M. Chardin, et s'en trouvoit bien. Cependant,*

un jour que M. Chardin, par ses réflexions, le seroit de près, M. Aved lui dit avec vivacité: "Tu t'imagines que cela est aussi aisé à peindre que des langues fourrées et des cervelas!" M. Chardin fut extrêmement piqué de cette repartie. Cependant, il se contint et n'en témoigna rien dans ce moment. Mais dès le lendemain il entreprit un tableau de figures: c'étoit celui d'une servante qui tire de l'eau à une fontaine." Cochin probably gave the year of the first Salon at which Chardin exhibited genre paintings, although the painter had already shown genre paintings at the *Exposition de la jeunesse* in 1734.

10 Pierre-Jean Mariette, 'Chardin', *Abecedario de P.J. Mariette et autres notes inédites de cet amateur sur les arts et les artistes*, vol. 1 (Archives de l'art français 2), Paris 1851–53, pp. 355–69, 357–58.

11 *Soap Bubbles by Jean-Siméon Chardin* (Masterpiece in Focus), Los Angeles County Museum of Art, Los Angeles, 1990; Paris, Düsseldorf, London and New York 1999–2000, pp. 208–11.

12 See further Berlin 2003–04.

13 Los Angeles 1990; Berlin 2003–04. Once, earlier in his life, Chardin had already ventured into what we would today call genre painting, when he painted a shopsign in the form of an overdoor (*plafond*) for a surgeon in Paris. Cochin relates its story and recounts the immense success of the work. Another early shopsign by Chardin is known today: see Jacques Wilhelm, '"La partie de billard" est-elle une œuvre de jeunesse de Chardin?', *Bulletin du Musée Carnavalet*, vol. 22, June 1969, pp. 7–13; Ottawa, Washington and Berlin 2003–04, pp. 178–79 (as an original by Chardin). It is more likely, though, that the painting in the Musée Carnavalet is an old copy.

14 See footnote 4. The evidence is not entirely conclusive that both paintings were originally intended as pendants. However, later in his life Chardin is known to have formed different sets of pendants from a stock of compositions.

15 See, most recently, Ottawa, Washington and Berlin 2003–04, pp. 224–25.

16 Dijon and London 2004–05; Hedley 2004, pp. 26–34.

17 Donald Posner, *Watteau: A Lady at her Toilet* (Art in Context), London 1973.

18 Thierry Lefrançois, *Charles Coypel. Peintre du roi (1694–1752)*, Paris, 1994, pp. 231–32.

19 Christophe Leribault, *Jean-François de Troy (1679–1752)*, Paris, 2002, pp. 58–77.

20 *Ibid.*, pp. 264–65.

21 The drawing was acquired by Count Carl Gustav Tessin from Boucher in Paris in April 1741.

22 The best discussion of the terminology of genre painting is Gaehtgens 2002. An English summary was published as: 'The Theory of French Genre painting and Its European Context', in Ottawa, Washington and Berlin 2003–04, pp. 40–59.

23 Martin Eidelberg, 'Watteau, peintre de fêtes galantes', in Valenciennes 2004, pp. 16–27; Colin Bailey, 'Surveying Genre', in Ottawa, Washington and Berlin 2003–04.

24 Christian Michel, *Le célèbre Watteau*, La bibliothèque des lumières, Geneva, 2007.

25 Colin B. Bailey, *Patriotic Taste. Collecting Modern Art in Pre-Revolutionary Paris*, New Haven and London 2002, pp. 18–20. See most recently (with earlier literature) Hans J. van Migroet, 'The Market for Netherlandish Paintings in Paris, 1750–1815', in Jeremy Warren and Adriana Turpin (eds.), *Auctions, Agents and Dealers. The Mechanisms of the Art Market 1660–1830*, Oxford, 2007, pp. 41–51. A case study on Teniers is Margret Klinge, '"Chardin le Teniers Français". Genrebilder von David Teniers d.J. in Pariser Sammlungen 1700–1750', in Karlsruhe 1999, pp. 57–65.

26 John Ingamells, *The Wallace Collection Catalogue of Pictures IV: Dutch and Flemish*, London 1992, pp. 40–42; Sturla J. Gudlaugsson, *Geraert ter Borch*, 2 vols., The Hague 1959, II, pp. 173–74;

Dublin and Greenwich 2003, p. 19 and *passim*. The painting was in the collection of Blondel de Gagny in Paris by 1757. It might thus also serve as an example of French collectors' taste for this type of Dutch genre painting, although it is documented slightly too late to have served as a model for any of the works discussed here.

27 Regina Shoolman Slatkin, 'Abraham Bloemaert and François Boucher: Affinity and Relationship', *Master Drawings*, autumn 1976, pp. 247–60; Françoise Joulie in Dijon and London 2004–05, pp. 42–58.

28 See Bailey 2006 .

29 Bailey 2002, pp. 3–4.

30 John Ingamells, *The Wallace Collection Catalogue of Pictures III. French before 1815*, London 1989, pp. 219–20. The attribution of the original Dutch painting remains problematic. The name of Willem Kalf has been suggested.

Tea à la Mode: The Fashion for Tea and the Tea Equipage in London and Paris

ANN EATWELL

"As the tea begins to come into use with some people, we expect some jars of Chinese as well as Japanese tea with all ships": 2 January 1637.[1]

Tea arrived in Europe before coffee but after chocolate, as a consequence of the growing trade with China and other Asian countries. Originally driven by demand for imported luxurious and exotic goods like silk, porcelain and lacquer, tea had become proportionally and by value the most important such commodity by the middle of the eighteenth century. It has been estimated that on average tea constituted 70% of the total purchase of the Dutch East India Company between 1729 and 1793.[2] Tea drinking also required new equipment for its storing, making and serving. It was to China and Japan that Europe first looked to supply these utensils. The paraphernalia of tea and the social customs and ceremony surrounding tea drinking began to be celebrated, romanticized and sometimes caricatured in paintings, drawings, plays and poems. Chardin and Boucher's paintings can be seen as part of this European response to the influence of tea drinking in social intercourse, in personal aspiration, and in the growth and display of possessions.

Tea is made from the young leaves and unopened leaf buds of a number of varieties of the Chinese plant *camelia sinensis,* grown in China and in Japan (fig. 34) and later also elsewhere. The three main categories of tea are black, green and oolong. The difference between these three types lies in the extent to which the leaves are allowed to ferment or oxidize.[3] Travellers had brought the first news of tea in the early seventeenth century but it received little attention, being noted only as a herbal remedy. Jesuits and priests sent on missionary duty were an important source of information. The Italian Jesuit Matteo Ricci was the first to describe how tea was made and to distinguish between the steeping or infusing method, used in China from the sixteenth century, and the whipped, powdered tea

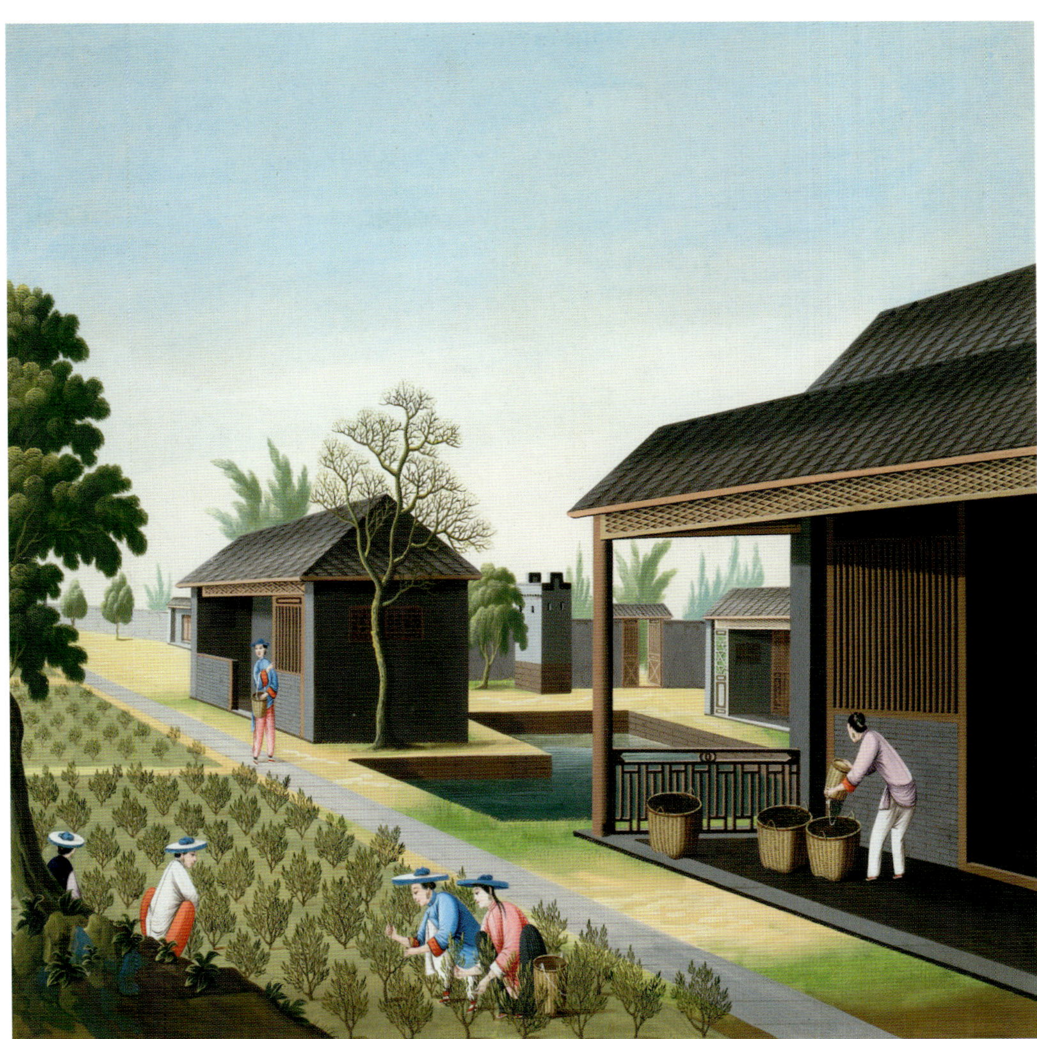

Fig. 34
Unknown artist, Guangzhou, China
Picking tea leaves, c. 1800
Watercolour and ink on paper, 40 × 54 cm
Victoria and Albert Museum, London
inv. no. D. 349-1894

preferred in Japan. Tea drinking in the East was recognized to be a social event rather than a medical prescription. Its bitterness and the hot water used to make it would have struck Europeans as novel, since cold beers, ale and wine were the most common drinks among them. Possets and herbal drinks such as myrtle tea were drunk hot, being taken for their health-giving properties, so it is not surprising that tea was initially promoted as a medicinal herb. Its bitterness may have been one reason why it was not considered a product worthy of trade for many years after it came to European attention, while lack of information about the making of the drink and suspicion concerning a country and a people insufficiently understood in the West may have been contributing factors.

The year 1610 is generally accepted as the date of the first occasion that the Dutch imported tea into Europe. It was from Holland that tea came to England, although France may have first tasted tea through returning Jesuit missionaries.[4] From 1637 the Dutch began a small commercial trade in tea

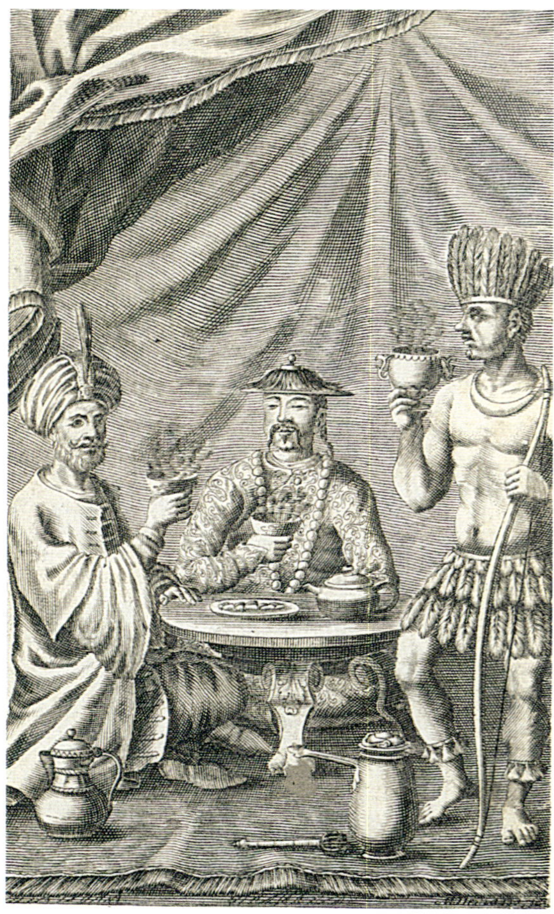

Fig. 35
A Chinaman, Turk and American Indian,
frontispiece from Philippe Sylvestre Dufour,
*Traitez Nouveaux et Curieux du café, du thé, du
Chocolat,* Lyons, 1685
Special Collections, University of Glasgow
Library
Sp Coll Hunterian BG59f-14

and were the source of the first regular supplies in England and France. Apothecaries were among the first vendors, selling tea by the ounce along with sugar, ginger and other spices. The trade must have been very small for a number of years, for the tea was very costly. In 1653 the Jesuit missionary Alexandre de Rhodes stated: "The Dutch bring tea from China to Paris and sell it at thirty francs a pound, though they have paid but eight and ten sous in that country, and it is old and spoiled into the bargain. People must regard it as a precious medicament; it not only does positively cure nervous headache, but it is a sovereign remedy for gravel and gout."[5]

There is some evidence that tea may have found its way to Paris before London.[6] Fierce debate about the efficacy of tea raged in French medical circles in the 1640s and 1650s. This did not stop some very influential statesmen developing a taste for tea. Cardinal Mazarin may have been inspired by Rhodes to use it for his gout, and a treatise on tea was dedicated to Chancellor Séguier in 1657. By 1659 tea had been accepted to such an extent that Dr Denis Jonquet appears to have voiced the general sentiment of the medical profession in Paris in calling tea a "divine" drink.[7]

In England, tea had been available for a number of years before the fashion-conscious and inquisitive Pepys recorded in his diary for 25 September 1660: "I did send for a cup of tee (a China drink), of which I never drank before."[8] In the same year tea had come to the attention of the government, along with coffee, sherbet and chocolate, and a duty of 18d was imposed on every gallon of tea. This tax presupposes a usage which would give an income worth collecting.

Though the medical effects of tea were the subject of a large number of contradictory tracts over the next hundred years, tea very quickly assumed a role in everyday life beyond that of a herbal remedy, particularly in Holland and England and also, though to a lesser degree, in France between 1660 and 1700. As the natural philosopher Margaret Cavendish, Duchess of Newcastle, explained in 1666: "... but I observe; that these latter drinks tea and coffee, are now become mode drinks, and their chief effects are to make good fellowship, rather than to perform great cures: for I can hardly believe, that such weak liquors, can have such strong effects".[9]

Tea was fashionable and this explains Pepys's desire to taste it only a few years before. A number of factors explain the swift uptake of the drink in London and Paris. Novelty was a strong incentive, of course, but the addition of sugar, making the drink more palatable, made a significant impact. The early manuals on the new hot drinks all advise adding sugar; many of these, including the first devoted to the subject, by Philippe Sylvestre Dufour in 1671, were written in France (cat. 24, fig. 35). Dr Duncan of Montpellier, writing in 1706, deplored the way sugar had increased the popularity of

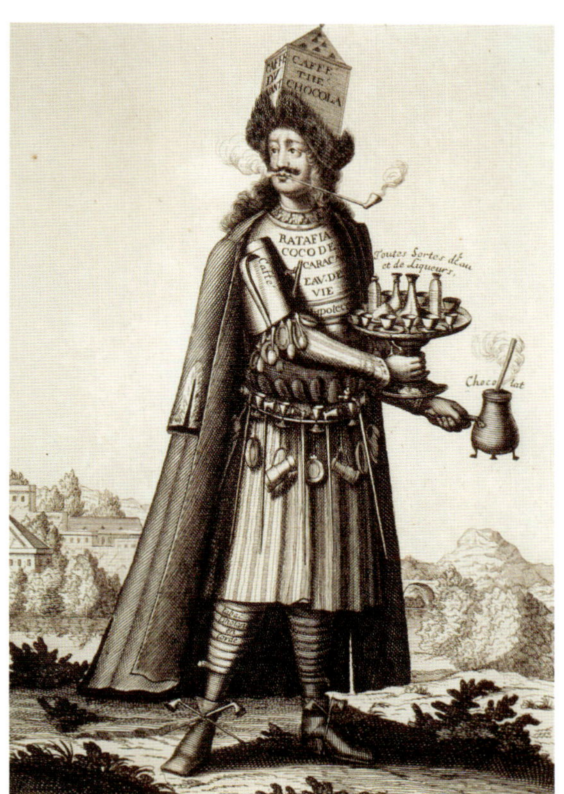

Fig. 36
Nicolas de Larmessin
Habit de Caffetier (Coffee seller costume),
c. 1690
Etching
Bibliothèque nationale, Paris
inv. no. Bnf OA 60 PET FOL

the drinks: "… coffee, chocolate and tea were at first us'd only as medicines while they continued unpleasant, but since they were made delicious with sugar, they are become poison".[10]

The lead of the courts of Charles II and of William and Mary, all of which may have experienced the passion for tea in Flanders and Holland, may have spurred emulation in England.[11] The first commercial import, of $143^1/_2$ pounds of tea by the East India Company, came to England in 1669, and from this date the Dutch domination of the tea trade diminished.[12] The market for tea in Europe was still small, however, and 4,713 *livres* imported by the English East India Company in 1678 reportedly created a surplus.[13] In France, all three hot drinks were fashionable at the court of Louis XIV. Saint-Simon's memoirs record that after dinner with the King, "*On était auprès de plusieurs cabarets de thé et de café ; en prenait qui voulait*" (There were several sideboards with tea and coffee nearby; those who wanted took them).[14]

Although Saint-Simon specifically states that Louis XIV did not drink tea, coffee or chocolate, as he preferred wine and flavoured waters such as orange flower, the ladies of the court took up the drinks with enthusiasm. The letters of Mme de Sévigné hold numerous references to tea drinking from 1673. She discusses how to make tea, praises its good effects and names some other ladies who regularly use tea. Writing to her daughter on 4 October 1684 she mentions Amélie, princess de Tarente, daughter of William, Landgrave of Hesse Kassel: "Every day she drinks fourteen or fifteen large dishes of tea; she prepares it as we do; first letting the leaves infuse, and then filling the cup half-full of boiling water: she says it has been the panacea of all her disorders; and she very gravely assured me, that the Landgrave, her nephew, drank forty dishes every morning".[15]

Parisian fashion prints portray women of the court drinking hot drinks. Sometimes the drinks are identified in the titles but more often it was enough to show that they were hot. Emulation of the court and wealthier citizens was a spur to tea drinking. The new hot drinks were being offered by street sellers in London and Paris (fig. 36), and this was one way in which they penetrated to all levels of society. Tea drinking amongst the poorer classes was probably associated with work.[16] Servants in England, for example, received part of their wages in tea by the early 1700s.

The wide dissemination of tea drinking in England has been attributed by some authors to the arrival of the coffee house: the first in London opened in 1652.[17] By 1657, Thomas Garway (or Garraway) was selling tea as well as coffee and chocolate. These establishments, which were largely male-orientated, numbered more than 550 by 1739.[18] The first Parisian coffee house or *café* opened later, in 1672. After a slow start, the exotic connotations of the hot drinks sold there helped create for them a unique identity. In 1698 an English traveller to Paris, Martin Lister, confirmed the availability of tea in *cafés*: "There are also very many publick coffee houses where tea also and chocolate may be had and all the strong waters and wine above mentioned".[19] By 1716 there were three hundred in Paris and over a thousand by 1789. Parisian *cafés* were resorts for the middle and upper classes of society. The furnishings were often lavish, including chandeliers, mirrors and silver and porcelain vessels.

This does not explain why in England *the* drink to be drunk in the home was tea whereas in France, by the early eighteenth century, it had become coffee. It was the huge surge of demand from families drinking tea at home in England which turned a fashionable drink amongst the few to a daily necessity for all levels of society. Here the choice of women may have been crucial.[20]

Tea was a pleasant, non-alcoholic alternative to wine and beer, and could be enjoyed in mixed company without the indelicacy of inebriation. It very quickly became associated with women. In *The Baccanalian Sessions: or The Contention of Liquors*, a poem written by Richard Ames in 1693, various drinks present their merits to Bacchus: "The next that attempted to put in his Plea, Was a Drink much admir'd by the Ladies, call'd Tea". English plays from the 1660s confirm the importance of tea in home life. "Come, come, man, you must e'en fall to visiting our wives, eating at our tables, drinking tea with our virtuous relations after dinner, dealing cards to 'em."[21]

In the seventeenth century wealthy English women were avid consumers of exotic goods sold in 'India houses'. Silks and porcelains but also tea could be purchased from them and evidence suggests that it was drunk in them.[22] Since Queen Mary was said to have visited an India house these establishments must have been respectable enough to allow women, before the opening of specialist tea shops in the eighteenth century, to sample tea and buy it for home consumption. Tea had been for sale from coffee houses since the 1650s, but these were almost entirely the domain of men. At India houses, apothecaries and later grocers and China warehouses women could buy tea for consumption at home.

Tea must have had a broader appeal in England than in France from the late seventeenth century. Although manuals devoted to the hot drinks were largely translated from French or Dutch, English playwrights and poets mention tea far more than their Contintental counterparts, suggesting that it was available to and important to more levels of society in England. It is interesting that Molière does not mention tea in his social comedies but, when his plays were translated for performance in England, tea-drinking scenes were added. The comparative absence of tea from

French texts may be explained by two quotations from the early eighteenth century. In 1710 Charles Cotolendi wrote: "For the rest, chocolate, tea and coffee are extremely fashionable, but coffee is preferred to the other two; it is said to be a sovereign remedy for low spirits".[23] In the 1727 edition of Furetière's *Dictionnaire Universel* it is stated under the heading for tea: "The use of this drink has become so common in Europe, above all in England and Holland, that, proportionally, its consumption by the English and Dutch is hardly less than the Orient's. In France coffee seems to have prevailed over tea."[24] Compare this with J. Ovington's opinion of tea drinking in England in the first English book devoted to the subject written in 1699: "And since the drinking of it has of late obtain'd here so universally, as to be affected by the scholar and the tradesman, to become both a private regale at court and to be made use of in places of public entertainment, which has greatly raised the character and gained it a singular repute …".[25]

There is no doubt that in eighteenth-century England tea became the centre of domestic ritual and a staple of the British diet. The size of the market can be seen in the tea imports. The facts and figures concerning the tea trade are notoriously contradictory, but the records of Flemish merchants may be taken as indicative of the wider picture of tea imports in Europe.[26] From 1719 to 1728, 41% of tea was sold to London, 41% to Ostend and Bruges, 13% to Amsterdam and 3.4% to France. Much tea brought to France was then smuggled into England at a great profit, so the import percentage does not truly represent the usage in France. From the 1720s the competition between the European trading companies led to a significant fall in the price of tea, but it was still a comparatively expensive commodity until the tax was cut in 1784.

It has been argued that tea drinking in France was restricted not only by the high cost of tea but also by the cost of the equipment. Research into French and English inventories has shown that, while the English were able to acquire luxury goods, such as table services in Chinese or Delft ceramics in the late seventeenth century, such items only appear in similar French households in the second half of the eighteenth century.[27]

Research by Annick Pardailhé-Galabrun into probate inventories in Paris over the period 1640–1790 has helped to build up an understanding of ownership. Ceramics were not common in Parisian households until after 1720: the earliest mention of Oriental porcelain is a tea service in Japanese porcelain in the house of a canon in 1720. By 1750, however, even modest households owned substantial amounts. The range of ceramic goods, from plates to sugar bowls, egg cups and saucers, became more diverse. In 1750 the painter Louis Boucher (d. 1750) owned 24 pieces of earthenware. His more famous namesake François owned more than thirty porcelain tea

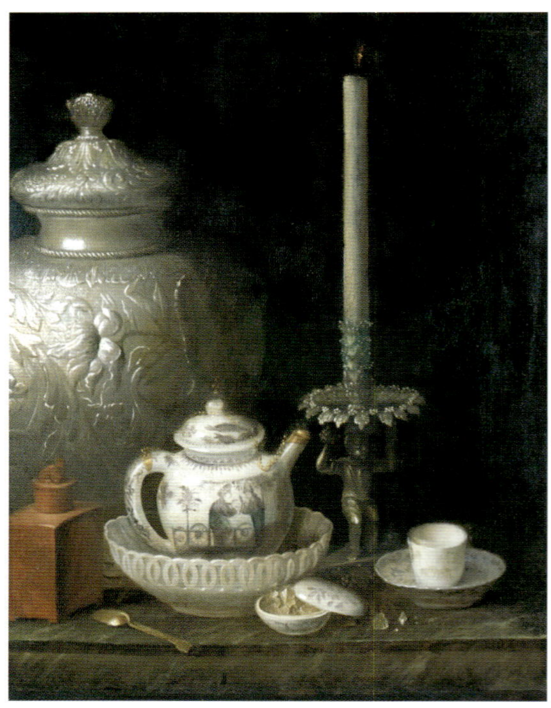

Fig. 37
Artist working in the style of
Pieter van Roestraten
Still life with teapot, silver jar and
candlestick, c. 1650–80
Oil on canvas, 68.6 × 54.5 cm
Victoria and Albert Museum, London
inv. no. P.2-1939

pots and twice as many teacups, as well as vases and pagodas. Services were still rare and found only in the wealthiest households, where several services might be stored in closets. In less wealthy homes the ceramics, such as teacups and coffee equipment, were displayed on mantelpieces. This had been the case much earlier in England. Seen from this perspective of ownership, based on inventory evidence, the comparative affluence of English families is marked.

Such was the cost of silver teapots, as of coffee pots, that, if found at all, they were often in the same households.[28] Porcelain teacups were also rare, owned only by the wealthy. In one of the richer parishes of Paris only 10% of households owned a teapot, whereas up to 37% might own a coffeepot. Pardailhé-Galabrun concluded that chocolate and tea remained expensive goods throughout the eighteenth century, used at home by comparatively few families.[29]

Pardailhé-Galabrun's argument presupposes that families needed or used teapots to make tea. An intriguing possibility is that this was not the case, so that tea usage may have been greater than the inventories suggest. In several editions of *L'Ecole parfaite des officiers de bouche* from 1715 to 1737, under the heading *Comment préparer le thé*, there is an instruction to make tea in a *caffetière*: "Take a pint of water, boil it in a *caffetière* …".[30] Tea can also be made by infusing the leaves in a cup – a method used in China to this day. Tea was drunk very much weaker than today and the French added more boiling water to the brewed tea.

However, even if these methods were used in France to make tea at home there is little evidence in the inventories of the storage of tea, and the smaller quantity of tea imported and its consequent higher price must presuppose that it was drunk in fewer homes than in England. Probate inventories in London show that tea utensils in the home outnumbered those of coffee by two to one in the period 1700 to 1730.[31]

The new equipment for tea drinking came initially from China and Japan. Oriental porcelains and red stonewares were at first viewed as costly and exotic objects in their own right and portrayed alongside expensive silver and sugar in Dutch still-life paintings of the late seventeenth century. (fig. 37). The most significant trade items were cups (tea bowls), saucers and plates.[32] There was no imperative in the eighteenth century that a tea set should be of identical pattern and material.[33] In England and France silver was the material of highest status but its ready conduction of heat made it unsuitable for tea bowls. Instead, it was used for the core utensils of the tea service – the teapot, milk jug, sugar bowl and tea kettle. Silver was especially valued in England for the status that it conferred, for its capability to be refashioned and as an instantly convertible reserve of wealth.[34]

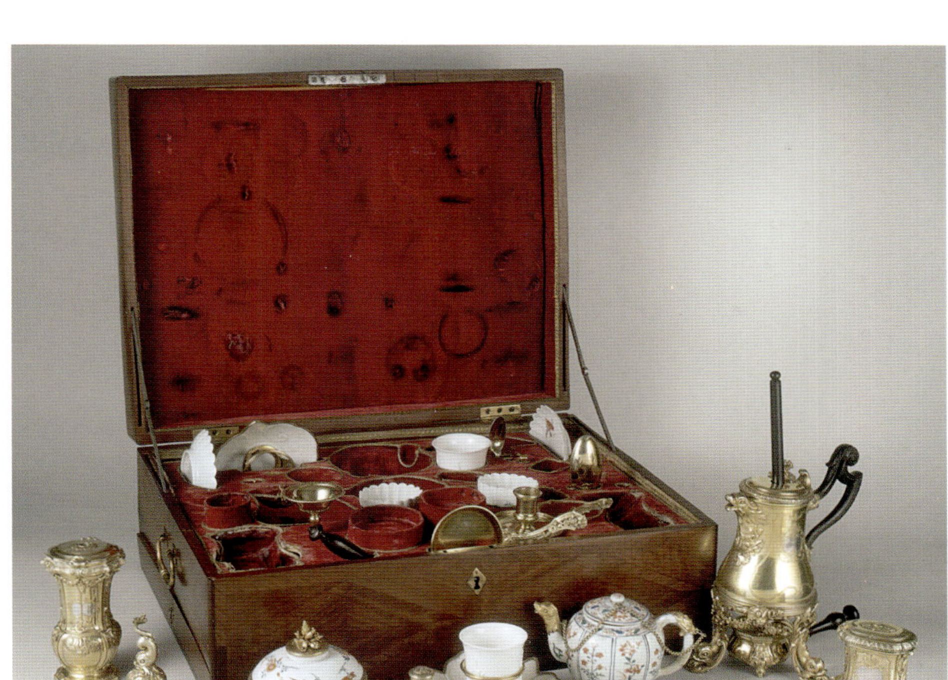

Fig. 38
Marie Leczinska's *nécessaire*, given to her on
the birth of the Dauphin by Louis XV, Paris,
1729–30, silver-gilt, Chinese, Japanese and
Meissen porcelain, gold, fabric and wood;
height of case 35 cm
Musée du Louvre, Paris
inv. no. OA9598

The *nécessaire* of Queen Marie Leszcynska, wife of Louis XV, made in
1729–30, shows this mix and match attitude to equipment, even at the
French court (fig. 38). Here a Japanese porcelain teapot has been supplied
with Chinese and German porcelain cups and Paris-made silver-gilt chocolate pot, tea canister and other equipment. It is a rare survival of a French
royal commission and a fine example of the creativity of the *marchands-
merciers*, skilled Parisian merchants who specialized in combining diverse
materials to create splendid and refined consumer goods.

Oriental porcelains reached seventeenth-century England and France
through the Dutch trade. The English East India Company did not start
importing porcelains in any quantity until the 1680s. The weight of the
porcelain made it an ideal ballast to the lighter tea and it had no rival in
the European market for practicality, aesthetic quality and cost until the
1760s, after which the Oriental trade diminished. In the eighteenth century the French supplemented imports from the Compagnie des Indes
with purchases in Holland. The royal collections had been enhanced by
gifts made by the King of Siam during his visit in 1686, which had included
teapots, but the first opportunity in France to buy porcelain and lacquer
in quantity came with the return of *L'Amphitre* in 1700 with 181 cases of
porcelain and almost as many cases of lacquer. Direct French trade with

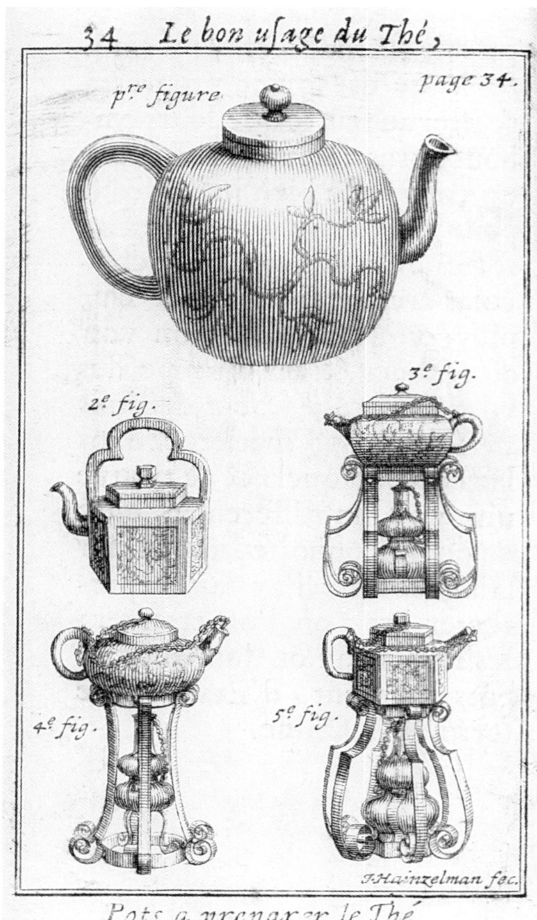

Fig. 39
Nicolas de Blegny (designer) and Johann Hainzelmann (printmaker), *Pots for preparing tea (teapots)*, print from *Le Bon Usage du thé, du café, du chocolat*, Paris, 1687
Bibliothèque nationale, Paris
inv. no. Bnf D3-8-TC24-16

the Orient seems to have been sporadic, but in 1722 and 1723 sales at Nantes by the Compagnie des Indes contained thousands of pieces of porcelain, largely consisting of cups and saucers of various sizes, forms and decoration. The total sales for these reached 683,032 *livres*.[35] The Compagnie des Indes did not sell tea services in sets until the 1730s.

Chinese and Japanese porcelain had long-standing prestige in the eighteenth century and for many consumers this was as important as price. Japanese porcelain was especially prized. The mystique of the distant origin of the earliest pieces to reach Europe, combined with their almost magical whiteness and transparency and the fabulous scenes painted on them in superb blue or enamel colours, created a powerful allure.[36] The wares were technically superior to most European ceramic bodies until the early eighteenth century and very practical for teapots and tea bowls which had to resist the shock of hot water. Mme de Pompadour had to replace one of her Sèvres teapots which may have broken for this reason. The hard-paste porcelain of the Orient was also impervious to liquids and, unlike the European tin-glazed earthenwares, resistant to wear and tear. The majority of pictures depicting tea drinking between the 1720s and the 1760s in England and France show Oriental porcelain. The tea bowls and saucers in Nicolas Lancret's *Morning*, painted before 1739 (cat. 6; fig. 27), are of a type of decoration with brown glazed exteriors known as 'Batavian' and would have been in the latest style at the time of the painting.[37]

How did the manufacturers in Europe respond to the challenge of the Oriental porcelains and the demand for utensils to store, prepare and serve the new hot drinks? The silversmiths, suppliers of luxury goods, were perhaps the first to attempt to match the expensive new drinks to new equipment. In the 1680s, publications such as Nicolas de Blegny's (fig. 39) illustrated designs for tea equipment. Surviving silver shows that silversmiths' designs were not limited to Oriental models. The earliest hallmarked silver teapot (fig. 40) is based on the multi-purpose London coffeehouse pot, which probably served all three hot drinks. Its tall, tapering cylindrical form, domed lid and leather handle, which would not conduct heat, made it a functional object. The shape may have evolved from Middle Eastern brassware for the serving of coffee.[38] A number of forms were tried, some copying Oriental models, until a pear-shaped teapot emerged about 1700.[39] Often this was supplied with a lamp and stand (fig. 41). A rounded or bullet form became common from the 1720s.

The milk jug, sugar bowl and tea canister, all essentials for the well-equipped tea-table of the mid eighteenth century, were European innovations. Milk, though mentioned by Thomas Garway in an advertisement for his coffee house of 1660, did not become a regular accompaniment to tea

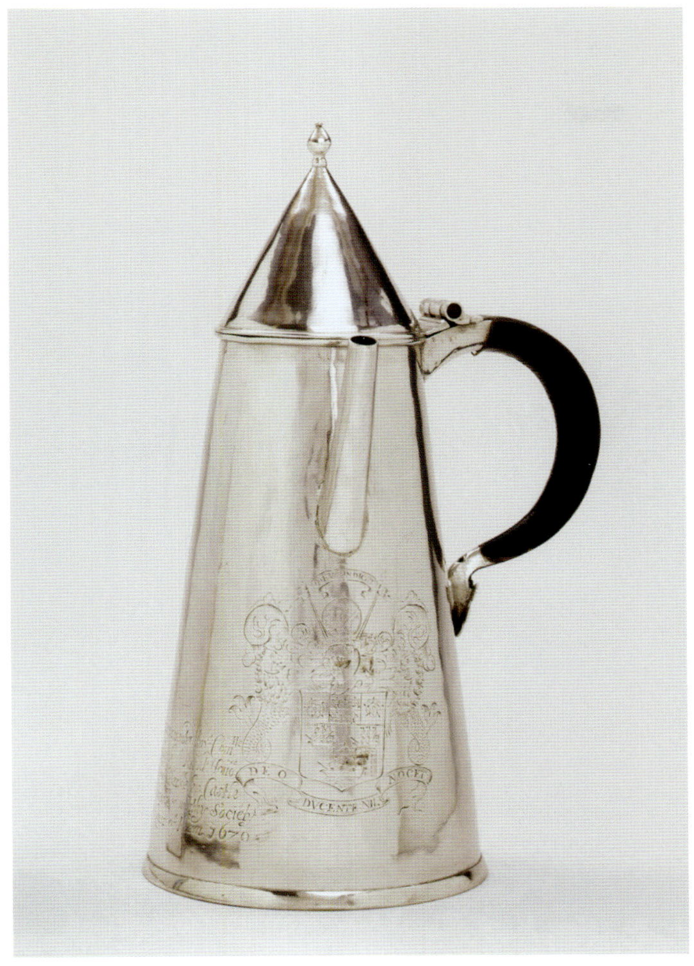

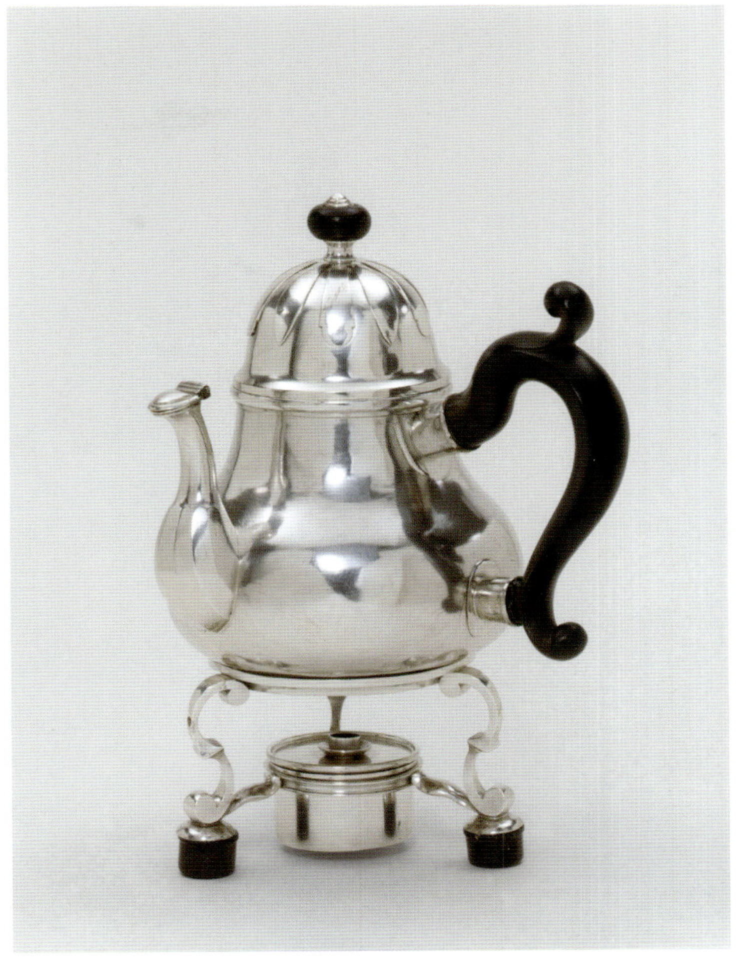

Fig. 40
Teapot, silver, engraved with the arms of the
East India Company and of George, Lord
Berkeley, and inscription recording
presentation of "This silver tea-pott" to the
Company in 1670–71, London, mark TL;
height 33 cm
Victoria and Albert Museum, London
inv. no. M.399-1921

Fig. 41
Simon Pantin, Teapot with stand and burner,
1705–06
Silver and ebony, London; height 17 cm
Victoria and Albert Museum, London
inv. no. M.172-1919

until the 1680s–90s. The French have been credited with the innovation.
Mme de Sévigné wrote to her daughter from Paris on 16 February 1680:
"It is true, Mme de Sablière takes tea with her milk; she told me so the other
day; it is her preference."[40]

In England Rachel, Lady Russell, was the first, in 1698, to mention a specific vessel for milk: "Yesterday I met with little bottles of milk to pour milk out for tea". Four years later she describes drinking green tea with milk.[41] At this time milk jugs in porcelain were imported from the East. The earliest surviving models are of pear shape with a cover. This design was popular in silver and in European porcelain. Vincennes was making milk jugs, sugar bowls and tea caddies from the 1750s.[42]

The forms of the silver hot-water jug, tea canister, sugar bowl and cover and fluted slop-bowl (for dregs) in Richard Collins's *Family at Tea* of about 1725 (fig. 42) demonstrate the ingenuity of the silversmiths in developing a vocabulary of shapes for tea wares. The forms are very reminiscent of the

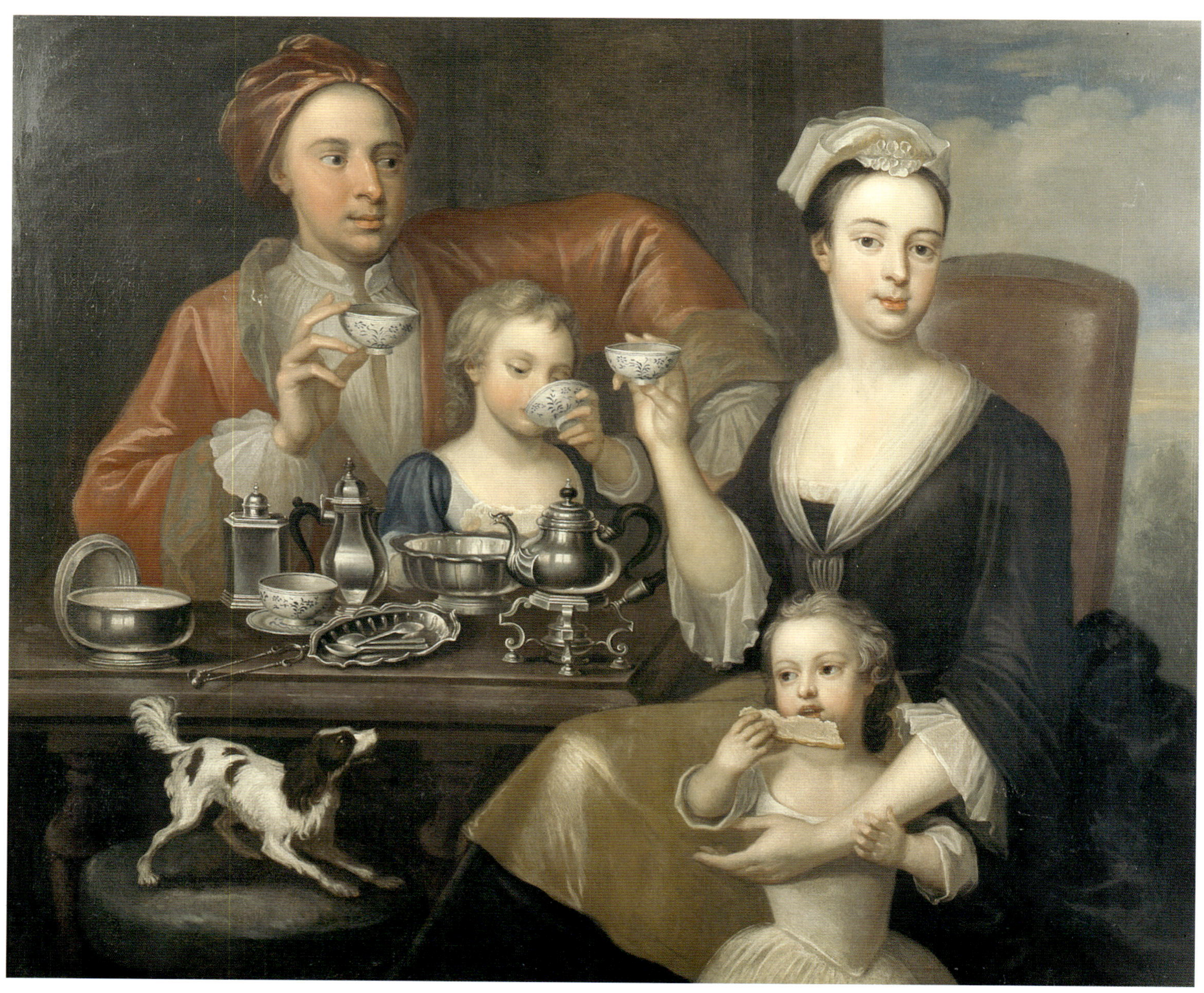

equipment for powders and potions in toilet services which had evolved in the late seventeenth century. Even the sugar tongs at the front of the table were inspired by contemporary fire furniture.[43] The first mention of a tea canister is in an advertisement for 1711, but tea could also be stored in wooden chests, in lead-lined compartments, or in silver canisters for green tea, black tea and sugar respectively. Green tea may have been preferred to black tea until the 1720s, when black teas such as Bohea became more popular in England, perhaps because more commonly diluted with milk. In France, tea was drunk weaker and often taken with lemon.[44] Locks on

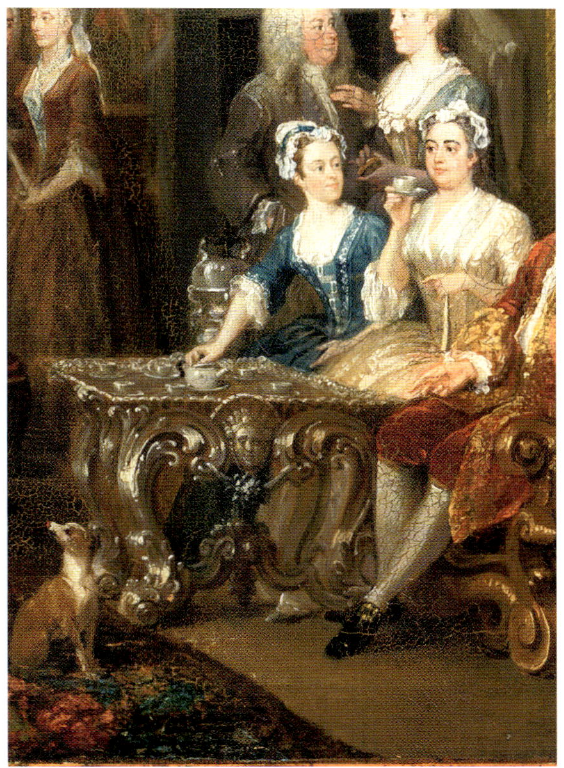 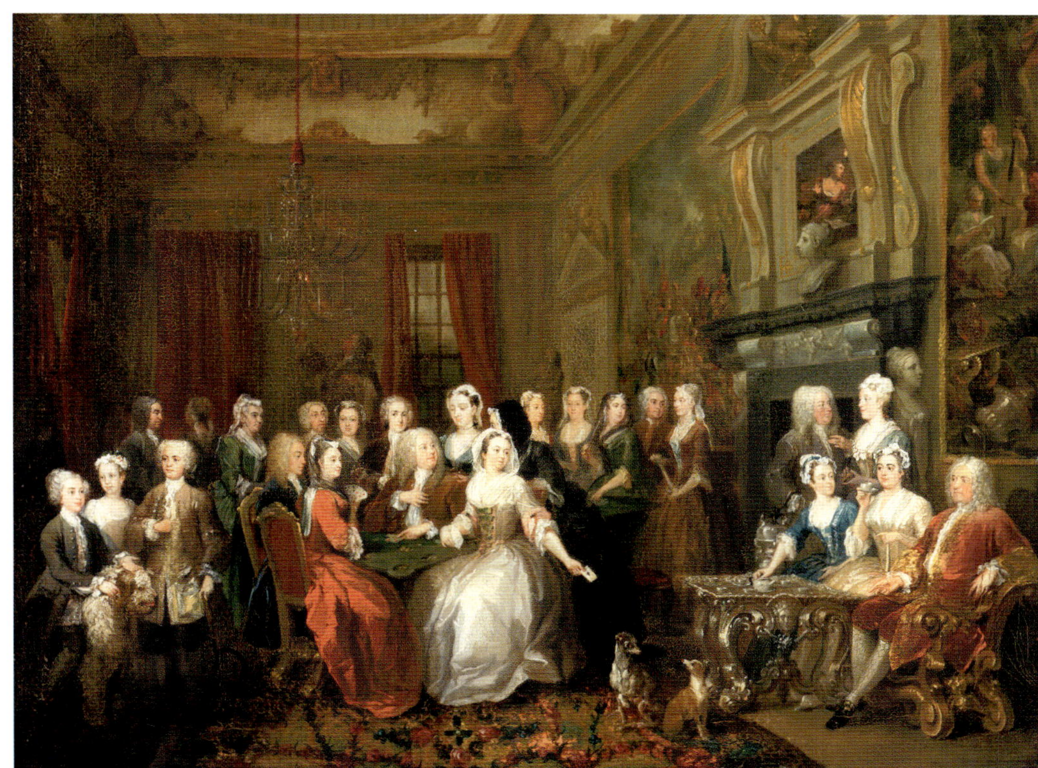

Figs. 43 (detail) and 44
William Hogarth
An Assembly at Wanstead House, 1730–31
Oil on canvas, 64.7 × 76.2 cm
Philadelphia Museum of Art
inv. no. M12928-1-13

the chests and on some silver tea-canisters (visible in a number of representations in paintings) show how valuable the commodity was.

The most expensive items for the service of tea were the kettle and the tray. The kettle stood on a silver or wooden stand providing a supply of hot water. It was later replaced by the tea urn, in conformity to the Neoclassical style. A silver tray to hold the tea items was still more expensive. George Wickes, the Royal Goldsmith, charged £40 for one in 1740. In the same year he supplied a tea service of a tea kettle and stand, coffee pot (often seen as part of the service), teapot, two tea canisters and a sugar dish in case for £58 10s 6d. This would be about ten years' wages for a maid servant at the time. The silver tea-table depicted in Hogarth's paintings would have been the top of the range (figs. 43 and 44); simple wooden tripod tea-tables were most common. Manufacturers experimented with numerous ideas and more specialist, complicated designs with tip-up indented tops and brass inlay for easy storage were also made. In France, small side-tables, sometimes in lacquer, were used, but the fashion for *le thé à l'anglaise* had led by the 1760s to the import of tea tables from England that were then copied in Paris.

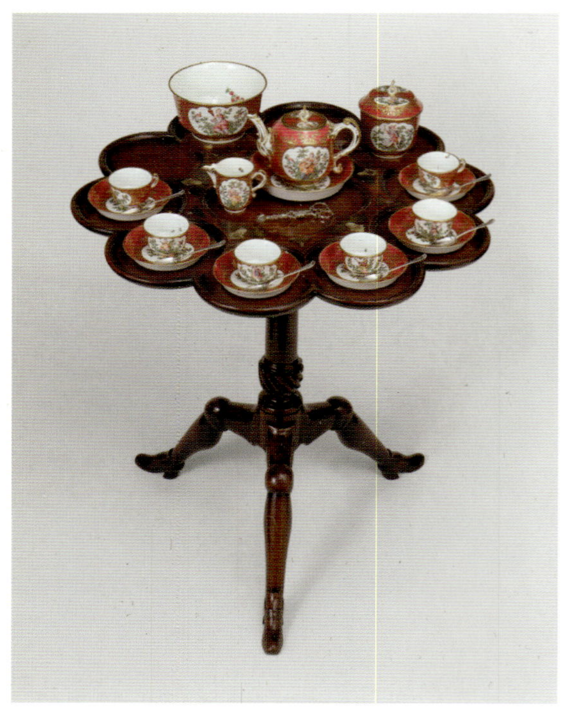

By the 1750s the desire for table wares and hot-drink utensils created such an extensive market that ceramics became common in English homes. Manufacturers in Europe had responded to the China mania. Innovations such as the slip-casting technique enabled objects like teapots, in complex shapes, to be made in quantity from the 1740s.[45] The manufacture of porcelain had begun in Europe in the 1690s at Saint-Cloud and Rouen in France and at Meissen in Germany in 1710. Factories soon sprang up all over Europe to meet the demand: some, like Vincennes/Sèvres and Chelsea (fig. 45), served a high-class market, while Bow and Worcester competed with Chinese goods for the middle range. The imports were still significantly cheaper. A typical Sèvres service sold for 400 *livres* at Lazare Duvaux, a *marchand mercier*, but for the same price the Compagnie des Indes could sell a dozen services.[46]

Teacups with handles began to be manufactured at Continental porcelain factories from about 1730 or 1740. Earlier handled cups existed as models but were not widely copied for the Oriental trade as tea bowls could be more easily packed and shipped and were perhaps preferred as more authentic. There are over fifty models of teacup recorded at Vincennes as well as 24 teapot models. Later evidence from the Sèvres factory indicates that the same style of handled cup was used interchangeably for coffee, tea and chocolate.[47]

The early productions of the manufactories closely copied Chinese prototypes, and it has been estimated that the huge amount of printed and painted decoration on English porcelains of the 1750s and 1770s featuring Oriental figures or landscape scenes (of European invention) account for about a quarter to a third of all surviving designs.[48]

Red stonewares had been made in London, Staffordshire and Holland since the late seventeenth century. Red-stoneware teapots, perhaps Chinese or copies of Oriental imports, are central to many English tea-drinking paintings. Francis Hayman's painting of Jonathan Tyers and his family of about 1740 (fig. 46) shows a type of red-stoneware teapot with facetted sides and a lion (dog of Fo) finial which was copied in Staffordshire (fig. 47). It was believed that tea drunk from red stoneware teapots tasted best of all.[49] Jonathan Tyers was the proprietor of the Vauxhall Gardens, one of a number of English gardens where men and women could walk, take tea and listen to music.

Despite the dependence on Oriental design for tea wares, teapot shapes and decoration in silver and ceramics did respond to underlying design trends in England and France. All the elements for the tea table, including the teapot, were made, for example, in Régence, Rococo or Neoclassical forms. The teapot in *Le Déjeuner Anglais*, a print by Gérard Vidal after Nicolas Lavreince (fig. 48), published in 1785, is Neoclassical, as would be expected at that date.

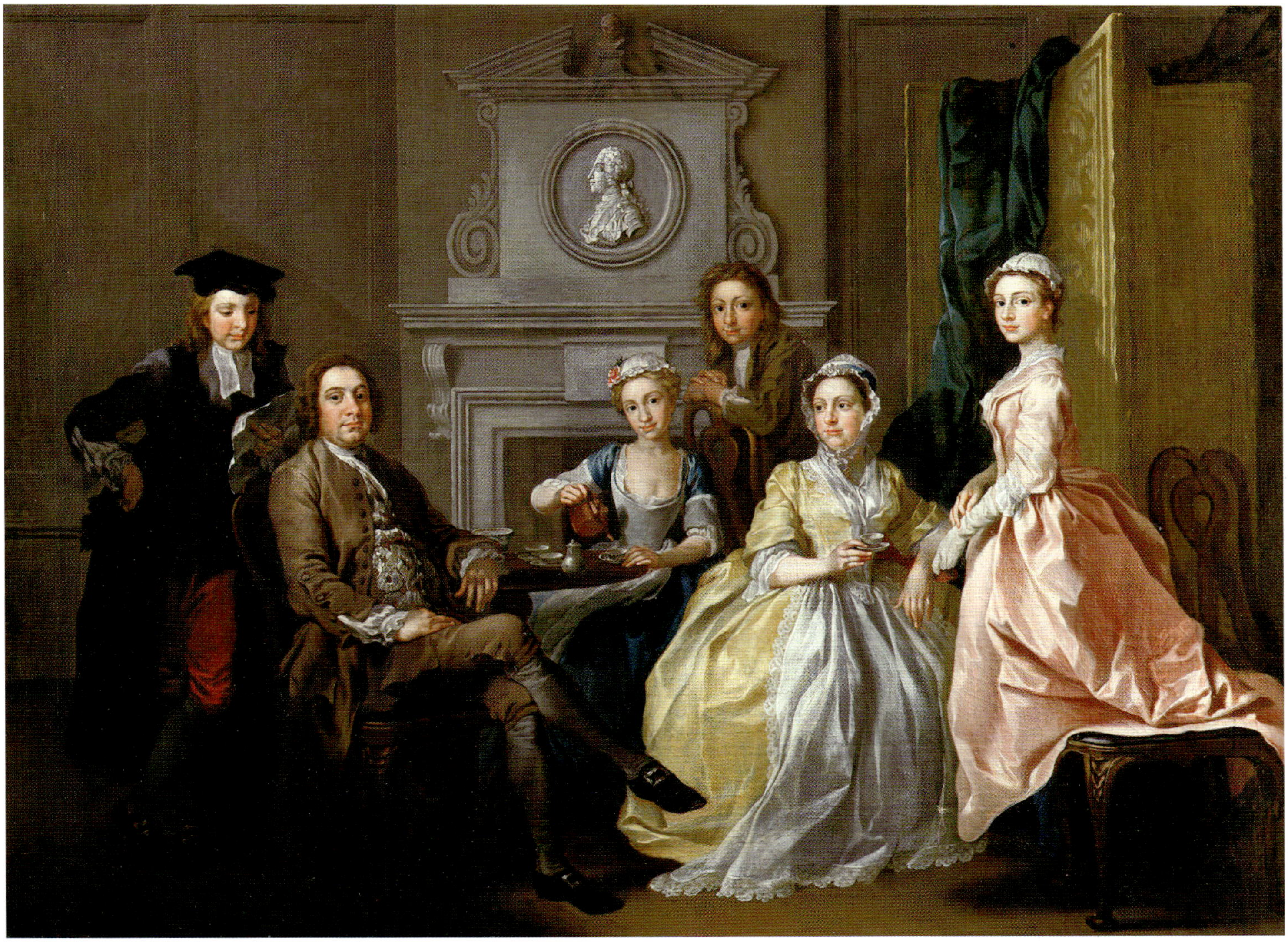

Fig. 46
Francis Hayman
Jonathan Tyers and his Family, 1740
Oil on canvas, 77.8 cm × 106.2 cm
National Portrait Gallery, London
inv. no. NPG 5588

Fig. 47
Teapot, Staffordshire, about 1740
Red stoneware, height 14 cm
Private collection

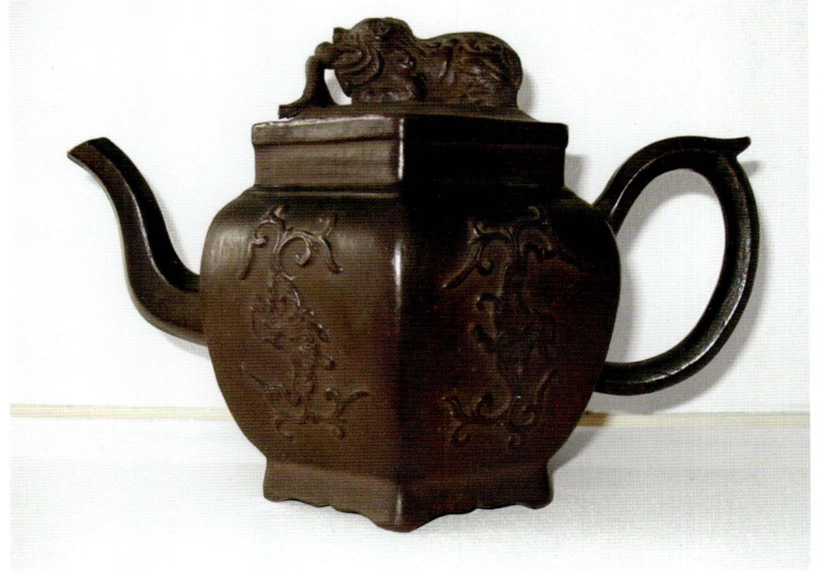

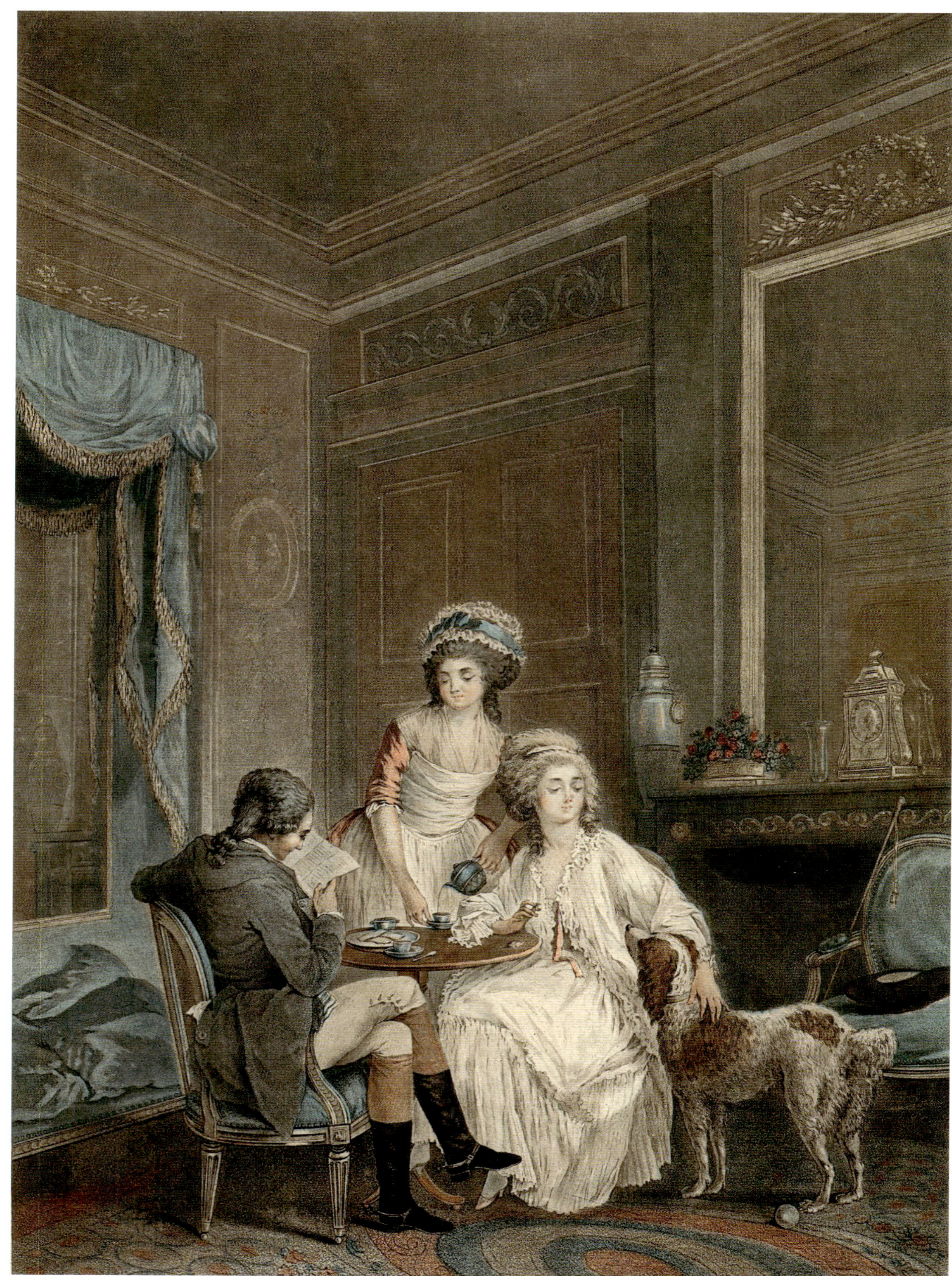

Fig. 48
Gérald Vidal after
Nicolas Lavreince
Le Déjeuner Anglais,
colour acquatint
published 1785,
345 mm × 252 mm
British Museum, London
inv. no. P&D 1894,
0611.10

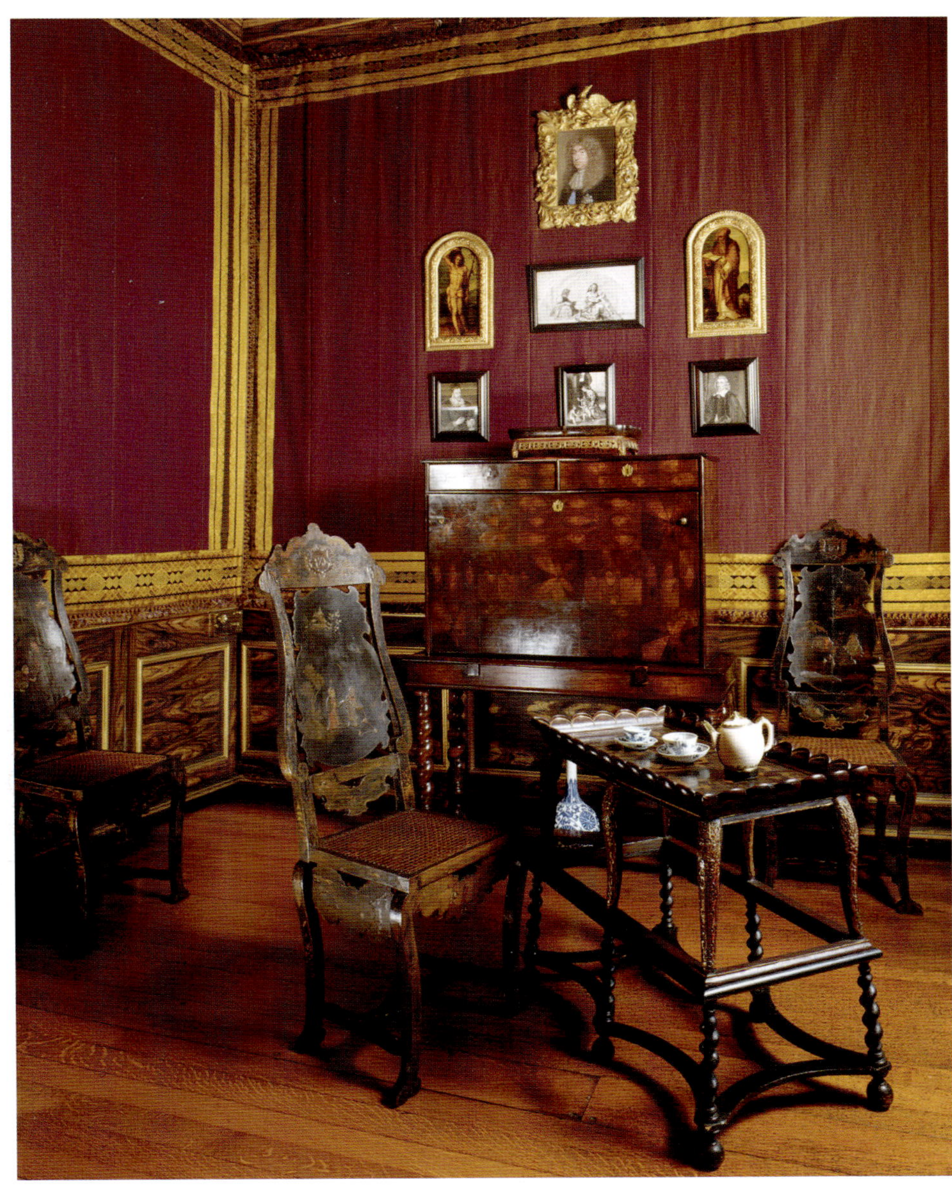

The large number of paintings, prints and drawings which show tea drinking and date from the 1720s to the 1760s reflect, particularly in England, the high status of the activity. The location in the home of tea drinking confirms the point. In the seventeenth century it was in the bed-chamber, the most important and lavishly furnished of all the apartments in a house, that French and English ladies took tea.[50] The wealthiest members of Dutch and English society, such as the Duchess of Lauderdale at Ham House in London, furnished rooms especially for tea drinking (fig. 49), although there is no evidence of this in France. The Earl of

Warrington, who was very old fashioned, had a separate Tea Room at Dunham Massey as late as the 1750s. English playwrights of the early eighteenth century place their tea parties in dining rooms. London inventories record that the tea kettle, lamp and stand were usually kept in the dining room, indicating that tea equipment, rather than being put away in cupboards, was proudly displayed at the front of the house.

The social activity of serving tea was similarly arranged to display the expensive equipment. While the servant brought hot water to the table it was the mistress of the house, or often a daughter, who would take the tea from the canister, put it in the teapot and add freshly boiled water to make the tea in front of the guests. In the nineteenth century this activity was relegated to the kitchen and only the filled teapot came into the drawing room.

A poem of 1747 eulogies the tea party: "The tea chest brought, where the best hyson [green tea] lies/ The sugar's whiteness, new-dropt snow outvies;/ The bread and butter cut exceeding thin,/ The water newly drawn, brought boiling in;/ The crystal stream, while thus severely hot,/ Runs murmuring from the Kettle to the pot;/ Soon receiv'd, 'tis changed in Quality,/ From simple water to celestial tea."[51] A specific etiquette grew up around tea drinking. Writers advised on the way to handle the tea bowl and what to talk about at a tea table: "Then as many postures must be us'd in drinking a dish of tea, as taking a pinch of snuff: some holding the rim at the bottom of the dish, betwixt their thumb and the first, second and third fingers, others holding the top and bottom of the dish betwixt the thumb and middle finger only, with the palm of the hand outwards so that one skilled in chiromancy may easily tell their fortune."[52] Inverting the bowl, putting the spoon across the cup, or leaving it in the cup, assured the hostess that the guest did not wish for more tea.[53]

In England and Holland tea drinking had become an essential part of social life. It reinforced polite behaviour and provided a forum for meeting people of different genders, ages and social rank. Despite the expense of tea, it was less trouble to make than a meal and yet showed hospitality. It allowed women a space and control which they adopted with enthusiasm. They used tea drinking not just for hospitality but sometimes for business. Tea was also a staple in the English diet.

"Breakfast at nine, two dishes of tea and one thin slice of bread and butter, dine at three, eat moderately, drink a sober pint, tumble into bed till 4, tea at six, walk till 9 eat some cooling fruit and to bed. There is regularity for you."[54] Tea in the mid eighteenth century was drunk at home for breakfast, at mid morning and after dinner between 3 and 4 pm. It may also have been the catalyst for the custom in England of ladies withdrawing from men's company after dinner to take tea elsewhere, while men sat over their pipes and bottles.

Contemporary illustrations of tea drinking do not reflect all these meanings. Nor do they show the enormous growth of tea drinking at all levels of society that was much commented upon and often criticized in print as unaffordable, unpatriotic folly. "But still to add to this luxury, there is a new whim come up of late call'd tea; which because it is far fetch'd, and dear bought it is therefore Drink for beaus: And so common it is become amongst us now that every servant wench before she handles her mop and pail, must have forsooth a dish of this Indian or Chinese liquor: there is scarce a Trull in any market about London, or mechanics Drab, but what must have her load of hot water and sugar, five or six times a day, to the small change of the poor contented cuckolds their husbands, when they consider, that a japann'd tea-table, a tea kettle, a stand, a teapot, a canister, a sugar box, china dishes, silver spoons and a fork cannot be had for nothing; besides what it costs in tea, sugar and bread and butter, for the support of this fantastick and useless equipage; in so much that a tradesman, had better trust his hand in the mouth of a lion, his substance to the management of a whore, his conscience to a horse courser, or his religion to a synagogue of Jews, than his purse in the hands of his wife, that's a tea drinker, unless it is his ambition to make the mint his asylum."[55] Women were, as this commentary shows, often berated for their love of tea and its accoutrements, but this is not a usual subject for early images of tea drinking. It is in the late eighteenth and early nineteenth century that tea drinking is caricatured.

The genre of 'conversation' portraiture emerging in England in the 1720s revolved around sociable groups enjoying polite entertainments. Tea drinking was frequently represented. The serving of tea was a means of demonstrating civilized social interaction and was almost always associated with card games or making music from a harpsichord. The family group was most important. The surroundings may be quite grand, for example a formal drawing-room or hallway with classical figures or pillars, but more homely and intimate studies and dining rooms are also frequent. Some of the grander backdrops, with swags of rich curtaining or screens, appear imagined rather than real. Even in the more restrained painting of Jonathan Tyers and his family (see fig. 46), the sculpted portrait over the mantelpiece is known never to have existed.[56] Some artists employed stock backgrounds and studio props rather than depicting the family's own possessions. William Hogarth's teapot, which seems to have a replacement handle, appears in several of his paintings showing tea drinking (fig. 50; see cat. 9, 10, 19). This is a puzzling object. It can look like silver, and so

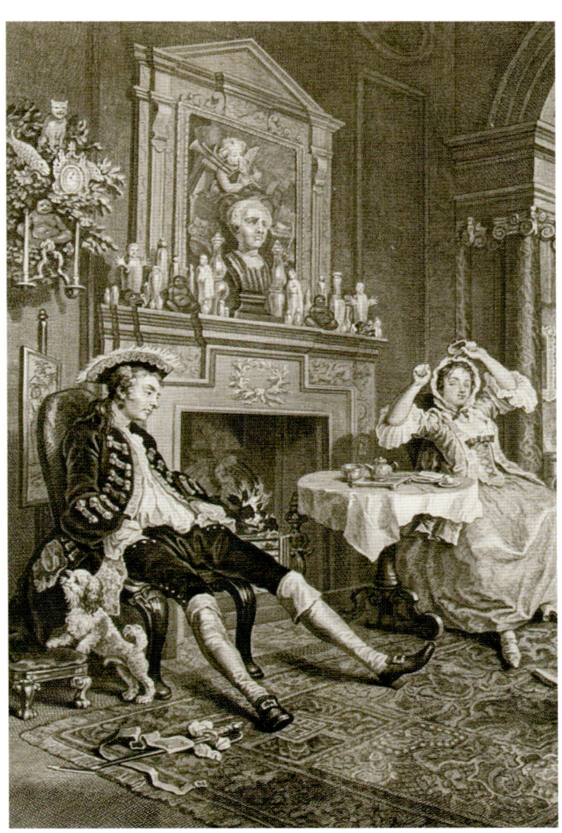

Fig. 50 (detail)
William Hogarth
Marriage A-la-Mode
Plate II, *The tête à tête*, 1745
Engraving and etching, 38 × 46.2 cm
Hunterian Museum and Art Gallery, Glasgow
inv. no. GLAHA 16023

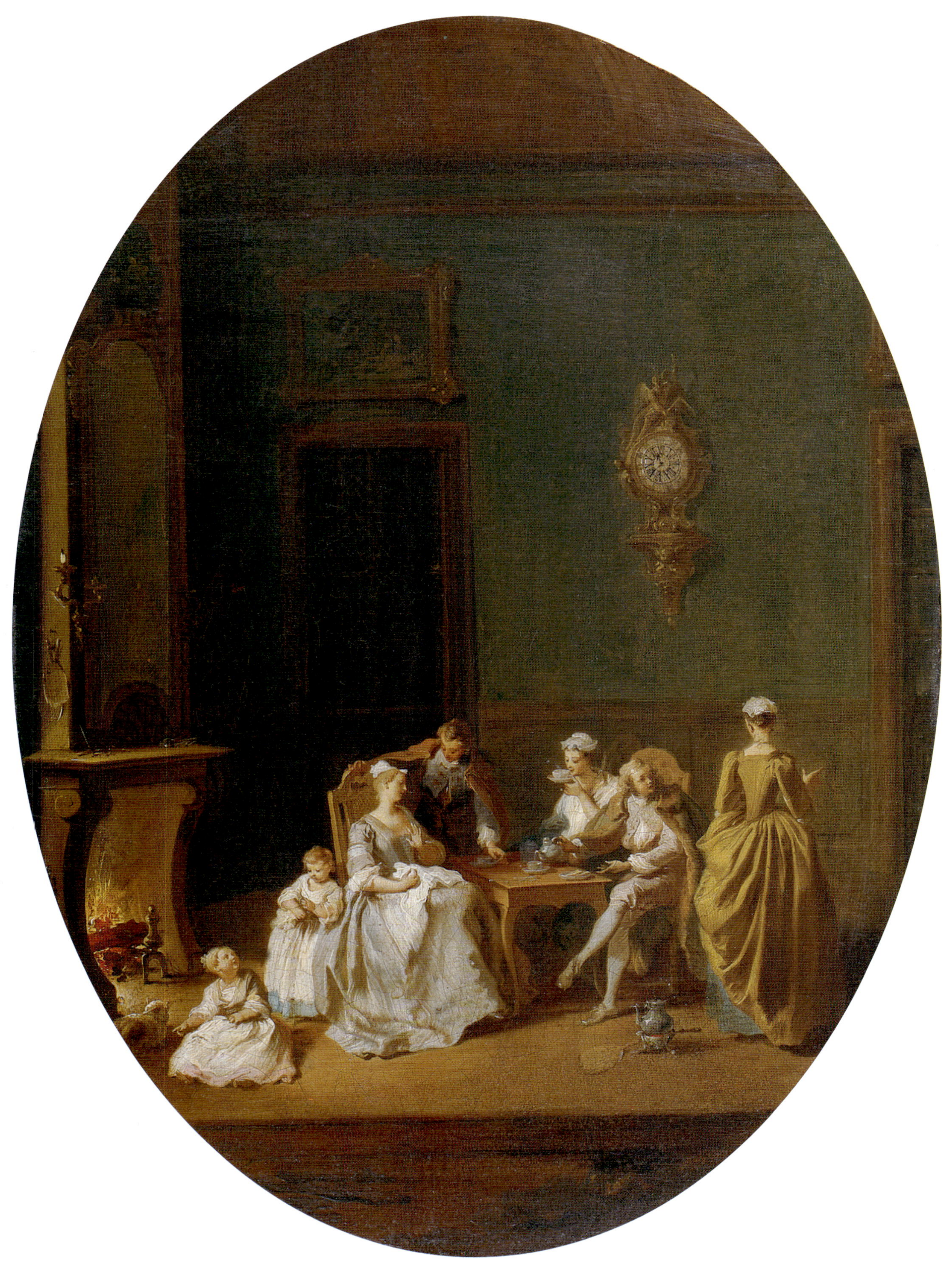

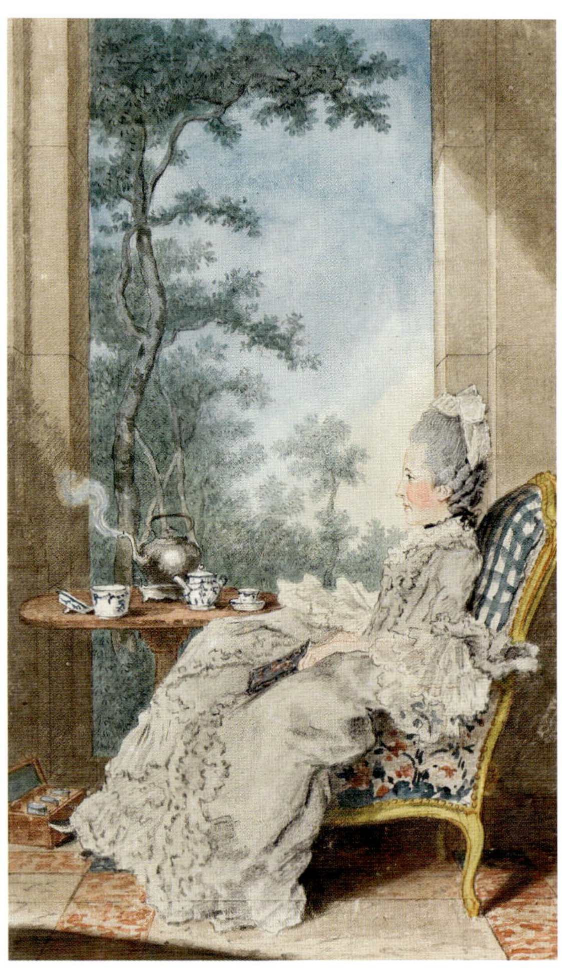

Fig. 52
Carrogis Louis, called Carmontelle
Mme la comtesse de Boufflers (with French
porcelain and a silver tea kettle), 1760
Graphite, gouache, sanguine, watercolour,
315 × 190 mm
Musée Condé, Chantilly
inv. no. Car220

facing page
Fig. 51
Pierre-Antoine Quillard
The Four Seasons: Winter, 1725–29
Oil on canvas, 42.5 × 33.5 cm
Museo Thyssen Bornemisza, Madrid
inv. no. CTB.1930.91

should have a wooden handle, but in some paintings it is clearly porcelain with blue decoration. Was it supposed to represent a treasured heirloom? If not, then why represent a high-status activity with damaged goods? The distinctive and ostentatious silver tea-table, which appears in a slightly different guise in three paintings, could not have been owned by Hogarth but must represent an expensive type of equipment which would flatter his sitters.

Comparable French images survive in smaller numbers (fig. 51). While tea finds a place in every form of English writing, in novels, poems, plays, letters, journals, newspapers and advice manuals and seems to permeate every aspect of English life in the eighteenth century, among French sources it is harder to trace. There is evidence that tea was drunk at the court of Louis XV. Although the king preferred coffee and served it himself to guests at his *petits cabinets*, he owned a small tea service or *déjeuner*. Mme du Hausset, lady's maid to Mme de Pompadour, remembered that once the king had a bout of indigestion in the middle of the night and, after taking medicine from the doctor and recovering, she says: "I called up one of the girls of the wardrobe, to make tea, as if for myself; the King took three cups …".[57]

Tea was thought to be good for the digestion, but here there is an element of drinking for the comfort of a hot drink and for companionship, as the king had already taken his medicine. The king's mistress, Mme de Pompadour, owned teaware. An enthusiastic patron of the arts, she secured state support for the Vincennes/Sèvres porcelain factory, and small porcelain tea services (*déjeuners*), sometimes with a matching tray, were made by the firm from 1753. Mme de Pompadour and several of the King's daughters bought the services. Only a few of the *déjeuners* had a teapot, but this was sometimes requested later. The small sets containing either one or at most two cups and saucers suggest that by the second half of the eighteenth century tea drinking, at this level of society, was seen as a solitary, reflective activity or, with a friend or lover, an intimate one. This is, too, in many respects, the idea that the surviving images of tea drinking in France convey, for example Carmontelle's portrait of the Mme de Boufflers (fig. 52). Chardin's *Lady taking Tea* (see fig. 1) is shown quietly contemplative as she stirs her tea. Was Chardin's painting a precursor for later French paintings in this genre? Certainly, solitary French ladies taking tea outnumber those having tea with companions, in contrast to the conviviality of English portraits featuring tea drinking.

By the mid eighteenth century tea, in many circles in France, was associated with England. Tea drinking appears to be linked to groups who had close ties with England and espoused a growing *anglomanie*. From the 1730s there had been an interest in English ideas, notably their freedom of thought, which was followed by imitation of English dress, tastes and amusements. Tea drinking in France is most frequently associated with people who had visited England. Mme de Mirepoix's tic, whereby she continually shook her head, was blamed on "the use of tea of which she drank several cups a day, a habit she had picked up in England where her husband had been ambassador".

The cultivated and artistic society of the Paris salons is known to have adopted tea drinking. A painting by Barthélemy Ollivier records the tea served at Mme de Boufflers's salon (fig. 53), at which, in 1766, the young Mozart played the harpsichord. The tea is served, not by servants, but by Mme de Boufflers herself, following the English tradition. The tea wares look thoroughly European in form and decoration, perhaps made at Sèvres. Mme de Boufflers, official mistress of the prince de Conti, was an inquisitive and passionate traveller who also encouraged foreign visitors to attend her Parisian salon. Her journey to London in 1763 contributed to the spread of the fashion for English culture.[58]

Tea was also associated with the exotic Orient in France. Artists such as Boucher used tea as a metaphor for the East by introducing tea wares, as well as lacquer screens, into their paintings. Chardin and Boucher owned tea wares and painted them in use. Can we conclude that they also drank tea themselves and that it was the custom in artistic circles? Artists travelling between London and Paris, such as Antoine Watteau (who visited London in 1719–20) or Hogarth and Hayman (who travelled to Paris with a group of artists in 1748), may very well have spread tea drinking within these social circles. Inventories in Paris show that a number of musicians and artists owned tea equipment.

Care needs to be taken in making these assumptions. The objects have a role to play in the painting and may have been collected with this in mind: after all, artists are concerned with images and ideas as well as description. Atmosphere and emotion are key to the work and condition the physical presence of the objects. The teapot in Chardin's *Lady taking Tea* is almost impossible to classify. It seems very large for a teapot of the time, although such a size is not unknown. The shiny surface would indicate a lead glaze of an eathenware body, perhaps the *terre de flandre* noted in his 1737 inventory.[59] The colour is so dark and the form so finely potted that the pot seems likely to have been of Chinese red stoneware, but the shape and especially the lid looks very European. Could it be – even though the handle appears too high – a Dutch- or German-made red stoneware in imitation of Chinese examples?[60]

Since the 1670s porcelain had been collected in France and England not merely for its functional properties but in pursuit of an aesthetic and

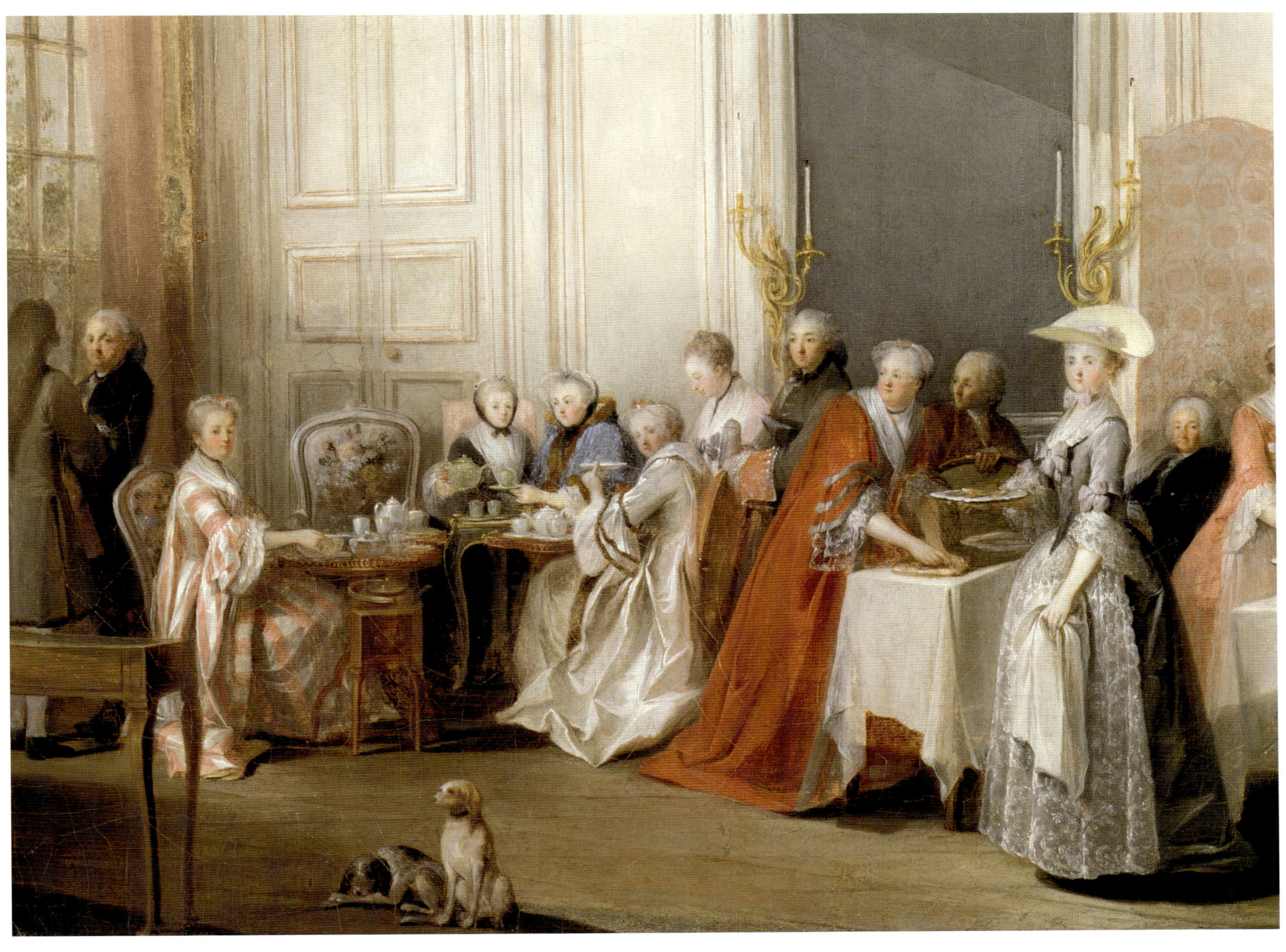

Fig. 53

Barthélémy Olliver

Le Thé à l'anglaise in the Salon des Quatres Glaces at the Palais du Temple in Paris, 1766

Oil on canvas, 53 × 68 cm

Musée du Louvre, Paris

inv. no. MV3824

acquisitive agenda.[61] Men and women indulged in this China mania. Porcelain became less of a curiosity and more of a fashionable furnishing material. The inventory taken at Burghley House in 1688, some months before the arrival of William and Mary, confirms that Oriental porcelain was already very much part of the decorative display of the nobility. Greater imports in the 1700s spread the acquisition of porcelain. A poem of 1725 identifies women as the main accumulators:

> "*China's* the passion of her soul;
> A cup, a plate, a dish, a bowl
> Can kindle wishes in her breast,
> Inflame with joy, or break her rest."[62]

Tea wares had always been fashionable interior decoration. The Dutch set out porcelain on finely carved wooden racks or in glass cases from about 1615. The tops of cupboards, mantelpieces or, on the walls, brackets displayed the porcelain. These design ideas and the prints of Daniel Marot may have given rise to the China closets of European princes, such as Augustus the Strong.[63] Arguably, the influence of Louis XIV's mounted hardstones on wall brackets at Versailles would have been crucial, because of the lead France gave to Europe.

In Boucher's painting, *Woman on a Daybed* (fig. 2), a bracket on the wall provides a second area of focus for the viewer after the initial interest of the woman's face and pose. The bracket holds a small tea set of Chinese porcelain, painted in blue enamel colour, and a coloured seated figure of a Putai (the god of good luck), sometimes also called a 'pagod' or 'pagoda'. French interpretations of Oriental *blanc de chine* models were very free and often painted in colours. This figure could well have been made in France. Hogarth satirizes the fashion for Oriental figures in *Marriage A-la-Mode* (*The tête à tête*) with a number of unlikely and ungainly small sculptures (cat. 19, fig. 50). Boucher uses a teapot on an elaborate bracket in *The Déjeuner* and the tea set in *Lady fastening her Garter* (see fig. 15) appears similar in form to the one in *Woman on a Daybed*, suggesting that he, too, owned tea wares for use as studio props. Porcelain was expected to decorate a room in England. In 1750, Mrs Montagu recommended that a friend could furnish her house "in the present fashion, of some cheap paper and ornaments of Chelsea china or Bow, which makes a room look neat and finished".[64] Hogarth and Boucher were following the current trends for furnishing rooms with tea ware and porcelains but there are differences between the meanings of those objects in their paintings. For Hogarth the objects were expected to tell their own supplementary stories. Some of the

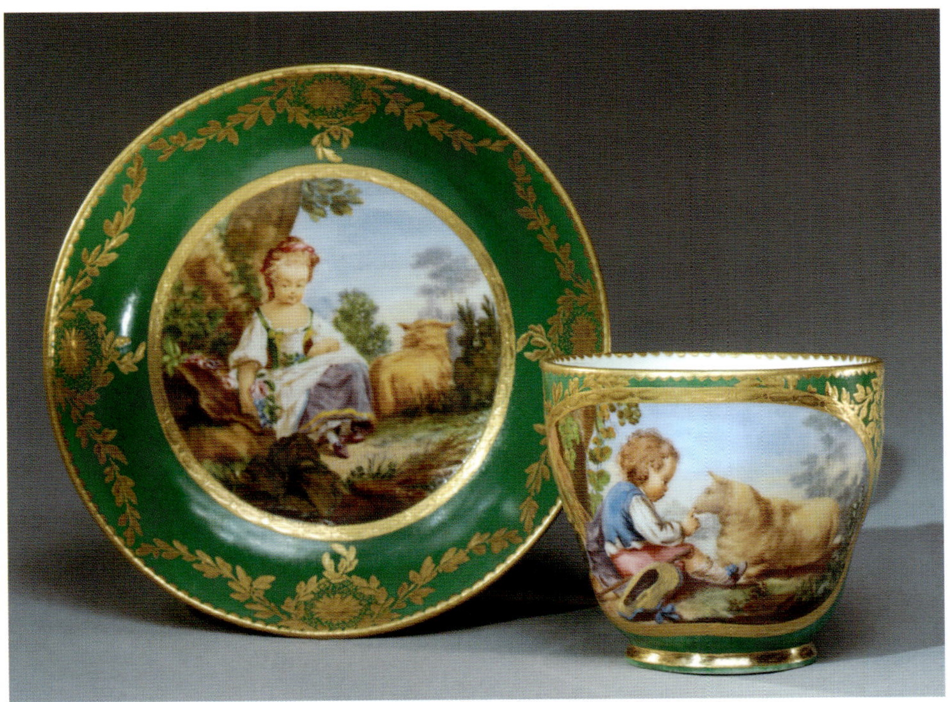

figures on the mantelpiece in *Marriage A-la-Mode* (*The tête à tête*) seem to be holding up their hands in horror at the behaviour of the married couple.

Notions of design and the idea of a designer emerged in England in the 1730s. Architects and painters were the obvious choice for the role of designer in new European industries such as ceramic production or in older established trades such as silversmithing and tapestry-making. In England, the architect William Kent published designs in 1744 which were exploited by silversmiths but it was often to France and French artists, such as the engraver and draughtsman, Hubert François Gravelot, or to prints and models by French artists and factories, that English manufacturers looked for inspiration. Prints after Watteau and Boucher could be copied in paint on Chelsea or, using transfer printing techniques, at Worcester. Tea drinking itself became the subject for the engraver Robert Hancock.

In France, Boucher designed both tapestries and tea ware. Through his patron Mme de Pompadour he gained favour with Louis XV and appointments at the Gobelins tapestry works. His first designs at Vincennes were for figures in biscuit porcelain. It may have been through the influence of Mme de Pompadour or through that of the firm's artistic director, Jean-Jacques Bachelier, that his designs began to be used at Vincennes from 1749. His images of children, cherubs, landscapes and mythological scenes, reinterpreted by the porcelain painters, were used at Vincennes/Sèvres (fig. 54).[65]

According to the 1771 sale catalogue of Boucher's possessions three quarters of his ceramic collection came from the Orient. He owned elaborate garnitures of vases with gilt-bronze mounts bought from *marchands-merciers* like Lazare Duvaux. Could one of these be the mounted vase on the mantelpiece in his painting *Lady fastening her Garter*? His ownership of European ceramics and of pieces that he had designed was very small. It appears to demonstrate a preference for and fascination with China and *chinoiserie*, the European idea of the East which he did much to promote.

Tea and the tea equipage assumed a place in the English way of life which became of far greater importance than in any other European country. The earlier conversation paintings reflect this, although the English could not help recognizing and poking fun at their obsession by the end of the eighteenth century. It is significant that Chardin and Boucher were portraying the objects for tea drinking in their paintings at a time when, according to the inventory evidence, it was only just becoming possible for the French consumer on modest incomes to afford them. Chardin illustrates these possibilities in his paintings. The objects shown are often the least expensive, such as earthenwares, tea bowls, a cup and saucer. However, porcelains and even the earthenwares were still aspirational in France and, in contrast to Chardin, Boucher appears to treat them in this way, as elements of luxurious interiors of elegance and richness.

1 Letter from 17 directors of the Dutch East India Company to the Governor General of Netherlandish East India at Batavia, quoted in Ukers 1935, I, p. 30.

2 Jörg 1982, p. 77, and Appendix 8.

3 Green tea is unfermented, oolong partially fermented and black tea fully fermented. The rolling of the leaves induces fermentation, which is then controlled and arrested by heat.

4 Brussels 1999, p. 71.

5 Father Alexandre de Rhodes, *Voyages et Missions Apostoliques*, Paris, 1653, quoted in Ukers 1935, p. 33.

6 Various accounts of the introduction of tea to Paris quote 1635 or 1636 as a possible date: see Ukers 1935, I, p. 33. Alfred Franklin (*La Vie privée*, vol. 13: *Le café, le thé et le chocolat*, 1893, p.130) prefers a later date, quoting a letter of Gui Patin from 1648 in which Patin refers to tea as "the impertinent novelty of the century".

7 Ukers 1935, pp. 34–35.

8 Cited in Jorge Tavares da Silva, 'Catarina de Bragança, the tea-drinking Queen?', in Brussels 1999, p. 19.

9 Margaret Cavendish, Duchess of Newcastle, *Observations Upon Experimental Philosophy etc.*, London, 1666, 'Of Several sorts of Drink and Meat', p. 86.

10 Dr Duncan, Faculty of Montpelier, *Wholesome Advice Against the Abuse of Hot Liquors: particularly of Coffee, Chocolate, Tea, Brandy and Strong Waters*, translation, London, 1706, p. 12.

11 While recent research has found no evidence for Queen Catherine's role in the spread of tea drinking, she certainly owned teapots, and Charles II received several gifts of tea from the East India Company: in 1664 the company records a gift to him of 2 lbs of tea and one of 23²/₃ lbs in 1666. See Jorge Tavares da Silva in Brussels 1999, pp. 15–27, and Sir George Birdwood, *Old Records of the India Office*, London, 1891, p. 26.

12 Sir George Birdwood, *ibid.*

13 Butel 1989, p. 53.

14 *Mémoires de Saint-Simon*, vol. 6, chapter 5: http://rouvroy.medusis.com/docs/0605.html?qid=sdxgo.

15 Marie de Rabutin-Chantal Sévigné, *Letters of Madame de Sévigné to her Daughter and Friends*, London, 1811, p. 268.

16 Sidney W. Mintz, 'The Changing Roles of Food in the Study of Consumption', in John Brewer and Roy Porter (eds.), *Consumption and the World of Goods*, London 1993, pp. 265–66.

17 Butel 1989, pp. 53–54.

18 Ellis 2005, p. 172 and note 27.

19 Martin Lister, *A Journey to Paris, 1698*, London, 1699, p. 166.

20 For a discussion about the contemporary perception of the centrality of the female tea drinker and the way it defined a woman's place in the domestic economy in England see Kowalski-Wallace 1994.

21 William Wycherley, *The Country Wife (A Comedy)*, London, 1675, Act II, Scene 1.

22 In 1693, Thomas Southerne's comedy *The Maid's Last Prayer* is partly set in the India house of a woman dealer called Siam. The men and women have tea at 5 pm, look at silks, game and gossip.

23 "*Au reste, le chocolat, le thé, & le caffé, sont extrêment à la mode, mais le caffé est préferé aux deux autres; comme un remède qu'on dit être souverain contre la tristesse*": Charles Cotolendi, *Saint Evremoniana ou Recueil de diverses pieces curieuses*, Paris, 1710, p. 377.

24 "*L'usage de cette boisson est devenu si commun en Europe, surtout en Angleterre et en Hollande, qu'à proportion il ne s'en fait pas moins de consommation par les Anglois et les Hollandois que par les Orientaux. En France le café semble l'avoir emporté sur le thé*": Antoine Furetière, *Dictionnaire Universel*, 1727.

25 J. Ovington, *An Essay on the Nature and Qualities of Tea*, London, 1699, p. 2.

26 Parmentier 1996, p. 110.

27 Ruggiu 1997, pp. 200–01.

28 The marquis de Savine had a silver coffee pot valued at 174 *livres* and a teapot at 140 *livres* in 1748: Annik Pardailhé-Galabrun, *The Birth of Intimacy* (first published 1988), trans. Jocelyn Phelps, Cambridge, 1991, p. 93.

29 Ten per cent owned a teapot in the wealthy parish of Saint-Eustache but only 2% were owners in the parish of Saint-Germain-l'Auxerrois. In contrast, a full 37% of homes in the same parish of Saint-Germain-l'Auxerrois between 1768 and 1790 owned a coffee pot. Even 15% of poorer households in Faubourg Saint-Antoine between 1760 and 1762 owned a coffee pot. See Pardailhé-Galabrun 1991, p. 93.

30 "*On prend une pinte d'eau, on la fait bouillir dans une caffetière*": *L'Ecole parfaite des officiers de bouche*, Paris, 1715 (17th edition), p. 203.

31 Earle 1989, p. 387, note 45; Weatherill 1988, p. 31. Lorna Weatherill found, using material from eight areas of England, that by 1725 60% of London inventories included utensils for hot drinks, although in rural areas the figure was 6%.

32 A supercargo (company agent) recorded in 1726 that they [the supercargoes] had noted that the majority consisted of dinner plates, bowls and tea sets, large consignments of which have been shipped to Europe, where they did not make much of a profit. They thus concluded that it was better to buy plates, cups and saucers, plus a certain number of chocolate cups, as these were most in demand in Europe and sell for the best price; quoted (in translation) in Parmentier 1996, p. 108.

33 As late as the 1820s the trade catering to a middle market in England did not expect to sell full, matching tea sets. See Ann Eatwell and Alex Werner, 'A London Staffordshire Warehouse 1794–1825', *Journal of the Northern Ceramics Society*, vol. 8, 1991, pp. 91–124.

34 Daniel Roche (Roche 1998, pp. 632–33) has advanced the theory that the French had a preference for porcelain. He contends that the meaning of porcelain for the wealthy French was wealth unconstrained by prudence, luxury freed from the tyranny of the useful, whereas silver was wealth constrained, a comforting luxury. These ideas caught on first with established and enlightened families, while *nouveaux riches* and *petits bourgeois* continued to insist on silver as proof of their new status. Older families, who already owned silver, looked to porcelain as proof of their intellectual curiosity, aesthetic predilections and sophisticated tastes. Porcelain signalled rapid rise, desire for new sensations. Exotic as well as fragile, porcelain reassured Enlightenment society of its possession of the world.

35 See Sargentson 1996, p. 64.

36 In 1783 Mrs Papendiek, assistant keeper of the wardrobe to Queen Charlotte, commenting on the preference of the gentry for Oriental or 'India' china, also clarified the hierarchy of materials for elegant drinking and dining: "Our tea and coffee set were of common India china, our dinner service of eathenware to which, for our rank, there was nothing superior, Chelsea porcelain and fine India china being only for the wealthy. Pewter and Delftware could also be had but were inferior."

37 It has been suggested that these wares were rather coarser than others and may have been used in the 1740s and 1750s

in commercial premises like coffee houses rather than the home: Kilburn and Sheaf 1988, pp. 112, 147.

38 The engraved inscription records that it is a teapot and that it was presented by Lord George Berkeley to the East India Company Committee. It may have been intended for an institutional use for which the shape was felt to be more appropriate.

39 The only known surviving Parisian silver teapot from the earliest period, in the collection of the Metropolitan Museum, New York, dates from about 1699–1700. The large, disproportionate handle is at right angles to the round body, like that of a chocolate pot. The design is close to a drawing by Nicolas-Ambroise Cousinet of a teapot for the duc d'Aumont. Later French silver teapots often had bulbous bodies with straight necks, while in porcelain the shapes were ovoid, globular or straight-sided.

40 "*Il est vrai que Madame de Sablière prenoit du thé avec son lait; elle me le disoit l'autre jour; c'étoit son goût*": Marie de Rabutin-Chantal Sévigné, *Letters*, 1811, p. 256.

41 *Letters of Rachel Wriothesley, Lady Russell*, London, 1773. However, there was a "blue and white milk cup with a handell and spout" in the 1678 inventory of the Duke and Duchess of Marlborough: Phillip Allen, 'Visit to Boughton House on Tuesday 28 June 2005', *Oriental Ceramic Society*, 2004–05, vol. 69, pp. 87–95.

42 A milk jug attributed to Saint-Cloud is shown in New York 1999, pp. 134–45.

43 Spoons are shown on the silver spoon tray in the Collins painting but the more sophisticated tea chests had compartments for tea spoons, strainer spoons (to remove debris from poured tea), knives (for cutting sugar) and sugar tongs.

44 Faulkner 2003, p. 94.

45 For information on this technique see Young 1999, pp. 116–17.

46 Sargentson 1999.

47 Savill 1988, pp. 489–90.

48 Young 1999, p. 75.

49 "The Chinese teapots are made from a reddish clod of earth or impressed clay, in which they think that the tea is best made perfect": Peter Muguet, *Tractatus Novi de Potu Caphe de Chinensium Thé et de Chocolata*, 1685.

50 In 1690 Mary Evelyn Mundus wrote in *Muliebris or The Ladies Dressing Room Unlock'd* (London, 1693, p. 11) that women were as expensive to out fit as ships and required: "… tea and chocolate pot,/ with molinet and caudle cup/ restoring breakfast to sup up/ Porcelain saucers, spoons of gold dishes/ that refin'd sugars hold".

51 Elizabeth Teft, *Orinthia's Miscellanies*, London, 1747.

52 *Whipping Tom or Red for a Proud Lady*, II, 'Of the expensive use of drinking tea', 1722 (5th edition), p. 17.

53 See Emmerson 1992, p. 23.

54 Letter from Charles Churchill to John Wilkes, 13 July 1762, in *Original Letters Illustrative of English History*, London (several edns), 'Letters to Mr John Wilkes'.

55 *Whipping Tom* (see note 52), p. 16.

56 Snodin 1984, p. 82, F2.

57 *Mme du Hausset: Memoires – or The Private Memoirs of Madame du Hausset: Lady's maid to Madame de Pompadour*, 1825, p. 25.

58 Benedetta Craveri, *Madame du Deffand and her World*, London, 1994, pp. 85–86.

59 See above, essay by Anne Dulau, pp. 20–21. A view of a similar handle on an object which may be a teapot, in a red earthenware, can be seen in Chardin's painting, *The Fast Day*, 1731 (Paris, Louvre), and a white-glazed earthenware teapot is shown in *Still Life with Teapot* (Boston, Museum of Fine Arts).

60 See also cat. 12a–c.

61 Sargentson 1996, p. 62 and note 5.

62 *To a Lady on her passion for Old china*, London, 1725, p. 2.

63 Jörg 1982, pp. 148–49.

64 Quoted in Charles Saumarez Smith, *Eighteenth Century Decoration*, London, 1993, p. 128.

65 Savill 1982.

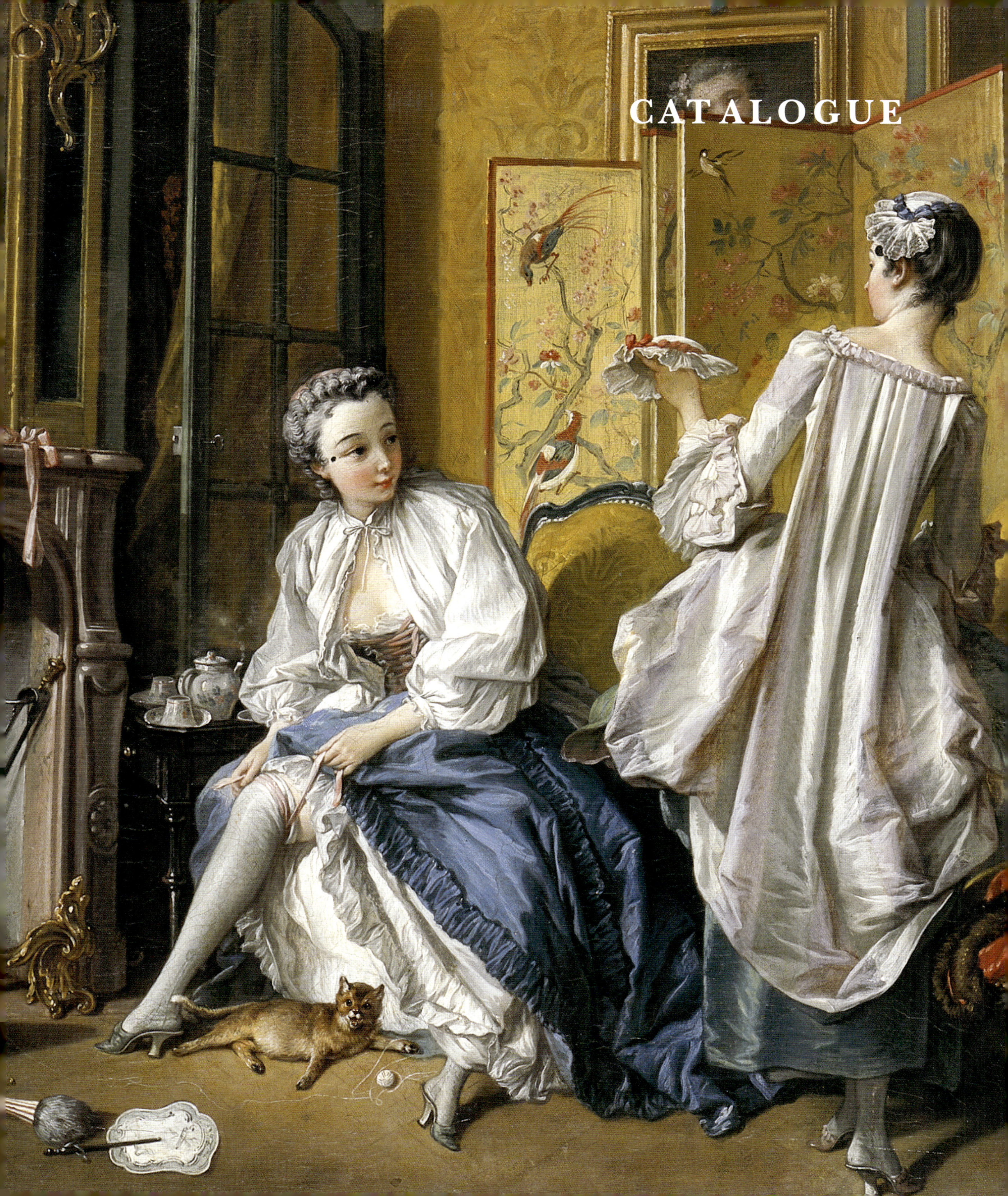
CATALOGUE

There is a small group of works by Boucher and Chardin that have many features in common with *Lady taking Tea* and *Woman on a Daybed* – costume, elements of interior decoration, objects, the paraphernalia of pastimes, the fascination for things Chinese, the drinking of tea. They include three works, *The Morning Toilet, Woman fastening her Garter* and *The Milliner*, which were commissioned either directly or through an intermediary by the eminent art collector Count Carl Gustaf Tessin. Swedish ambassador to the court of Louis XV from 1739 to 1742, Tessin indulged his love of French art during his Parisian stay, buying and commissioning a number of paintings by modern masters. Impressed by Boucher and Chardin's genre scenes, he commissioned each to depict a morning toilet. The resulting works, Chardin's *The Morning Toilet* (1741) and Boucher's *Woman fastening her Garter* (1742), were both viewed by contemporaries as quintessences of contemporary life and its daily occupations and were reproduced in print form before they left for Sweden and Tessin's collection. In Sweden they were admired by the Princess Royal, Louisa Ulrika of Prussia, whom Tessin was assisting in building up a picture collection. This led to the commission of the third painting, Boucher's *The Milliner*, which, showing a fashionable Parisienne at her toilet in the latest French interior, was to represent 'Morning'.

This introductory section examines Boucher and Chardin's individual interpretations of their world and how each put them on canvas, and compares and contrasts their common features.

INTERIORS

Both Chardin and Boucher illustrated many features we consider typical of interiors in the first half of the eighteenth century, encompassing small tables, upholstered furniture, dressing tables, daybeds, chimneypieces, screens and furniture with *pieds de biche* (curled back ends) and slender curved legs. With the exception of some Oriental objects found in Boucher's paintings, the furniture represented is of a kind one would have expected to find in the home of a reasonably fashionable and well-heeled Parisian family. Of no interest to collectors, furniture of this kind has rarely survived.

Floors

In all three interiors Boucher depicted a simple pine floor. Such floors are more characteristic of modest dwellings and secondary rooms such as an artist's studio than of reception rooms. By contrast Chardin chose a fine oak chequered parquet for *The Morning Toilet* (cat. 3; see p. 90) of a kind fashionable from the early years of Louis XV's reign (fig. 55).

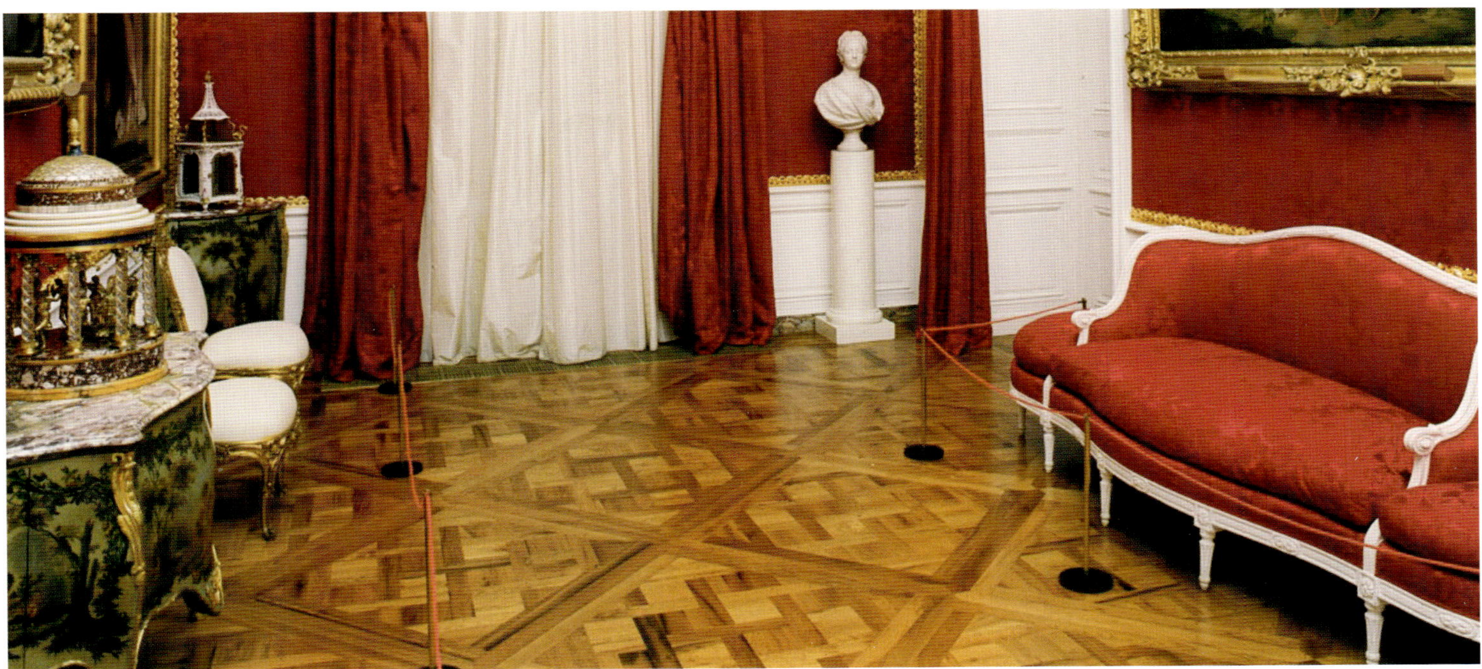

Walls

Boucher's walls illustrate the latest fashions in an age when portable wall decorations like tapestries were being replaced by permanent features – opulent damask in *Woman on a Daybed* (fig. 2) and *Woman fastening her Garter* (fig. 15, p. 21) or fashionable *rocaille* boiserie of *The Milliner* (cat. 5; see p. 91) – complete with an overdoor picture of a type Boucher had made his speciality.[1] Chardin opted for those blurred, muted backgrounds that he did so well, a solution which allowed him perhaps to focus better on the moment depicted. Had he chosen to describe his backgrounds more accurately he would likewise have depicted materials, inspired perhaps by the walls of his bedroom and cabinet, hung with Bruges satin and Aubusson tapestry.[2] The *Morning Toilet* shows skirting boards, though they are barely discernible, and there is some suggestion of panelling in *Lady taking Tea*.

Chimneypieces

"The chimney-piece with its gilt-framed mirror and its gilt-bronze fire irons is perhaps, more than any other parts of the wall-decoration, one of the successes of Paris art."[3] Generally of marble or stone, fireplaces (fig. 56) were the sole source of heating, inefficient and liable to smoke in an ill wind. The fireplace of *Woman fastening a Garter* (fig. 57a) is of a simple but modish type common in the early years of Louis XV, with console supports, tall mirror and matching sconces with twin candles – similar to the

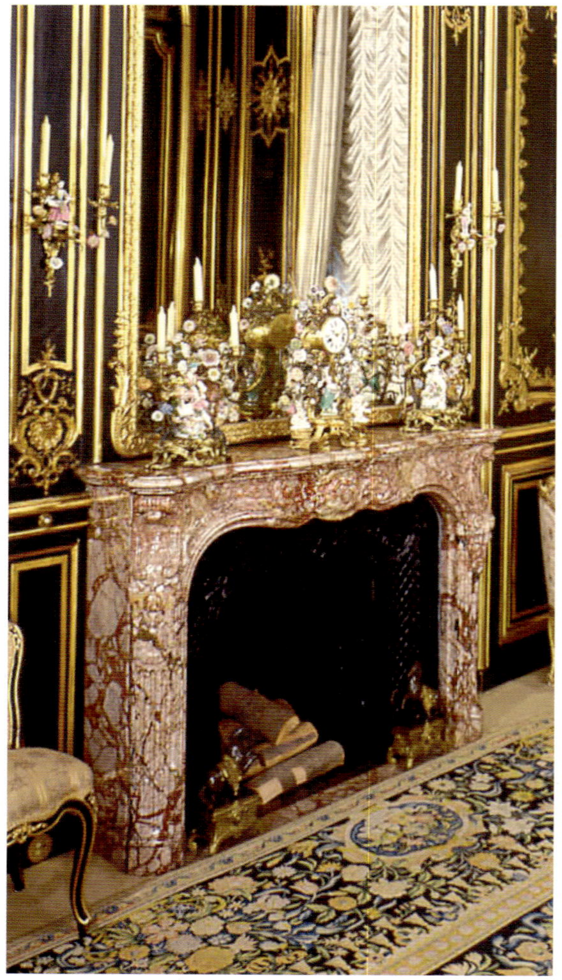
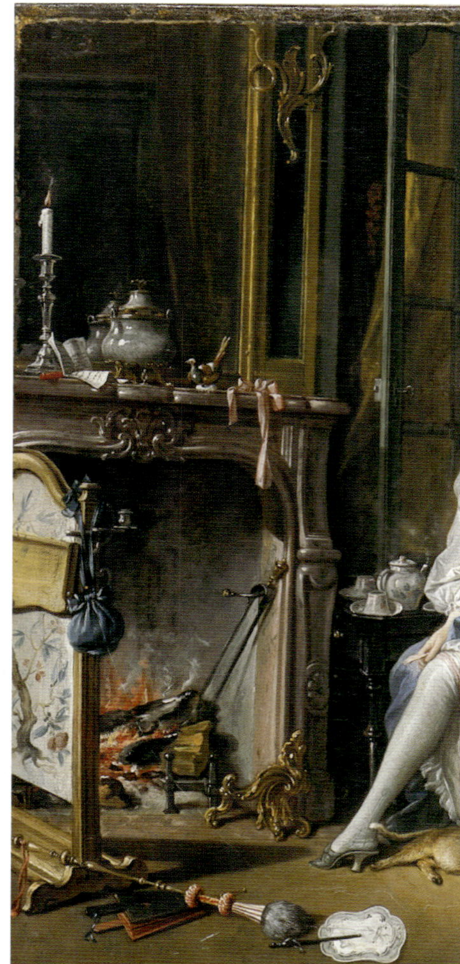
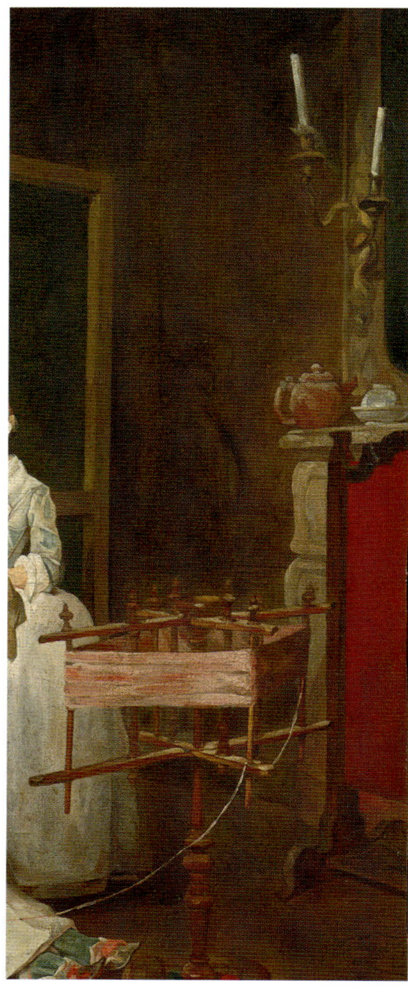

Fig. 56
Fireplace from the Green Boudoir,
Waddesdon Manor, Waddesdon

Fig. 57a (detail)
Boucher, *Woman fastening her Garter*

Fig. 57b (detail)
Jean-Siméon Chardin
The Diligent Mother, 1740
Oil on canvas; 50 x 39.5 cm
Nationalmuseum, Stockholm
inv. no. NM 784

one depicted by Chardin in *The Diligent Mother* (fig. 57b) of 1740. But, as often in these scenes of daily life, Boucher concentrated on details – the grain of the marble or the light caught on its scroll motifs – which Chardin would leave to the imagination in favour of "*les masses générales, ces tons de la couleur, la rondeur, les effets de la lumière et des ombres*" (the general masses, shades of colour and curves, effects of light and shadow).[4] While Boucher's aim is to impress and to seduce the eye, Chardin's is to simplify, to create an environment true to nature whilst providing an appropriate context for his exploration of human interaction.

High mirrors

High mirrors were an essential element of fashionable interiors and a costly commodity, partly because pieces frequently broke during manufacture or in transit. Tessin wrote to his wife in 1741: "We are unlucky with our

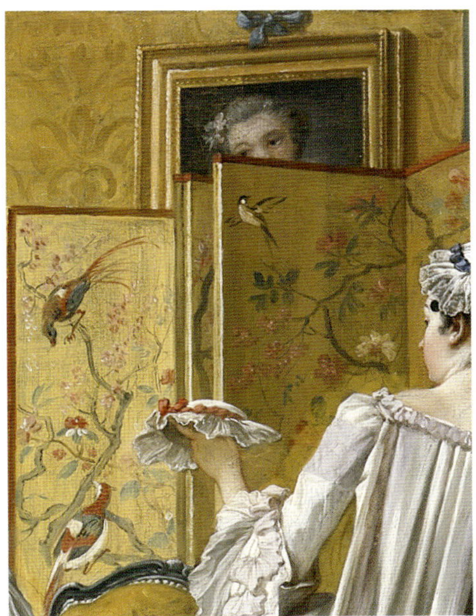

Fig. 58 (detail)
Boucher, *Woman fastening her Garter*

mirrors; I have scolded the packer, but that does not give us back our looking glass".[5]

Screens and curtains

Folding and fire screens were a necessary protection against heat, cold and drafts and could be used to create more intimate spaces. Boucher depicted a magnificent Oriental screen in *Woman on a Daybed* and *Woman fastening her Garter* (fig. 58) that makes a profound fashion statement with its eight leaves and exotic décor of birds and foliage. Such an item would have been seen in the most luxurious interiors, but its appearance in both paintings suggests it may have been Boucher's own. The fire screen in *Woman fastening her Garter* (see fig. 57A) includes a small collapsible table and a candlestick holder. This clever addition – which besides offering protection from the fire could be used for reading, writing or needlework – shows the ingenuity of eighteenth-century furniture makers. Such multi-functional fire screens were popular and appeared in other contemporary paintings, including the now lost *Instant de la Méditation* (Moment of Meditation) by Chardin.

Another device for keeping draughts at bay was curtaining for windows, as in *The Milliner* (cat. 5; see p. 91). These made their appearance in the early eighteenth century, proliferating after Louis XV had hung them everywhere in the Cour des Cerfs. This recent vogue for curtains is evident in Mme Chardin's inventory: they appear in every room including the kitchen. Doors were frequently fitted with drapery in winter, attached directly to the door as in *Woman fastening her Garter* (see fig. 15; p. 21) or above it as in *Woman on a Daybed* (fig. 2, p. 11). Again, Mme Chardin's inventory alludes to this practice and informs us that Chardin had his studio door covered with Caen *damas*.

THE BEDROOM AND THE TOILETTE

Three of the paintings – *The Morning Toilet*, *Woman on a Daybed* and *The Milliner* – depict bedrooms, but only Boucher included beds – a daybed in *Woman on a Daybed* (fig. 2, p. 11) and an alcove with a bed in *The Milliner* (fig. 59). Numerous contemporary designs have survived for alcoves with tightly drawn curtains, which would retain warmth at night (fig. 60).

That the *toilette* was an all-important moment in the life of the eighteenth-century woman was acknowledged by the *Petit Dictionnaire de la Cour et de la Ville*: "A charming woman uses more subtlety and politics in her dressing than there are in all the governments of Europe."[6] Contemporary artists, well aware of the importance of *la toilette*, depicted it in genre scenes and portraits. Boucher completed at least three other paintings, besides

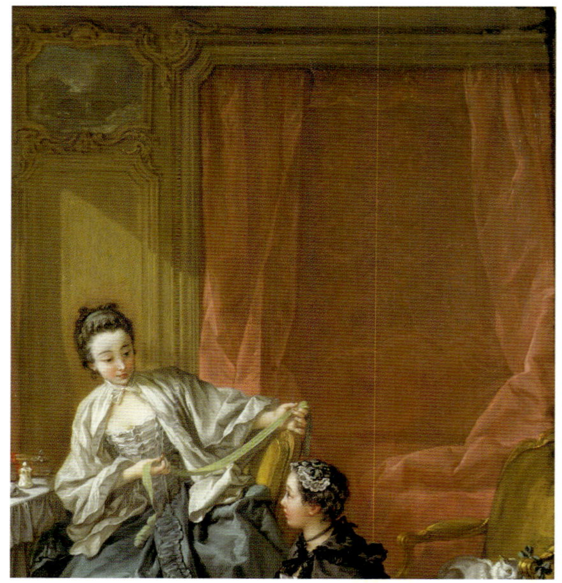

Fig. 59 (detail)
Boucher, *The Milliner*

Fig. 60
Office of Jean-François Blondel,
Design for the alcove wall of a bedroom,
c. 1710–25
Pen and ink, wash and graphite,
161 x 286 mm
Waddesdon Manor, Waddesdon

Fig. 61
Silver *toilette* or dressing set, Louis XV style
Dunham Massey

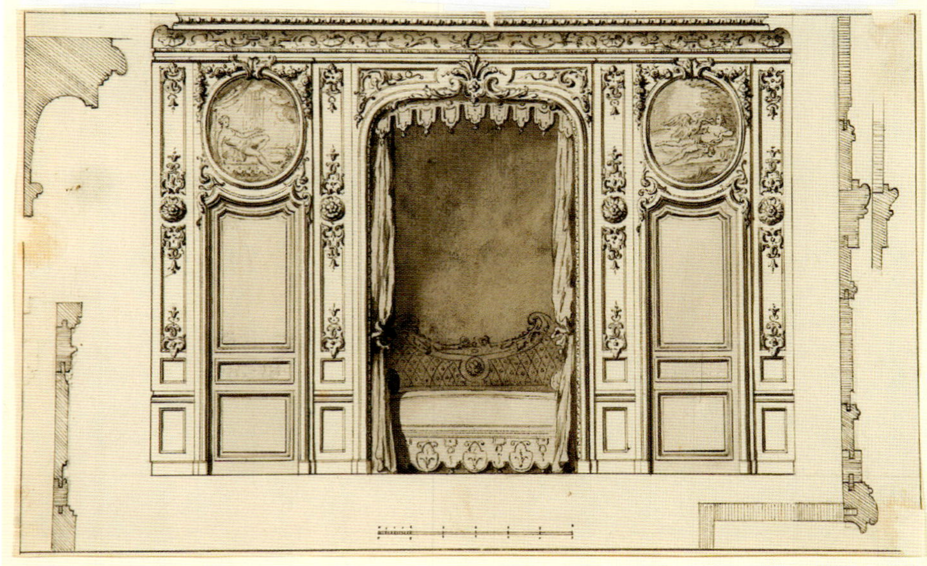

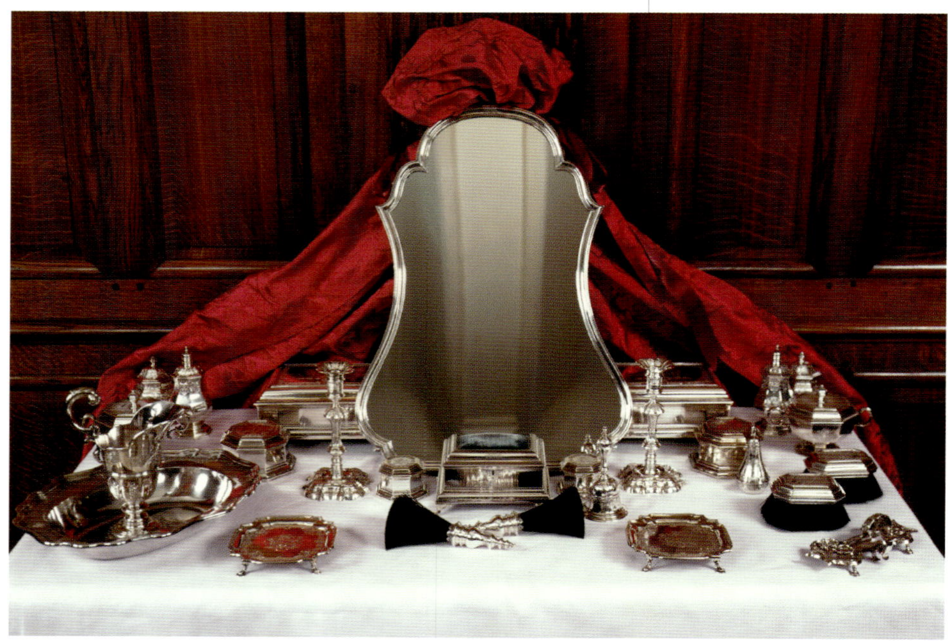

The Milliner and *Woman fastening her Garter*, on this subject. The appropriate dress for this leisurely procedure at which friends could be present and business affairs discussed was a *négligé du matin*, a loose robe worn over a chemise and stays. A powdering mantle, as depicted by Boucher, would protect the outfit from cosmetics, hairpowder and pomades.

The dressing tables and standing mirrors depicted by Boucher and Chardin are similar in style and simple. Usually kept in a clothes closet, consisting of a frame draped with silk, lace or muslin, often mounted on

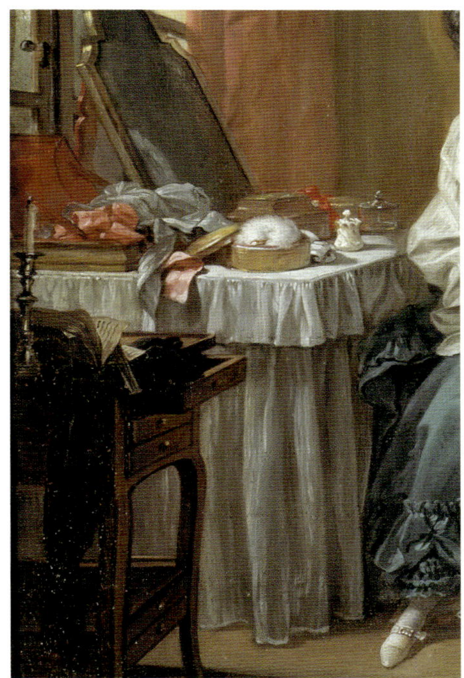

Fig. 62 (detail)
Boucher, *The Milliner*

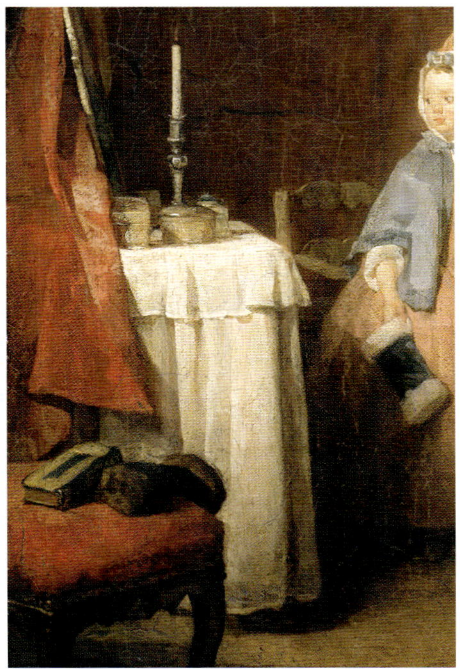

Fig. 63 (detail)
Chardin, *The Morning Toilet*

casters, they were brought into the bedroom each morning and evening. The mirror, framed and raised on an easel-like stand, was sometimes half draped with material, as in Chardin's *Morning Toilet* (fig. 63) or standing alone as in Boucher's *The Milliner* (fig. 62). Such dressing sets would have been silver, plate or pinchbeck. Relatively simple, they are early Louis XV in style (fig. 61). As the 1737 inventory of the first Mme Chardin included a toilette mirror covered with red silk (*miroir de toilette … dans sa bordure cintrée … couverte de soie cramoisie*),[7] it is likely to be the one used as a studio prop in *The Morning Toilet*.

FURNITURE AND DECORATIVE ART OBJECTS

Candles were essential after dark, and an expensive commodity (under Louis XVI, the cost of a candle was equal to a week's pay for a field labourer). The candle holders depicted by Boucher and Chardin in their genre scenes appear to be of silver and are strikingly similar. Like the dressing sets they are typical of the Louis XV period and not unusual. Likewise, the rest of the furniture, though modish, is not extravagantly so; the stool in *The Morning Toilet* and the daybed in *Woman on a Daybed* have Régence frames; the straight-legged black cabaret table of *Woman fastening her Garter* is also less up to date than other pieces; both reappear in Boucher and Chardin's contemporary genre scenes. Boucher's chairs and armchairs with their *pieds de biche* are of a more recent style but less intricately carved than most surviving contemporary furniture (fig. 64). Chardin's style of chair, simple yet enduring, is still in use today.

Small side-tables, easy to carry from room to room, were an important feature of interiors. Boucher, who, in common with his fashionable clients, crammed his interiors with furniture, depicts three different types in his paintings – the black-lacquered cabaret table from *Woman fastening her Garter*; in *The Milliner* a *chiffonnier* with three upper and two lower drawers to hold the small objects women used every day; and a very simple table with one drawer and slender curved legs in *Woman on a Daybed*. By contrast Chardin would include only furniture which served his purpose: in the three paintings examined here, *Lady taking Tea* alone called for the top of a small, simple, fashionably lacquered cabaret table, the same with which he would also furnish a still life in the 1750s (see figs. 19, 20, pp. 23, 24).

Shelving like the pale blue wall-cupboard in *Woman on a Daybed* seems to have been a favourite with Boucher, and can be connected with his activity as a collector, since such furniture was designed for the display of collectibles. Similar shelves appear, for example, in *Le Déjeuner* of 1739 (Louvre, Paris)

Also to be noted are the corner cupboard and the clock in Boulle style in Chardin's *Morning Toilet* and the *châtelaine* (ornamental chain) watch

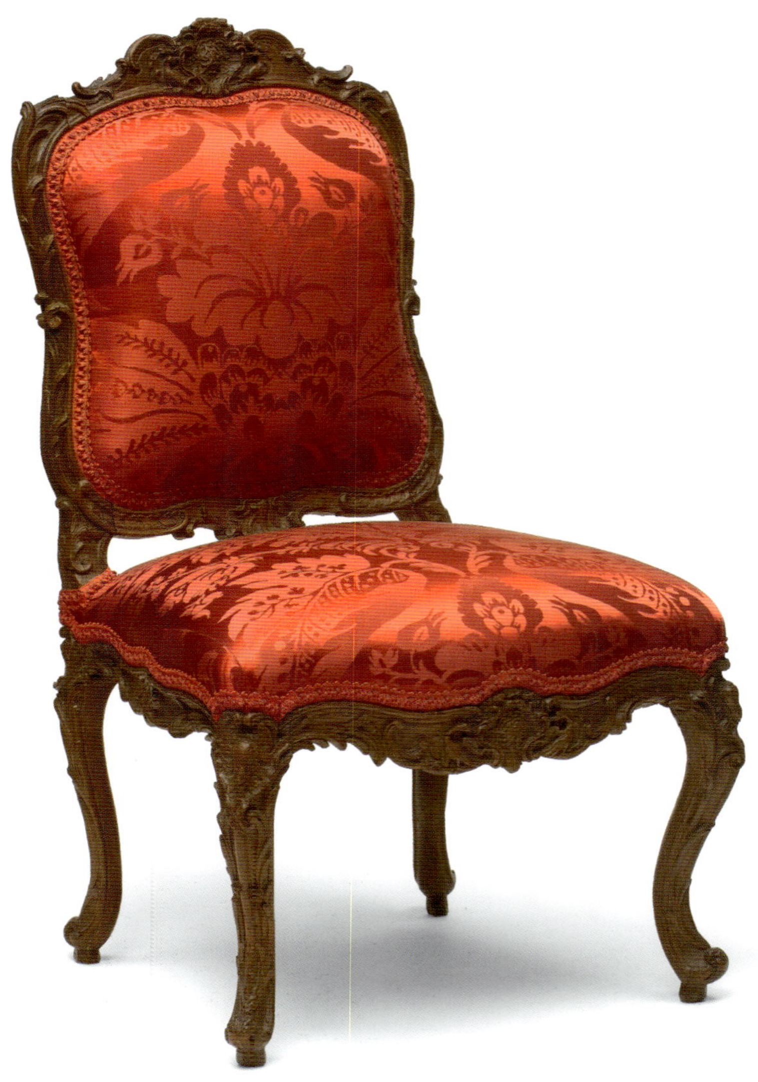

beside the cupboard in Boucher's *Woman on a Daybed* (see frontispiece). The corner cupboard or *encoignure* was a popular piece specifically designed to fit into a right angle to make the most of available space. Clocks, barometers, thermometers and *châtelaines* were much in demand among Boucher and Chardin's contemporaries. Allying science to art, they had recently taken on an ornamental role and could be found in most comfortable interiors. Bracket or mantel clocks such as that depicted by Chardin were introduced by André-Charles Boulle around 1700. Their design was so popular that countless variations were produced throughout the eighteenth century.

Most of the furniture in *The Morning Toilet* putatively matches pieces in Chardin's own interior. The stool might be one of his two "*cabriolets de crin de velour cramoisy*" (stools covered with crimson velvet) and part of a set that included a *bergère* and two armchairs of "*bois de hêtre*" (beech) embellished with cushions of "*velour cramoisy*" (crimson velvet).[8] It reappears in *La Bonne Education* (*The Good Education*), commissioned from Chardin by Princess Ulrika in 1745 (she commissioned four paintings from Boucher and two from Chardin in that year).[9] Chardin had four *encoignures*, two in "*bois de palissandre*" (rosewood) in the sitting-room and two of unspecified wood in the bedrooms.[10] Chardin's possessions in 1737 included a clock by Fiacre Clément in the Boulle style.

Trifles, trinkets and daily occupations

Fashionable interiors contained domestic items in an inexhaustible variety of shape and form, and purely decorative objects were increasingly sought after. The trifles and trinkets that abound in Boucher's interiors are largely absent in Chardin's. It is the abundance of fashionable detail in fans, porcelain pheasants, crumpled scarves and ribbons, Oriental porcelain, opened books and letters, vases and knotting bags with escaping threads that give Boucher's scenes their narrative, for the bland expressions of his sitters reveal little. The porcelain trinket in the shape of an artichoke on the

Fig. 64
Jean-Baptiste I Tilliard,
'*Chaise à la reine*' (queen chair), Paris, *c.* 1730–40
Carved beechwood,
height 96 cm, width 60 cm
Musée des arts décoratifs, Paris
inv. no. 36422

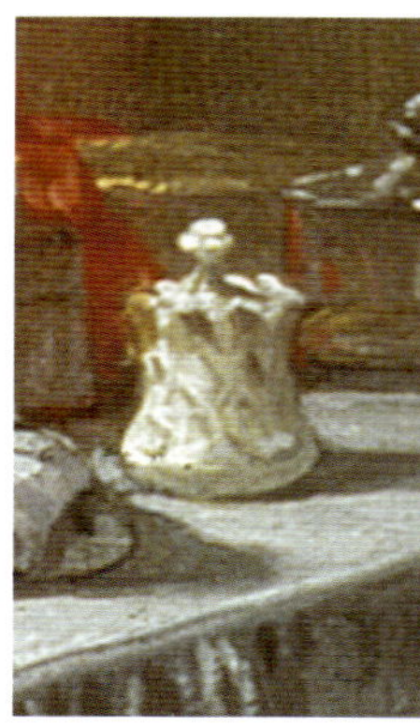

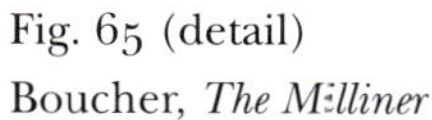

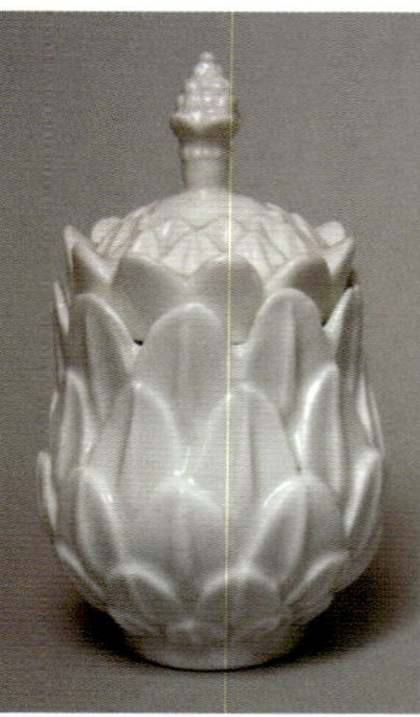

Fig. 65 (detail)
Boucher, *The Milliner*

Fig. 66
Pot in the shape of an artichoke, *c.* 1730–50
Saint-Cloud factory
Private collection

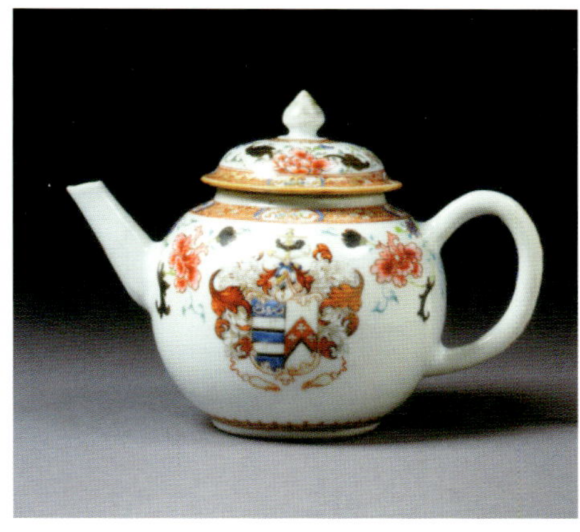

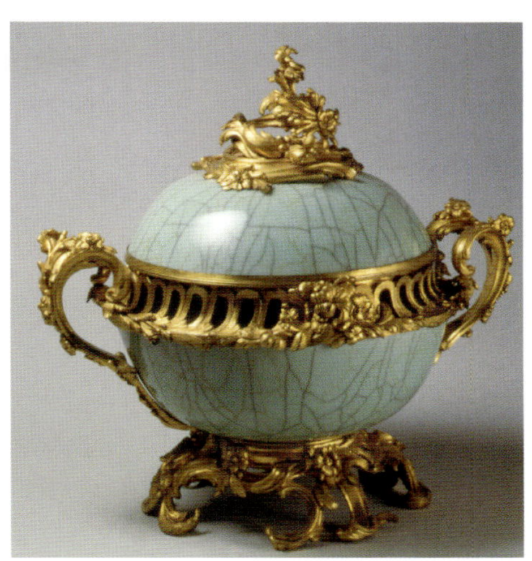

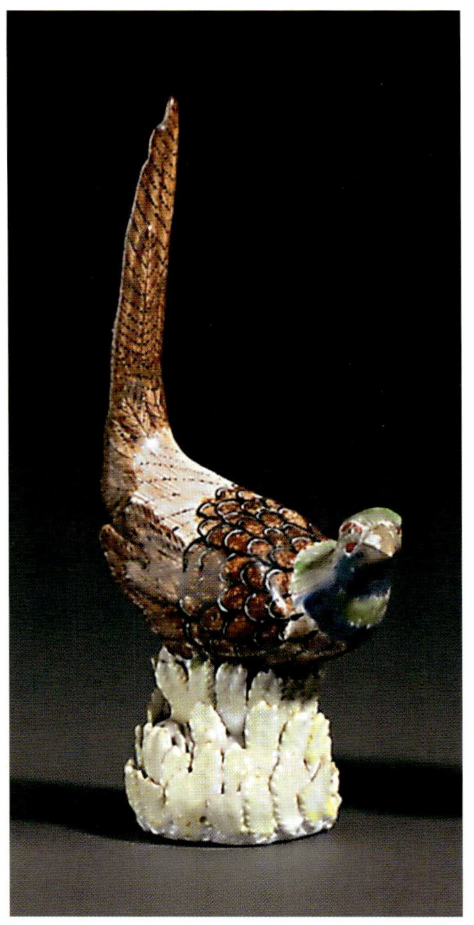

dressing table of *The Milliner* (fig. 65) may be an example of the china lately manufactured at Saint-Cloud (fig. 66).

Porcelain and the Far East

Whereas Chardin's interest in Oriental porcelain would become more apparent in his later still lifes, Boucher's *tableaux de mode* of the late 1730s and early 1740s bear testament to a fascination for China. This is nowhere more apparent than in *Woman fastening her Garter*, in which a steaming teapot with matching cups, probably Chinese Imari porcelain or *famille rose* style (like the example in fig. 67), sit on a lacquered tea-table, and a mounted Chinese grey crackle-glazed *cassolette* or *pôt-pourri* and a pheasant likely to be Meissen grace the mantelpiece. Such objects would have adorned the households of connoisseurs like Mme de Pompadour and the duc d'Orléans, who purchased crackled-glaze wares in the 1750s. Several lots in the 1771 sale of Boucher's collections contained objects like one now at Waddesdon (fig. 68), which matches the description of lot 808, "*Deux beaux vases bleuatres, richement garnis en bronze doré*" (two beautiful bluish vases, richly garnished with bronze gilt). Like the ornate screen in *Woman on a Daybed*, this type of vase, *pôt-pourri* or *cassolette* reappears in other works by Boucher painted at this time.[11] These regular studio props must have been in Boucher's possession in those years, just as the red cabaret table or blue and white teacups would be Chardin's own. The little Meissen pheasant, a good example of the European-manufactured objects supplying the craze for anything Oriental, is also of a type still found in today's collections (fig. 69).[12]

The match with surviving examples confirms that Boucher did indeed depict real objects. As for Chardin, most of the furniture he painted in two of the works at the heart of this study, *Lady taking Tea* and *The Morning Toilet*, are probably pieces described in inventories of his own interior. We can be certain that they both offer a tantalizing glimpse of the sort of objects with which they were themselves surrounded and occasionally used as studio props.

Fig. 67 '*Famille rose*' teapot, *c.* 1730, porcelain, height 12 cm
Victoria and Albert Museum, London, inv. no. FE.112&A-1978

Fig. 68 Chinese covered bowl mounted as pot-pouri, mount French, *c.* 1725–50, height 37 cm
Waddesdon Manor, Waddesdon

Fig. 69 J.J. Kändler (modeller), *Pheasant*, *c.* 1750, Meissen, porcelain, height 19 cm
Private collection

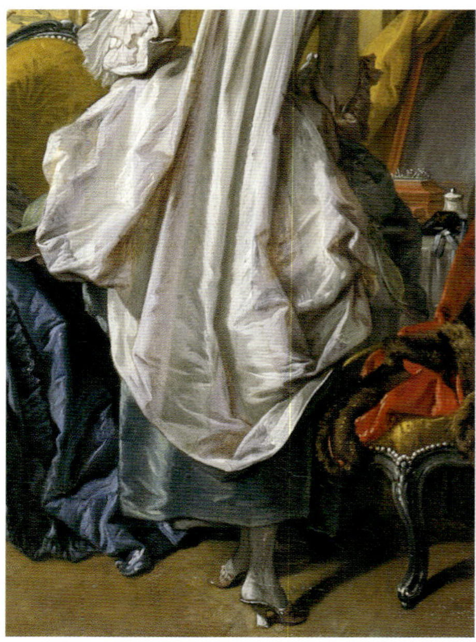

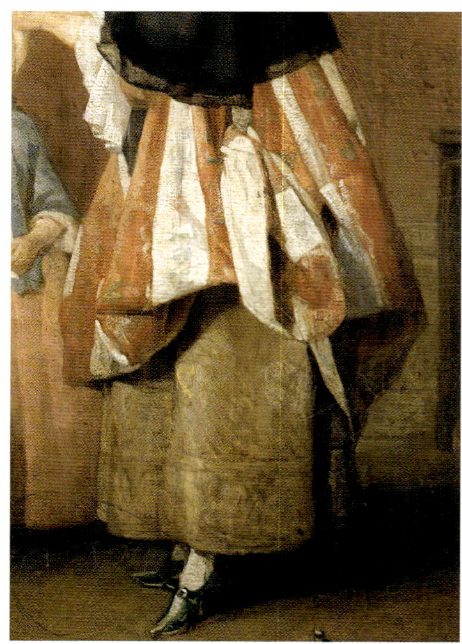

Fig. 70 (detail)
Boucher, *Woman fastening her Garter*

Fig. 71 (detail)
Chardin, *The Morning Toilet*

FEMININE FASHION

Between them Boucher and Chardin illustrate most of the important characterics of female fashion in the 1730s and 1740s. Both used clothing as a compositional tool and to convey a mood. The details of Chardin's dresses are sometimes obscured, half-hidden by a hood, head-scarf, apron or cape. By contrast, Boucher revelled in the subtleties of the latest fashionable details.

Robes volantes and *robes à la française* or sacque robes

The dress of the *Lady taking Tea* was known (from its flowing, lilting movement) as a *robe volante* (flying dress). Deriving from the *négligé* popular towards the end of the reign of Louis XIV (1634–1715), it consisted of a bodice with large pleats widening from the shoulder blades to the ground over a round petticoat supported by stays and a hoop. Such a garment was a necessity according to the *Mercure de France* for March 1729: "the *robes volantes* are all the rage and one hardly sees any other dress …".[13] In the early 1740s the *robe volante* was replaced in fashionable circles by the sacque dress, immortalized by Boucher. In his paintings he shows variations of a plain silk sacque dress fitted at the waist and worn with a stomacher and with tantalizing lacing at the bosom, perfect for seduction. Although exquisite details such as small rouches beautify their outfits, they remain simple compared to those found in contemporary portraits of *bourgeoises* and aristocrats. So while the garments depicted by Boucher in his genre scenes have come to epitomize the gracefulness of Rococo dress, no painter represented such simple examples in contemporary portraiture. This indicates that by the 1740s Boucher was turning away from faithful imitation to the creation of a pictorial vocabulary calculated to conjure up a personal interpretation of the current stereotype of a fashionable young woman.

In *Woman fastening her Garter* (fig. 70) and *The Morning Toilet* (fig. 71) both Boucher and Chardin reproduced the latest way of wearing the sacque dress, with its hem tucked into the pockets of the petticoat to achieve a swagged look in harmony with Rococo taste. This new fashion was referred to by Mme d'Epinay in 1749 when she described wearing her gown *"retroussée dans ses poches"* (tucked up in her pockets).

Hairstyle and head-dresses

Whenever the hair is visible, Boucher and Chardin's women wear the fashionable tightly curled style known as *tête de mouton* under a linen or lace head-dress adorned with ribbons that match their outfits, reflecting the variety of fashionable headgear of the time. This included the *commode* presented to the *Woman fastening her garter* and worn by the *Woman on a*

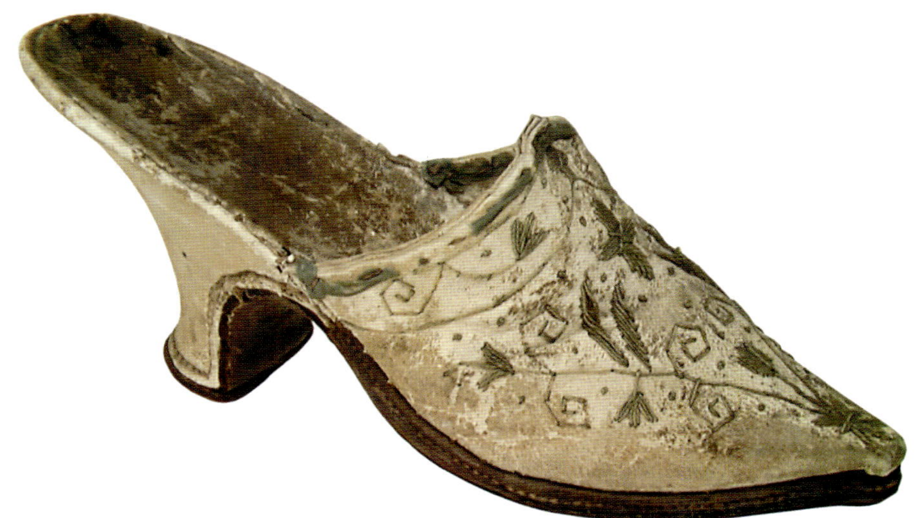

Daybed, or the smaller head-dresses made of linen or lace of the *Lady taking Tea* or *The Milliner*. Only the woman taking tea displays hair dusted with white powder, as the other sitters are either waiting to undergo this final stage of the *toilette* or are wearing head-dresses. Diderot, who praised Chardin's faithfulness to nature, would have been delighted, had he known the painting, by the sprinkling of white powder that has settled on the shoulder of Chardin's model .

Capes and shawls

Exquisite long and short capes, in lace, silk or trimmed with fur, reflect the need to keep warm. The ravishing black shawl lined with blue silk is among the most sophisticated items depicted by Chardin. Both Chardin and Boucher painted the *capucine* or short cape that sometimes included a hood. In *The Morning Toilet* the little girl is prettily clad in a soft pink dress and blue *capucine*. Her mother or governess wears a black version with matching hood, as does Boucher's *Milliner*. As always, Boucher gives vibrancy to the *capucine* by lovingly detailing the tiny ruffles of its edging. The full-length red velvet fur-trimmed *pelisse* draped over the chair of *Woman fastening her Garter* (fig. 70) and the fur-lined muffs of *The Morning Toilet* reflect the fashion for fur trimming, likely to have been inspired by the uniforms of Central European troops during the War of the Austrian Succession, which began in 1740.[14]

Shoes

All Boucher's women wear mules (fig. 72) with white leather heels designed for indoor use and commonly worn by middle- and upper-class Parisian women and their maids in the 1730s and 1740s. This type of white leather heel was particularly favoured by Louis XV's mistress, Mme de Pompadour, and later became known as the Pompadour heel.[15] Aileen Ribeiro has noted that "the backless mule, called a slipper, made of silk with embroidery or lace, and familiar through the intimate scenes by Boucher of ladies at their toilettes, is perhaps the most characteristic shoe of the Rococo, typifying the softness and sexual allure of this most 'feminine' period in the history of dress".[16]

Patches

Like hoops, *robes volantes*, sacque dresses, mules and *têtes de mouton* hair, patches made of black taffeta covered with gum arabic were another French fashion vulnerable to caricature when worn by the undiscriminating. The language of allusion was precise in the positioning of these black signals; according to le Camus, a patch "at the exterior Angle of the Eye" – as worn by the *Woman fastening her Garter* – was "killing".[17]

Needlework and associated pastimes

Needlework in all its forms was enthusiastically pursued at all levels of society. In the higher echelons it was viewed both as a constructive pastime and as an opportunity to show off the gracefulness of the fingers. Sewing bags frequently appear in contemporary paintings and Boucher includes a blue one in each of the present three paintings. Their popularity owed much to their secondary use as receptacles for small accessories such as gloves and fans. In *Woman fastening her Garter* the small rounded shape of the bag suggests it might be used for knotting, a hobby popular from the end of the seventeenth century consisting in knotting linen or silk threads with a small shuttle into a decorative braid which would be sewn on to fabric and small textile objects.

The briefest journey through these beautiful paintings uncovers a wealth of information on the milieu inhabited by Boucher and Chardin. The approach of each to the portrayal of daily female life gives us real insight into the way painters so similar in background could depict such different worlds, two scene-settings offering the same *tableaux* from opposite ends of the telescope. Boucher conveyed luxury in opulent, fashionable rooms with rich materials and a plenitude of detailed frippery. The furniture, however, is typically bourgeois. Chardin's muted backgrounds, fastidiously plain and carefully composed, give his interiors what the Goncourt brothers described as the "perfume of honesty and decency that emanates from his interior scenes, that breathes from … the arrangement of the furniture, the sobriety of its forms, the rusticity of the chairs, the nudity of the walls …".[18]

1 For example the overdoors for the residences of the king at Choisy and Versailles, or the hôtels of Soubise and Mazarin.

2 See the 1737 inventory in Pascal and Gaucheron 1931, pp. 64–70.

3 Verlet 1967, p. 91.

4 Cochin 1780, in Roland-Michel 1994, p. 267.

5 Whitehead 1992, p. 108.

6 Anonymous, *Le Petit Dictionnaire de la Cour et de la Ville*, Paris and London, 1788

7 See the 1737 inventory in Pascal and Gaucheron 1931, p. 68.

8 See the 1779 inventory in Wildenstein 1933, p. 145.

9 Merit Laine, 'An Eighteenth-century Minerva: Louisa Ulrika and her Collections at Drottningholm Palace 1744–1777', *Eighteenth-century Studies*, vol. 31, no. 4 pp. 493–503.

10 See the 1779 inventory published in Wildenstein 1933, pp. 144–45.

11 The grey crackle-glazed Chinese porcelain reappears in *L'Odalisque*, 1745? (Louvre); the screen is identical to that of *Woman on a Daybed*, 1743.

12 I am grateful to Errol Manners for identifying these two objects and locating surviving examples.

13 Ribeiro 2002, p. 37.

14 *Ibid.*, p. 150.

15 Nancy Bradfield, *Costume in Detail: Women's Dress 1730–1930*, Harry N. Abrams, New York, 1987, p. 27.

16 Ribeiro 2002, p. 162.

17 *Ibid.*, pp. 152–53.

18 Goncourt 1948, p. 130.

I

Boucher and Chardin's representations of women in domestic interiors

1 Jean-Siméon Chardin (1699–1779)
Lady taking Tea, 1735
Fig. 1 and details
Canvas, 80 × 101 cm
Signed and dated: *J.S. Chardin/1735*.
Inscribed on verso: *ce tableau/a este
fait/en/fevrier 1735*
Bibliography: Kemp 1978; Baxandall 1987,
pp. 80–104; for more recent bibliography
see Rosenberg 2000, no. 46
Hunterian Art Gallery and Museum,
University of Glasgow,
inv. no. GLAHA 43512

Lady taking Tea was Chardin's second essay at depicting a woman. Although exhibited at the 1739 Salon and engraved a few years later by Pierre Filloeul (1696–after 1754) it seems to have gone unremarked by contemporary critics. Since its rediscovery by scholars it has been thought to be a portrait of the artist's first wife, yet analysis shows that Chardin in fact depicted an archetypal face and dress then in vogue, creating with images from his own home (the tea table, pot and cups are all listed among his first wife's possessions) a neutral set for the evocation of the intimate daily life of a fashionable woman.

In 1735 Chardin was still new to depicting the human figure, for which he had no formal training. This is perhaps why, although he conformed to certain archetypal precedents, he chose to focus on a single, daydreaming figure rather than to adopt the anecdotal and detailed style of his contemporaries. The resulting image, a

strikingly modern work, was the first to associate tea with contemplative solitude.[1]

Interestingly, images of women drinking tea are relatively rare in contemporary French painting.[2] In those years the French preferred coffee or chocolate and tea tended to be restricted to the morning toilet.

Chardin's inspiration behind this unprecedented focus on a solitary cup of tea may lie within his personal life. By 1735 his wife, who died on 13 April of that year, had been suffering for some time with her lungs and was very ill. She liked tea and may have sought comfort in the warm beverage that was neither as heavy as chocolate nor as strong as coffee and thought to alleviate "shortness of breath" and other ailments.[3]

2 François Boucher (1703–1770)
Woman on a Daybed, 1743
Fig. 2 and details
Canvas, 57.2 × 68.3 cm
Signed and dated: *f. Boucher, 1743*; signed on the letter on the upper shelf: *f Bouche[r]*
Bibliography: Ottawa, Washington and Berlin 2003–04, no. 53
The Frick Collection, New York,
inv. no. 1937.1.139

Dated 1743, *Woman on a Daybed* belongs to a small group of pictures Boucher painted between 1739 and 1745 depicting young women of the *beau monde*. Neither exhibited at the Salons nor engraved, this too, like Chardin's *Lady taking Tea*, seems to have been overlooked by contemporary critics and later been erroneously associated with the artist's wife. Like *Lady taking Tea*, it is a painting of arresting modernity, conceived specifically to answer the contemporary demand for "embellished and modernized" Dutch works. Apart from the references to contemporary fashion, as suggested by Colin Bailey, *Woman on a Daybed* could be viewed as a

transposition of an Old Master theme to a modern context.

The setting in which the *Woman on a Daybed* reclines is the last of Boucher's *tableaux de mode* which illustrate France's contemporary fascination with China and Japan. Take the Oriental objects and sumptuous fabrics away and it shares much with Chardin's interiors depicting the daily lives of the *bourgeoisie*. Boucher and Chardin used the same raw material, transforming it with great skill to different purposes: while the woman on a daybed epitomizes the art of gracious living, *Lady taking Tea* refers to the simple pleasures of a warm drink and a moment of solitude.

Boucher's sharp eye discerns the intimacy of the ritual. Tea sets in contemporary France tended to be small, often of only one or two cups and saucers, and surviving French images from the 1730s and 1740s convey the impression that tea drinking was something to share with a friend or lover. Tea was also associated with the exotic Orient. All this is reflected in *Woman on a Daybed*, with its lacquered hanging cupboard displaying a pagoda, its blue and white tea set for two, and its pretty young woman who may well be pausing in the activities suggested by a disarray of letters, book and sewing kit to dream of a lover.

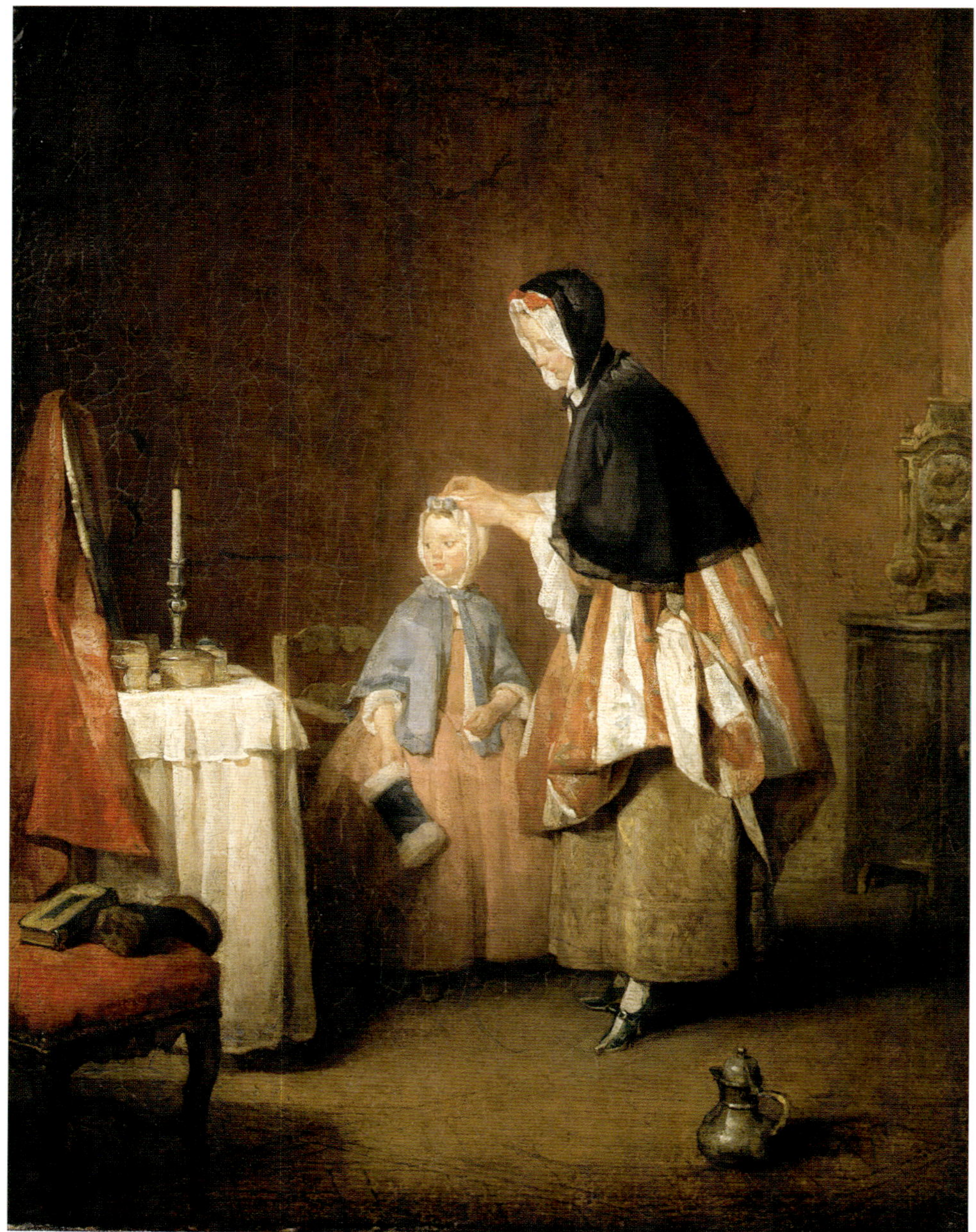

3

genre painting since *Lady taking Tea* representing a subject in vogue, Chardin turned again to his own home for a setting of modern life.

This time, however, he did not zoom in on the characters so exclusively. A fashionable corner cupboard with a Boulle-style clock and a dressing table with its accompanying silver set the scene. Adding fashionable accessories and details similar to Boucher's in his contemporary *tableaux de mode* – such as fur-lined muffs and a modish way to tuck up sacque dress into its pocket – Chardin created an evocation of the Parisian interior and feminine elegance that Europe so much admired.

Similarities with the work of contemporary painters end there. Departing from the usual treatment of such themes as in Boucher's *La Toilette* (cat. 4) or Lancret's *Morning* (cat. 6), and ignoring Tessin's original request for a woman in her *negligé*, Chardin focused his attention on a little girl and her guardian about to leave for Sunday Mass. Chardin avoids the traditional trinket and powder-puff vocabulary of the *toilette* and opts for a mixture of fashionable detail and psychological subtlety. Note the way he suggests the importance of one's appearance (inherent in his century) by means of a simple glance into a mirror and the careful positioning of a ribbon.

Visitors to the 1741 Salon were enchanted by *The Morning Toilet*, as was the Count Tessin. Surviving comments stress that visitors saw, as Philip Conisbee has put it, "… the image of an ideal of daily life to which they aspired".[4]

Engraved the same year by Jacques-Philippe Le Bas (1707–1783), this became one of Chardin's best-known works owing to the elegance with which it masters two essential features of great art – pleasing the eye while capturing truth.

3 Jean-Siméon Chardin (1699–1779)
The Morning Toilet or *The Négligé*, 1741
Reproduced above
Canvas, 49 × 39 cm
Bibliography: Rosenberg 2000, no. 63;
Ottawa, Washington and Berlin 2003–04,
no. 41
Nationalmuseum, Stockholm,
inv. no. NM 782

In 1740 Chardin's contribution to the Salon included *The Diligent Mother*, a scene of domestic life he intended to present to Louis XV which caught the eye of Count Tessin, the Swedish ambassador. After acquiring a studio copy of the painting, that eminent collector commissioned Chardin to paint a scene with a woman in her negligé and agreed to have the resulting painting, *The Morning Toilet*, included in the Salon of 1741 before taking it to Sweden. For his first

4 François Boucher (1703–1770)
Woman fastening her Garter or *La Toilette*,
1742
Fig. 15, p. 21
Canvas, 52.5 × 66.5 cm
Signed: *f. Boucher 1742*
Bibliography: Ottawa, Washington and Berlin
2003–04, no. 52
Museo Thyssen-Bornemisza, Madrid,
inv. no. 58

A year after commissioning *The Morning
Toilet* from Chardin, Tessin turned for an
interpretation of the same subject to
Boucher. Unfortunately little is known of the
circumstances surrounding the commission
except that Tessin came to own several
drawings and paintings by Boucher
representing women in their domestic
surroundings.[5] *Woman fastening her Garter* is
the second of four genre scenes by Boucher
– the first being *Le Déjeuner* (Louvre, Paris) –
painted between 1739 and 1745 and evoking
a contemporary Parisian interior.

The depictions of furniture by each
painter – the dressing table for example –
have much in common, and both paintings
offer an equal glimpse into eighteenth-
century life and values. However, they
differ significantly in overall appearance.
This unique episode in the two artist's
careers (the first and last time that each
was tackling the same subject) highlights
just how different interpretation of a
common subject can be.

In *Woman fastening her Garter*, the mastery
lies not so much in psychological subtlety as
in the skilful orchestration of the realistic.[6]
There is, for example, a steaming teapot,
suggesting imminent tea for two, a realistic
touch rare in Boucher's work. Interestingly,
although the world he created for the
woman and her maid is a fantasy, their
teapot and two teacups and saucers are a
down-to-earth recognition of tea's association
with morning and the intimacy of the *toilette*
in contemporary France.

Note the grey crackle-glazed Chinese
vase or *cassolette* and its ormolu mount, the
Meissen pheasant, the *famille rose* teapot and

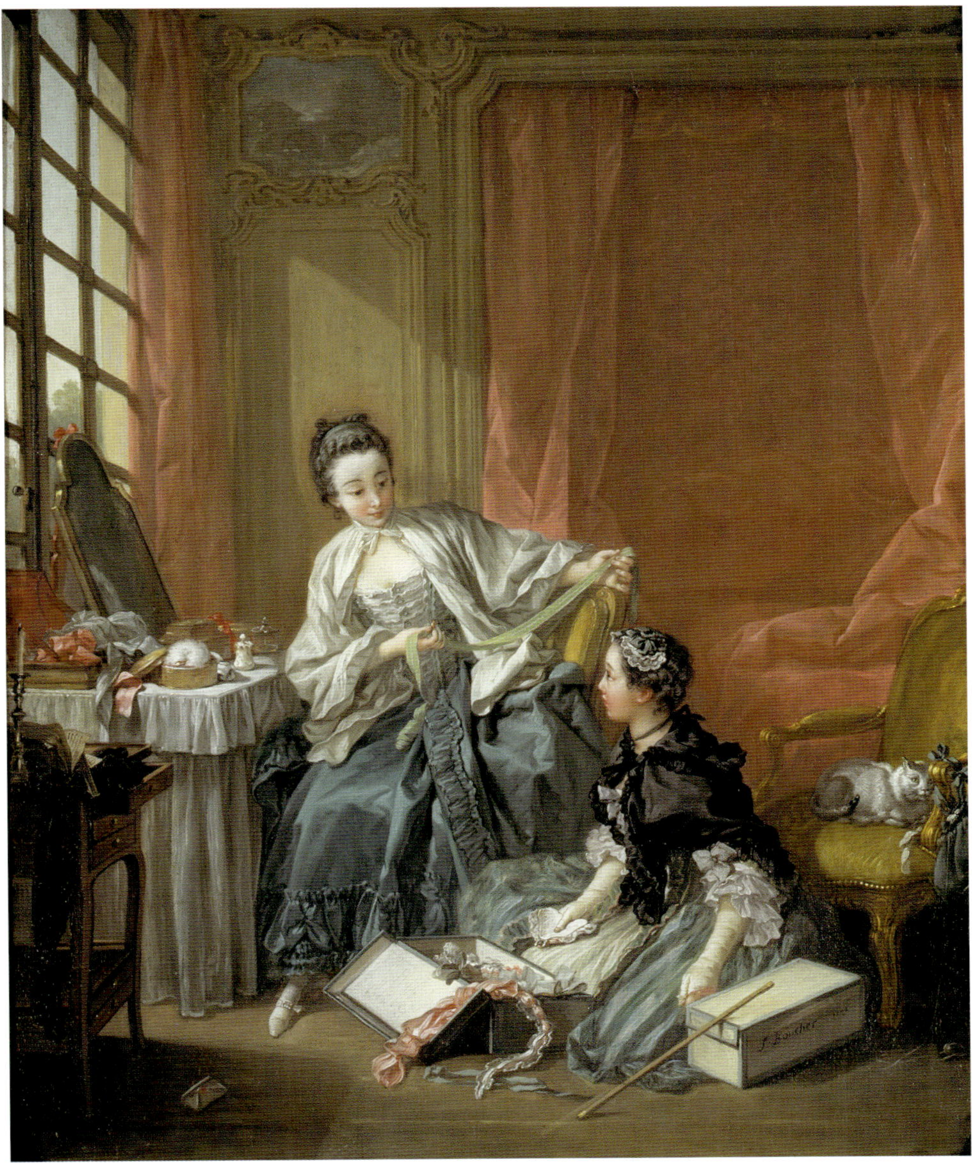

the Oriental screen, which all add a
brilliance that must have delighted Tessin, a
fellow collector of objects from the Far East.

5 François Boucher (1703–1770)
The Milliner, 1746
Reproduced above
Canvas, 64 × 53 cm
Signed on the bandbox: *f. Boucher 1746*
Bibliography: Ottawa, Washington and Berlin
2003–04, no. 54; Hyde 2006
Nationalmuseum, Stockholm,
inv. no. NM 772

In 1744 Count Tessin headed an embassy to Berlin to escort to Stockholm Louisa Ulrika, who was engaged to the Swedish Crown Prince. Enchanted by his collection of paintings by French modern masters, in October 1745 the princess asked Tessin to commission from Boucher four pictures, of *Morning, Midday, Evening* and *Night*, slightly larger than his own *Woman fastening her Garter*, "showing fashionable figures, with the pretty little faces that he is so good at". *Morning*, or *The Milliner*, was to be "a woman who has had her hair done, is still in her dressing gown, and amuses herself with looking at the trifles a milliner has spread out".[7]

To achieve his effect Boucher used as a backdrop an alcove with a bed and fashionable *boiseries* and a painted overdoor, of a type comparable to Blondel's design for the alcove wall of a bedroom (fig. 60, p. 82).[8] Not for the first time Boucher drew inspiration from designs by contemporary architects such as Blondel, as noted by Alistair Laing in the context of *Le Déjeuner*.[9] The overdoor painting itself is reminiscent of Boucher's own landscapes.

The rest of the interior has much in common with Chardin's *Morning Toilet* and Boucher's other depictions of modish women. Using the generic vocabulary he had developed from the late 1730s, probably inspired by his own home, this is Boucher's last known work dealing with the daily life of contemporary women.

The Milliner was delivered to Stockholm in 1746 but, in spite of endless reminders, Boucher never executed the three other commissioned works.

II
Taking tea and the taste for the Far East in French and British art 1720–1750

This group of works by French and British artists with subjects relating to the taste for tea and the Far East is complemented by a selection of examples of seventeenth- and eighteenth-century tea ware and Oriental figures from which artists such as Boucher, Chardin and Lancret in France and Hogarth in Britain would have drawn inspiration.

Between 1720 and 1750 Boucher and Chardin were unique in their multiple references to drinking tea, although French artists often featured porcelain and other Oriental objects in their work. Both included teapots and/or teacups and saucers in at least eight compositions.[10] Other French artists who painted subjects involving this novel drink included the little-known Antoine Quillard, who showed a family having morning tea in winter (*The Four Seasons: Winter, c.* 1725–29; fig. 51, p. 28). A decade later Lancret showed tea drinking in a fashionable set of allegories of the Seasons (*Morning*; cat. 6, fig. 27), whilst Jacques-André-Joseph Aved (1702–1766) hinted at sitters' inclination for tea in three of his portraits.[11] These works confirm what is known of French attitudes towards tea in the period. Coffee and chocolate were more common, and tea, an antemeridian delicacy, was drunk indoors in privacy.

By contrast, across the Channel the new drink was fast becoming a pivot of social life, coinciding in the 1720s with the rise of a new genre in painting, the 'conversation piece'. This typically British type of painting evolved to meet the demand of the emerging middle classes for informal small-scale group portraits depicting polite social activities. Symbolic of the social aspiration of their sitters, often bankers and merchants, conversation pieces increasingly centred on afternoon tea, either *en famille* or with visitors. Within the three decades 1720–50, over thirty conversation

pieces representing drinking tea were produced.[12]

As the 1730s unfolded tea would feature in another new British genre, the modern moral tale developed by the painter William Hogarth (1697–1764). Apprenticed to the silver-plate engraver Ellis Gamble in 1716, Hogarth witnessed first hand the popularity of tea among London's middle and upper classes when he was commissioned to engrave the Da Costa family coat of arms on a silver tea service designed by the renowned goldsmith Paul de Lamerie (1688?–1751) in the late 1720s.[13] By that time Hogarth had taken up printmaking and portrait painting and was about to become pre-eminent in the development of the conversation piece. Of the dozen or so such pictures he painted between 1730 and 1740 at least half were of families taking tea.

Simultaneously he was creating his first modern moral subjects, such as *Marriage A-la-mode* (cat. 19), with story-lines anchored in contemporary life. He had come up with a groundbreaking concept that was to be a triumph – a skilful conflation of the traditional vocabulary of Dutch seventeenth-century genre painting with related imagery by Boucher, Chardin and other French artists. His success was due in large measure to his accurate and critical observations of the life of his contemporaries, in which tea drinking and *chinoiserie* featured strongly as a symbol of misplaced ambition.

6 Nicolas Lancret (1690–1743)
The Times of Day: Morning, 1739
Fig. 27
Oil on copper, 29 × 37 cm
Bibliography: M.T. Holmes, *Nicolas Lancret 1690–1743*, Harry N. Abrams, New York, 1991, no. 16
National Gallery, London, inv. no. NG5867

A decade older than Boucher and Chardin, Lancret was instrumental in modernizing French genre painting in the wake of Watteau. He was the first French artist to depict episodes taken from the life of contemporary fashionable women, and his work was a source for Hogarth when he began work on his moral tales. This allegory of Morning was exhibited at the 1739 Salon, at which Chardin's *Lady taking Tea* was also shown. Together with *Woman fastening her Garter*, it is one of the few contemporary French paintings specifically dealing with the drinking of tea.[14]

Although the three paintings share a number of other elements such as the contemporary woman with a stereotypical face in a fashionable interior or a focus on the *toilette*, Lancret's *Morning* adopted a different approach. Exploiting without vulgarity the enticing quality inherent in a *toilette* scene, he mixed a wealth of contemporary detail with a light psychological study of what transpires when a pretty young woman *en déshabillé* shares a cup of tea with a French *abbé*.

Unlike Boucher and Chardin, Lancret painted his series illustrating *The Times of the Day* with a view to having them engraved in the following year. As pointed out by Mary Tavener Holmes, the inspiration for this allegorical subject was the seventeenth-century popular print. Allying sophistication and charm, *The Times of the Day* had great success at home and abroad, the prints influencing Hogarth's *toilette tableau* in Plate V of his *Marriage à la Mode* series painted in 1743–44 and engraved in 1745.

7 François Boucher (1703–1770)
Portrait of the Hon. Charlotta Fredikra Sparre
(1719–1795; later Countess von Fersen),
1740–41
Fig. 30
Red, black and white chalk on paper,
34.3 × 26.5 cm
Bibliography: J. Patrice Marandel, 'Boucher and Europe', in New York, Detroit and Paris 1986–87, p. 75
Day & Faber, London

Although today Boucher and Mme de Pompadour are inseparably linked, we rarely know the name of his other female sitters. This beautiful informal drawing of Charlotta

Fredrika Sparre (favourite niece of a most important patron, Count Tessin, and a celebrated beauty) is a rare example of Boucher's skills as a portraitist.

This drawing in coloured chalks (*trois crayons*) was apparently not commissioned and is one of a group Boucher is known to have made of great beauties of the day mainly for his own pleasure. Executed shortly before Boucher started painting *Woman fastening her Garter* for Count Tessin, it is as much a portrait of a stylish beauty as a genre scene capturing the fashionable pastime of having coffee.

With its sitter gracefully holding a large coffee cup, the drawing is also a reminder of the frequency with which coffee rather than tea appeared in contemporary French genre scenes representing genteel habits and of its popularity in France from the court of Louis XV to the humble household.

Boucher's portrait drawing remained in the family of the sitter until 2004.

8 Marcellus Laroon (1679–1772)
Group at Tea, 1729
Reproduced alongside
Pencil, 31.3 × 20.0 cm
National Gallery of Scotland, Edinburgh,
inv. no. D4682

This drawing of an elegant couple taking tea is one of many British works of art documenting the popularity of the infusion in fashionable London circles from the mid 1720s. Marcellus Laroon was an army officer and artist specializing in "painting & drawing in small with much variety & pleasant entertainment of musick".[15] His military career took him repeatedly to the Continent, where he became familiar with the latest artistic developments, and in his admiration of the French *fête galante* tradition he played a significant part in its transposition from outdoors to indoors, thus contributing to the creation of the British conversation piece.

Laroon's sketch – possibly a study for a larger conversation piece – exhibits a full awareness of contemporary French fashions and makes an interesting comparison with

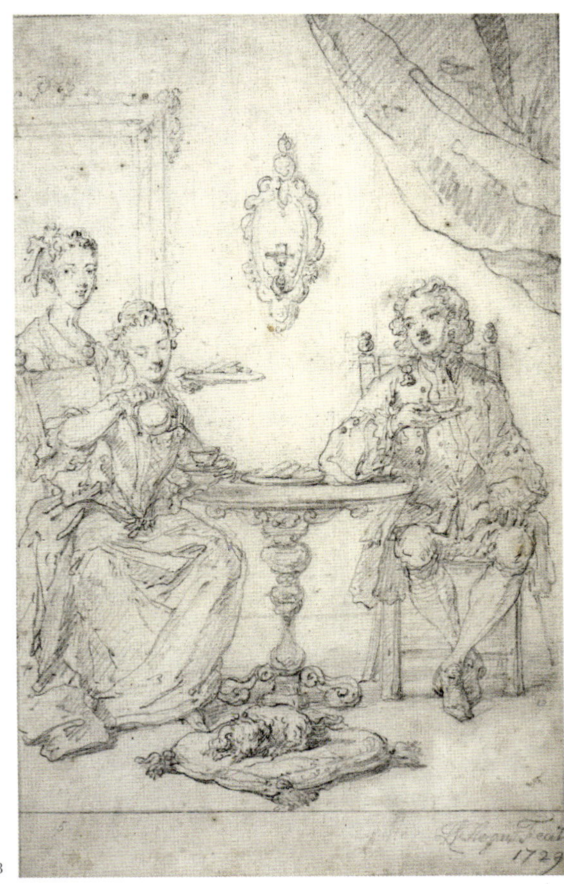

8

Nicolas Lancret's *Morning* (cat. 6). Both works show stylish contemporary interiors and a similar ritual for serving tea: the hostess holds the cup and its saucer in one hand and pours tea with the other while the maid stands behind, ready to pass it to the visitor. This represents the adoption by fashionable hostesses in France and Britain of the Japanese custom in which, according to Dufour, "even persons of the highest qualities are not ashamed, but on the contrary … take great pride to make with their own hands the decoction of this herb for their friends".[16]

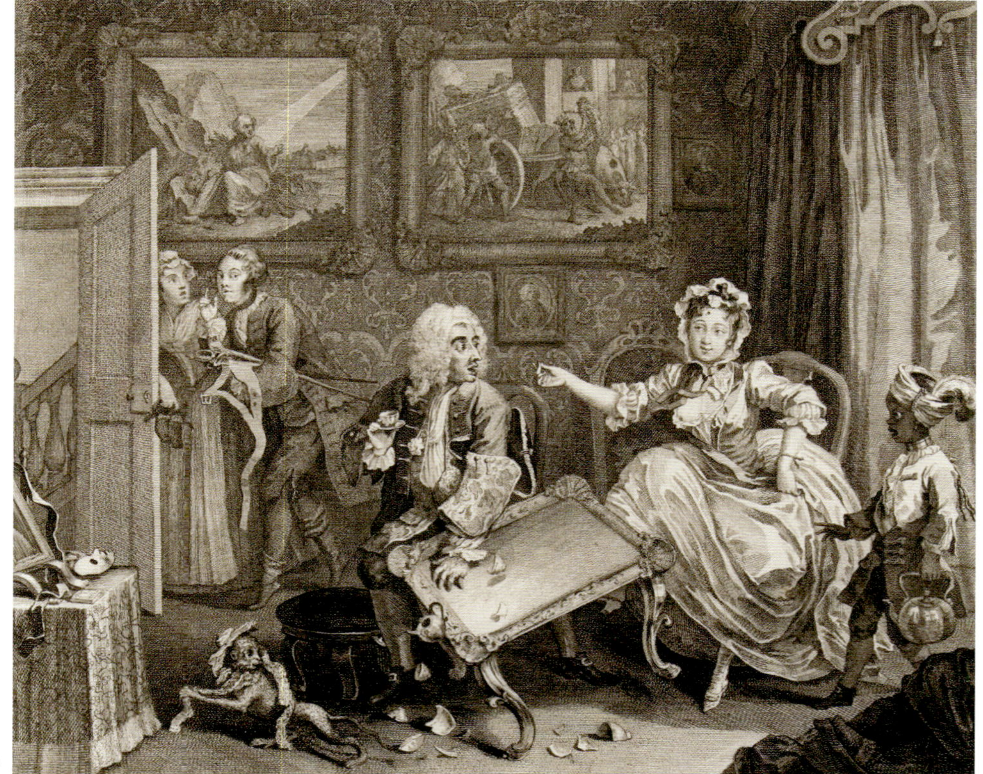

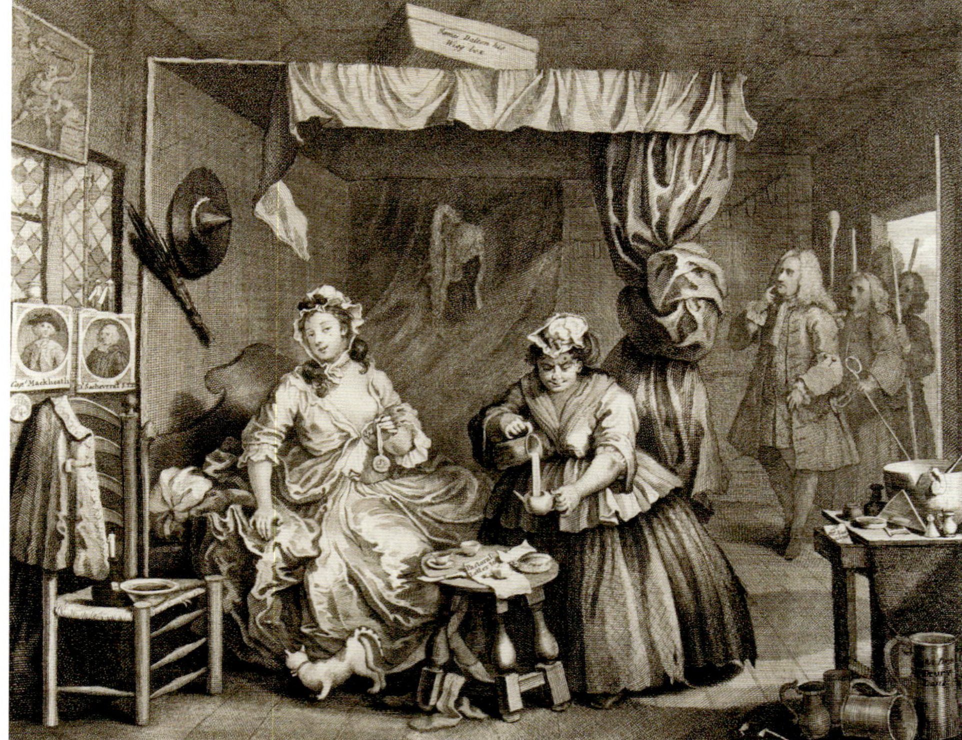

9 William Hogarth (1697–1764)
A Harlot's Progress, 1732
Plates II and III
Reproduced alongside
Engravings, 38 × 31.5 cm
The Hunterian Museum and Art Gallery,
Glasgow, inv. nos. 16002 and 16003

Hogarth's famous prints illustrate his view of tea drinking as a social symbol, his interest in French contemporary painting and his adaptation of a popular genre developed in France by de Troy, Watteau and Lancret among others. It also highlights his use of studio props such as a teapot with a broken handle repaired with metal that is also included in other works by the artist.

Hogarth's *A Harlot's Progress* was the first of his modern moral tales, a series of six paintings conceived in 1731 specifically to be engraved. They tell the story of country girl, Moll Hackabout, arriving in London and finding herself soon involved in a cycle of corruption, sex and decay, culminating in her death. Plate II shows a finely dressed Moll living with a rich Jewish merchant whose pretentions to grandeur are illustrated by the black servant-boy carrying a kettle of hot water and the silvered tea table. The damasked walls, dressing table, *pied de biche* furniture and heavy picture frames with scallop motifs echo contemporary Rococo fashions. In Plate III Moll has been abandoned by her rich protector and become a common prostitute. A squalid room with a simple wooden stool has replaced the silvered table, a coarse-looking hag the fashionable black page. This is a reminder that, as observed in her essay by Ann Eatwell, tea had already become a daily necessity for all levels of society.

Hogarth achieved remarkable success with this first series, partly owing to his clever marketing stratagems. Before he had completed the six episodes he had already advertised a subscription for their engravings, resulting in the sale of a great many sets and a far greater profit for the artist than if he had simply sold the paintings. Hogarth's approach would inspire a number of artists, among them Nicolas Lancret (see cat. 6) and Philip Mercier (see cat. 11).

10 William Hogarth (1697–1764)
The Western Family, 1738
Reproduced alongside
Oil on canvas, 71.8 × 83.8 cm
Bibliography: *Hogarth*, exh. cat., Tate, London, 2006, no. 55
National Gallery of Ireland, Dublin, inv. no. NGI 792

By 1738 Hogarth had become one of the most accomplished painters of the conversation piece. This famous portrait was commissioned by the prosperous London merchant Thomas Western (d. 1766) and shows Thomas holding a bird to indicate his recent participation in a hunt. His wife Anne and various other members of the family are visited by a clergyman – probably Archdeacon C. Plumptre.

The picture beautifully illustrates British tea drinking in its social context. Tea is seen to encourage civilized conversation among people of different ages and stations in life, temporarily bringing them together into a harmonious group.[17] The painting has passages that would have been at home in contemporary works by Chardin or Boucher, and highlights Hogarth's awareness of French painting.

The Western Family is one of half a dozen conversation pieces on the theme of drinking tea painted by Hogarth in the 1730s for members of the rising professional classes. Interestingly, among the genteel props through which Hogarth conveyed his story-line are a silvered tea-table and a blue and white Oriental porcelain teapot with what looks like a metal repair on the handle.[18] Both are of a type he had used before in *The Wollaston Family* (1730), *An Assembly at Wanstead House* (1728–31; fig. 44, p. 61) and *A Harlot's Progress* (1731–32). The pot reappeared on its own in several conversation pieces and moral tales of the 1730s and 1740s and one cannot help wondering if his socially aspiring

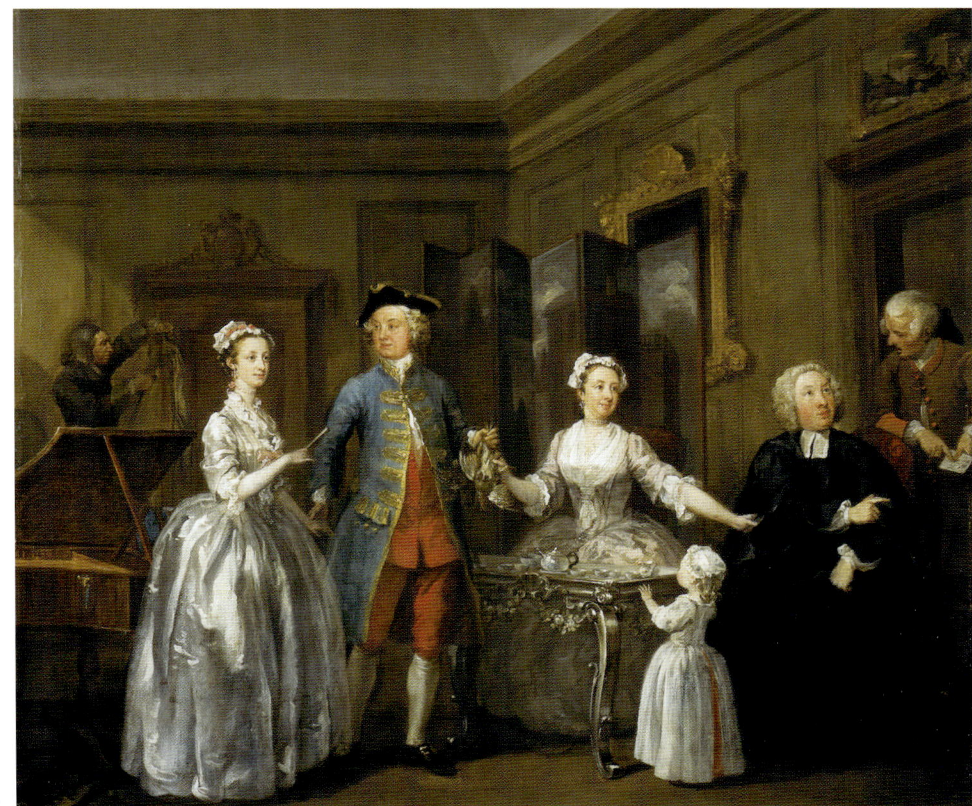

10

patrons noticed that they shared their teapot and such an ornately decorated tea-table with the rich Jewish merchant whose pretensions to grandeur Hogarth had ridiculed in Plate II of *A Harlot's Progress*.[19]

11 James McArdell (1710/28–1768)
after Philippe Mercier (1689–1760)
Woman taking Tea, c. 1750
Reproduced here
Mezzotint, 35.3 × 25.3 cm
Hunterian Museum and Art Gallery, Glasgow, GLAHA 51339

Although never a first-rate artist, Philippe Mercier nonetheless played an influential role in the development of British art. Familiar with the work of Watteau, after whom he etched a number of plates, Mercier introduced to London the *fête galante*, which he was the first to adapt to group portraiture. Keeping abreast of the latest artistic developments on the

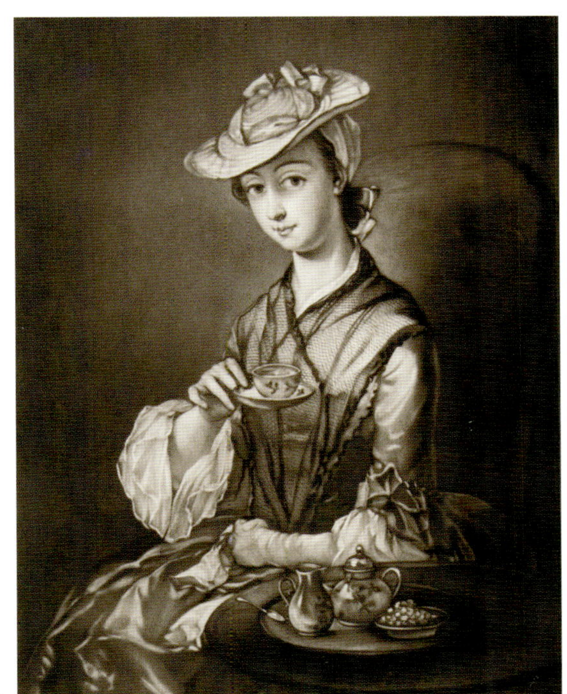

11

Continent, he exploited the popularity of the new genre developed in France by Chardin, creating around 1737 the type of a single genre figure later known as the domestic 'fancy' picture, painted specifically to be reproduced in print form.

Mercier was among the first to highlight the use of tea in a private setting rather than stressing its fashionable or social connotations.[20] Here his lady taking tea is wearing an outdoor hat and a glove, suggesting that she has just come in. Tea for one is served in a fashionable tea set reminiscent of the type of porcelain produced by the Chelsea or Bow factories.

Although Mercier's *Woman taking Tea* shares several elements of Chardin's composition, his figure looks into the eye of the viewer in an engaging manner more reminiscent of Boucher than of Chardin. Interestingly, Boucher seems to have owned several engravings by Faber of Mercier's compositions.[21]

12a Kangxi period (1662–1722)
Yixing teapot
Reproduced alongside
Hand-moulded stoneware, Yixing, China, height 9.5 cm
Private collection

Red stoneware Chinese teapots of this kind from Yixing in Jiangsu province were hugely successful when they arrived in Europe via Holland in the mid 1600s. If the pot in Chardin's *Lady taking Tea* was the *terre de Flandre* item listed in Mme Chardin's inventory, its prototype would have been a Yixing teapot such as this one and would probably have been of Dutch origin, since Delft potters were from the early 1690s renowned imitators of Chinese red stoneware. No red stoneware is known to have come from Flanders itself at the time and the term 'Flanders' would have included the northern Netherlands as well.

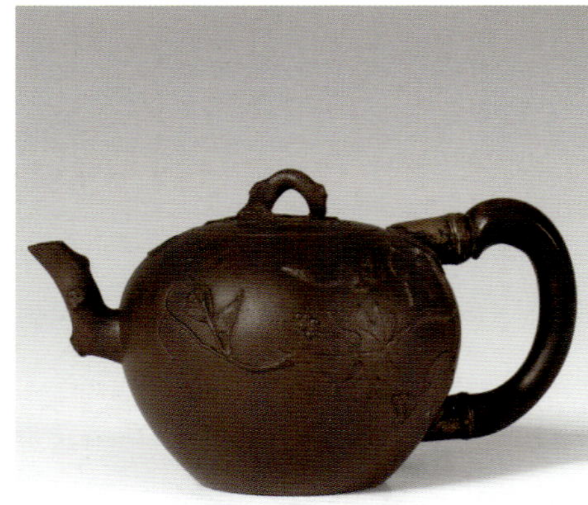

12a

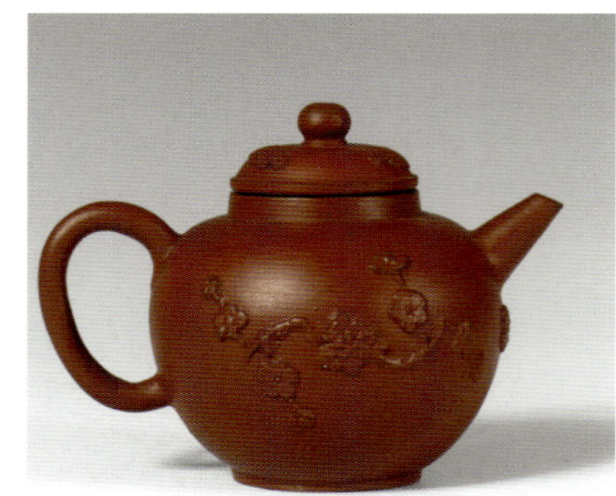

12b

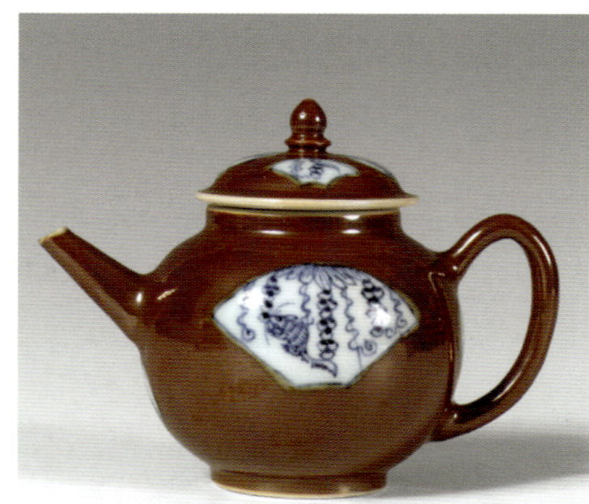

12c

12b Ary de Milde (1690–1720)
Red stoneware teapot
Reproduced alongside
Hand-moulded stoneware, Holland, height 11 cm
Private collection

Though at first less expensive, Dutch red stoneware teapots such as this were softer and less practical for day-to-day use than their Chinese prototypes. The production of these pots seems to have ceased around 1730.[22] If Chardin's teapot was indeed Dutch red stoneware, it would have been at least five to six years old when he painted *Lady taking Tea*.

12c Kangxi period (1662–1722)
Brown-glazed Chinese export teapot (so-called 'Batavian' ware), *c*. 1690–1720
Reproduced alongside
Porcelain, China, height 12.5 cm
Private collection

The shiny surface of the teapot in *Lady taking Tea* is puzzling, as Yixing and red Dutch earthenware were not glazed. Might Chardin's teapot have been of Chinese porcelain with a brown glaze of a type known as 'Batavian'? 'Batavian' ware is characterized by a lustrous brown glaze on the outside that varies in colour from light brown to a much darker colour. The most common 'Batavian' vessels are cups, bowls and other small items. Few examples of such teapots have survived.

13a Kangxi period (1662–1722)
Blue and white teapot
Reproduced facing page
China, porcelain, height 11 cm
Private collection

This Kangxi teapot typifies the under-glaze blue porcelain produced in eighteenth-century China and mass-imported into Europe. Commonly known as 'blue and white', the style is still popular today. Given the sketchy nature of Boucher and Chardin's depictions of tea ware, the tea set of *Woman on a Daybed* and tea bowl and saucer of *Lady taking Tea* could be either Chinese blue and white porcelain or a European imitation.

Tea ware of the same kind regularly appeared in numerous British conversation pieces painted in the 1730s and 1740s, for example *The Western Family* (cat. 10). They were often matched with a red stoneware teapot, as in *Lady taking Tea* or in Hayman's family portrait of Jonathan Tyers (fig. 46, p. 63).

13b Kangxi period (1662–1722)
Blue and white teacup and saucer
Reproduced alongside
Porcelain, China; cup, height 3.5 cm, diameter 7.4 cm; saucer, height 1.9 cm, diameter 11.4 cm
The Hunterian Museum and Art Gallery, University of Glasgow, GLAHA 54734; 54599

This blue and white Chinese teacup and saucer have a swirling floral pattern similar to that on the cup held by Chardin's *Lady taking Tea*, and a shape matching those displayed on the shelves behind Boucher's *Woman on a Daybed*. One fact merits more consideration. The large size of Chardin's cup has attracted the attention of Oriental porcelain experts. Although less common than the standard cup illustrated here, larger blue and white Chinese cups and saucers were available. Next to tea and coffee ware, bowls were among the most popular exports. They were accompanied by saucer dishes, and were sometimes mistaken for large cups. Perhaps the cup of the *Lady taking Tea* is in fact a small bowl?[23]

14 Saint-Cloud
Cup and saucer, *c.* **1700–20**
Reproduced alongside
France, porcelain; cup: height 11 cm, diameter 8.5 cm; saucer: diameter 12.75 cm
Private collection

European manufacturers started to copy Chinese blue and white porcelain in the late seventeenth century, and by the 1730s admirers of this type of porcelain could choose between authentic Chinese imports

and ware inspired by the Orient from the Saint-Cloud factory. This cup and saucer's blue and white motif represents a synthesis of French design and characters found on bowls made for Tibetan Buddhists. The large shape of the tea bowl of Chardin's *Lady taking Tea* and the depth of its matching saucer suggest it could well have been a Saint-Cloud cup and saucer similar to this one.

15 Kangxi period (1662–1722)
Pair of brown-glazed teacups and saucers
Reproduced alongside
China, porcelain; cups, height 4 cm, diameter 7.5 cm; saucers, height 2 cm, diameter 12 cm
Hunterian Museum and Art Gallery, University of Glasgow, GLAHA 54588; 54591; 54590; 54587

This pair of teacups and saucers with a rich brown glaze on the outside resembles the so-called 'Batavian ware' depicted by Lancret in *Morning* (cat. 6, fig. 27; see also cat. 12c). Decorated inside with lively representations of ducks, geese and dragonflies, they come from the collection of the painter James McNeill Whistler, who, like Boucher, was a keen collector of porcelain. Although inventories of mid-eighteenth-century sunken porcelain cargoes indicate that such wares were exported in large numbers,[24] they do not often appear in contemporary paintings.[25]

16 Chinese (*c.* **1680–1720)**
Pu-tai Ho-Shang seated, laughing
Reproduced overleaf
Porcelain, height 10.8, width 14.7 cm
Burrell Collection, Glasgow Museums, inv. no. 38.617

This laughing Chinese god known as Budai eshang or 'Hemp-bag monk' was worshipped as a harbinger of good news, or god of happiness, in eighteenth-century China. With its bare belly, droopy earlobes and smiling face it is a good example of the type of Chinese porcelain figure much favoured in

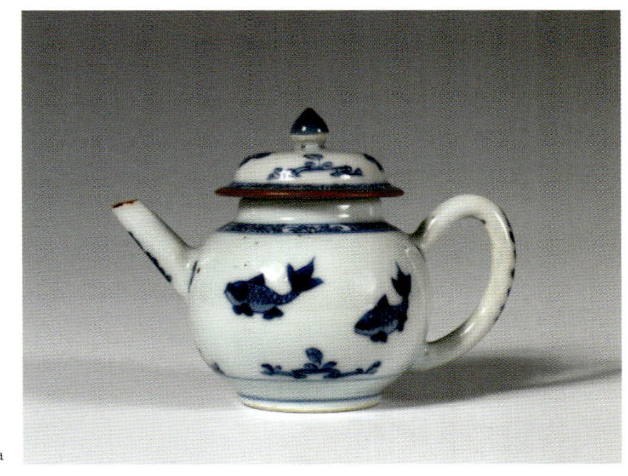

13a

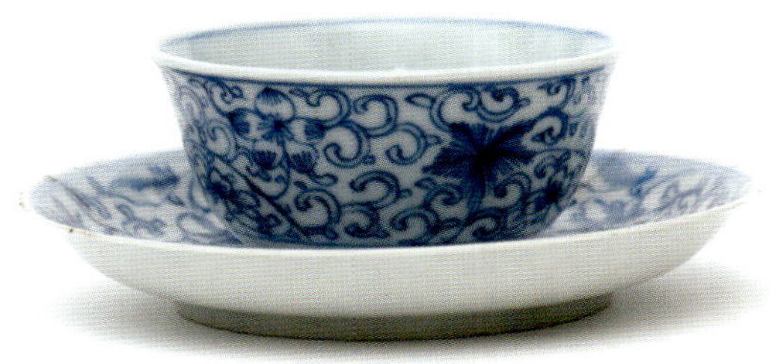

13b

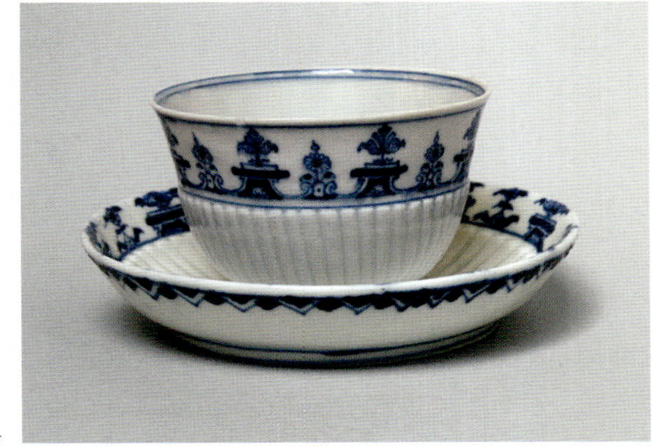

14

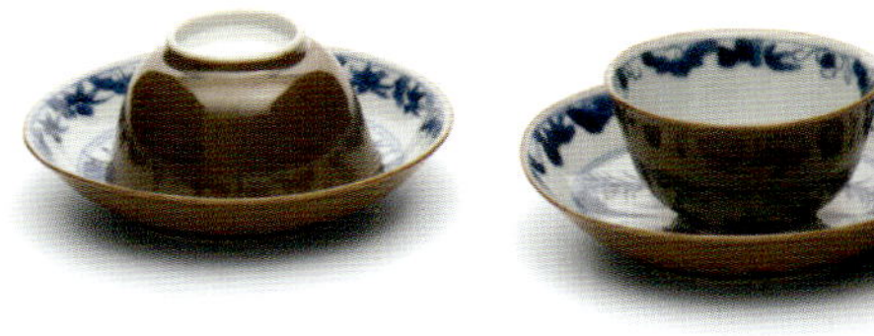

15

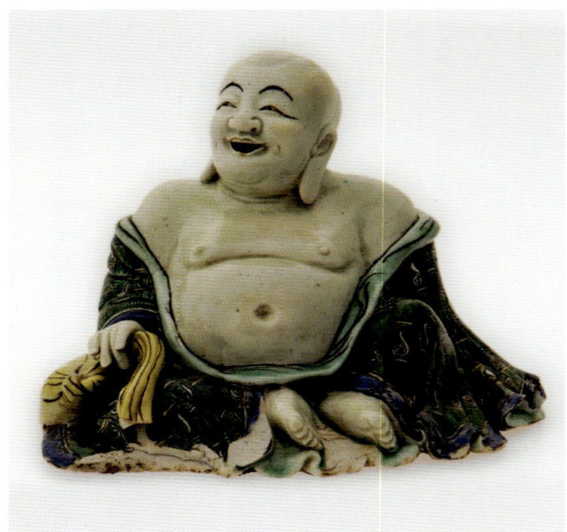

16

17 Pierre François Aveline (1702–1760)
after François Boucher (1703–1770)
The Four Elements: Fire, 1739–40
Etching, 33.0 × 26.6 cm
British Museum, London,
inv. no. 2004, 1031.10

Boucher discovered Chinese subjects when
making prints after Watteau's décor at the
Château de la Muette, and this work was
followed by a royal commission of exotic
hunting scenes for Versailles in 1735–39.
In 1740 the commission of designs for a new
set of Chinese tapestries for Beauvais led
Boucher to the creation of further Chinese
designs, many of which were engraved.[26]

This delightful impression of two
Chinamen having tea under the eye of a
pagoda dates from 1740, and is from a set of
four exotic designs of the Elements. It may
have been the popularity of such designs that
led Boucher to include tea drinking and
pagodas in several of his descriptions of
women in modern interiors, such as *Woman
on a Daybed* or *Woman fastening her Garter*.

Boucher's particular feeling for motifs
of *chinoiserie* greatly contributed to the
dissemination of the style in France and
beyond. In most decorative fields designers
adapted these motifs to create modish
interiors with a touch of the exotic, a fashion
sometimes leading to excess and ridiculed by
artists such as Hogarth with a sharp eye for
contemporary extremes.

**18 Unknown artist after William Hogarth
(1697–1764)**
Taste in High Life, 1746
Reproduced facing page
Engraving and etching, 21. 5 × 28.0 cm
The British Museum, London,
inv. no. 1868, 0822.1555

Conceived shortly after Hogarth's first visit to
France, this image concentrates on the folly
and superficiality of aristocratic taste with an
emphasis on foreign influences. Two effete
connoisseurs dressed in exaggerated French
fashions are cooing over a tiny teacup. The
plump, short woman sports a small lace head-

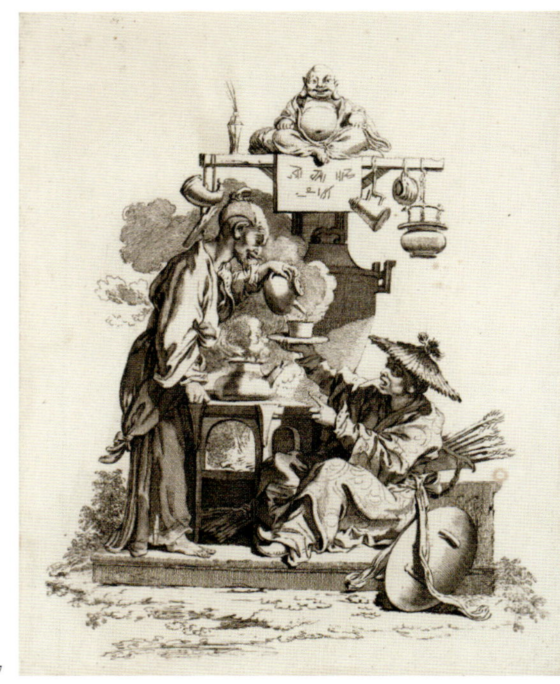

17

dress atop an ill-fitting *tête de mouton* hairstyle,
patches, ridiculously large three-quarter sleeves
over her small arms and an absurdly large
hoop under her sacque dress.

Hogarth's print eloquently ridicules the
fashionable outfits so beautifully depicted by
Boucher, Chardin and others. The same can
be said of his allusions to the contemporary
love of Oriental objects, symbolized by
porcelains like the diminutive teacup and
saucer admired by the two connoisseurs, the
minuscule pagoda held by a black page-boy,
the very large vase at the rear and the screen
with a Chinese motif.

Such works demonstrate Hogarth's
ferocious denunciation of the fashionable
excesses of his contemporaries. It also
confirms the meaning of tea and *chinoiserie*
in his work, which by the mid 1740s would
have been instantly recognizable to viewers as
symbols. He also mocks "duck's tongues,
rabbits' ears" and snails in the menu held by
the monkey in the foreground, an allusion to
the fashion for keeping French cooks.

The print, after a painting commissioned
by Mary Edwards in 1742, was made without
Hogarth's permission.

the West, known as a 'pagoda' or 'magot'. By
the 1720s their popularity was such that
European manufacturers were imitating
them in papier mâché and porcelain.
Boucher, a keen collector, owned over fifty
pagodas, both Chinese and European. Single
figures, pairs or groups, in porcelain,
soapstone and other materials, ranged from
the conventional to the bizarre. Boucher
appreciated pagodas for their exoticism
without knowing what they really
represented. His collection included a
smiling Chinese god like this one, described
in his 1771 sale as a "*medecin chinois*".

Whatever Boucher thought it to be, there
is no doubt that such a figure was behind the
stereotype of a smiling chinaman or child
which he developed in the late 1730s.
Throughout the 1740s the figure could
often be found perched on a shelf, as in
Woman on a Daybed (cat. 2) or *The Four
Elements: Fire* (cat. 17).

Other artists used the popularity of
'hemp-bag monk' figures and other pagodas
to express a taste for the Far East. In
Hogarth's work they often become tools
to mock the excess of Rococo. In Plate II
of *Marriage A-la-mode* (cat. 19; see fig. 50,
p. 67), a smiling god appears once on the
mantelpiece and again among the Rococo
decorative elements on the wall.

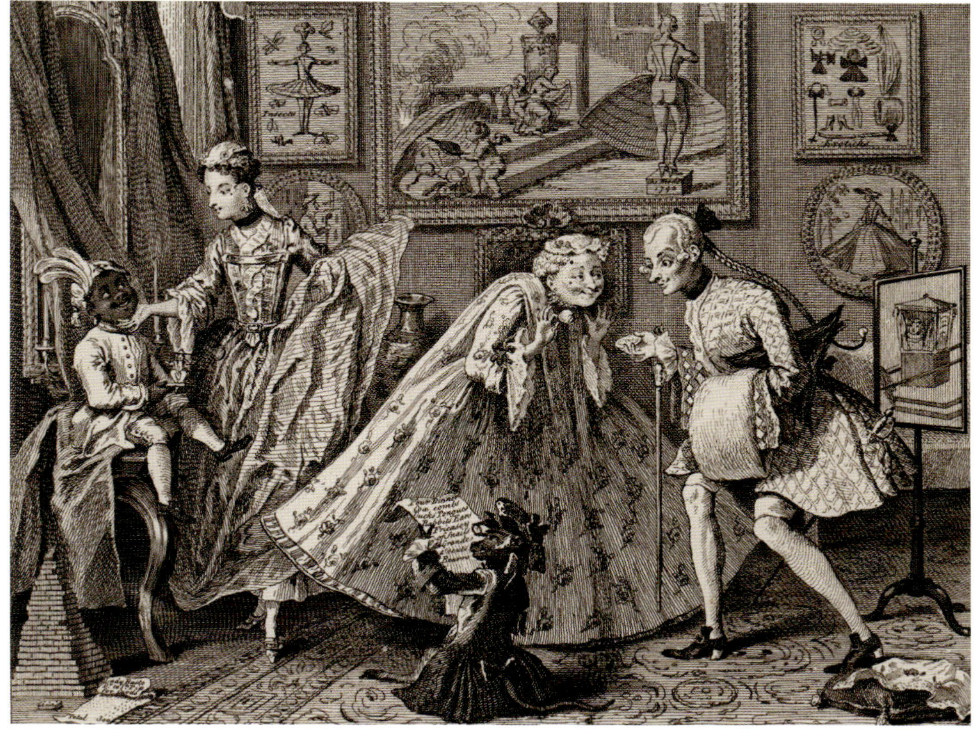

18

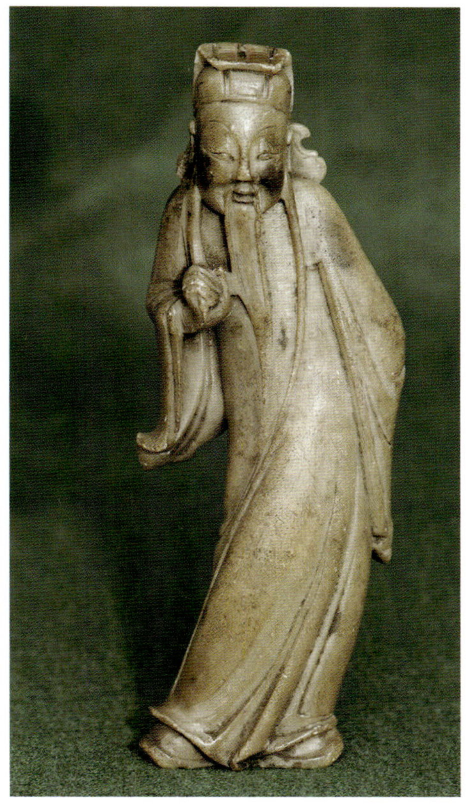

20

19 William Hogarth (1697–1764)
Marriage A-la-Mode, **Plate II, 1745**
Fig. 50 (detail)
Engraving and etching, 38.0 × 46.2 cm
Hunterian Museum and Art Gallery,
University of Glasgow,
inv. no. GLAHA 16023

In this satire of married life Hogarth's
interior is an extension of the personalities
of its owners. Rich in incidental detail, his
interior was created not for the pleasure
of the eye as Boucher's were, but for
the entertainment of the mind. With its
deliberately grandiose setting and meticulous
parade of components suggesting wealth
without breeding, it recalls the sort of
interior Horace Walpole would have called
"fine but without taste", as he remarked of
An Assembly at Wanstead House (fig. 44, p. 61)
in 1735.

Among the many details poking fun at the
bored couple's poor taste is the mantelpiece,
stacked with every possible type of Chinese

porcelain including a smiling god and a frog,
referring to the popularity of bizarre objects
that were in fashion for no other reason than
their exotic provenance. Hogarth was not
alone in mocking the want of discernment in
some of his contemporaries when it came to
the craze for *chinoiserie*. Elizabeth Montagu, a
celebrated London hostess, commented:
"Sick of Grecian elegance and symmetry, or
Gothick grandeur and magnificence, we
must all seek the barbarous gaudy gout of
the Chinese; and fat-headed pagodas and
shaking mandarins bear the prize from the
finest works of antiquity".[27]

The clock to the right of the mantelpiece
offers a brilliantly absurd parody of the
different elements central to Rococo
(*chinoiseries* and the vegetable and animal
worlds). The detail of an egregiously single
teacup and solitary teapot suggests the
couple have reached a state of such
indifference that they no longer share
their morning cup of tea and are living
separate lives.

20 China (Ming Dynasty)
Lu Dongbin with a sword on his back
Reproduced above
Soapstone, height 16cm
Hunterian Museum and Art Gallery,
University of Glasgow,
inv. no. GLAHM 106710

Lu Dongbin was one of the eight Immortals
at the heart of the Taoist religion, whose
portraits were to be seen everywhere in
China – on porcelain objects, fans,
embroideries or as figures made of wood,
stone, porcelain and metal. The magic sword
on his back, one of his great attributes, was
to combat evil. Numerous figures of the
Immortal were imported into Europe from
the seventeenth century onwards. They were
often made of soapstone, a popular material
for small statuettes because of its softness and
cheapness, with attractive varying colours.

In China, statuettes of the Immortals
would be found in middle-class houses.
While it was hoped that they would bring

their owner good luck, they also had a
private devotional role. In Europe, such
soapstone figures were thought exotic and
amusing, and found their way into royal and
aristocratic collections and into the hands of
collectors of *chinoiseries* such as Boucher,[28]
and on to the mantelpieces of fashionable
couples like those illustrated in *Marriage
A-la-mode*, Plate I (see cat. 19).

21 Jacques Gabriel Huquier *fils* **(1725–1805)
after François Boucher (1703–1770)**
The Chinese Fair and *The Chinese Emperor
holds Audience*, c. 1779
Reproduced alongside
Engravings, 44.5 × 68.5 cm
Hunterian Museum and Art Gallery,
University of Glasgow,
inv. nos. GLAHA 51841; 51842

In 1740 Boucher was commissioned to
produce preparatory oil sketches for a set of
Chinese tapestries to be woven at Beauvais.
As noted by Perrin Stein, the two to three
years Boucher spent designing the set
significantly influenced his development
of a pictorial vocabulary that would express
chinoiserie motifs.[29]

An immediate hit, the *Tapisseries chinoises*
were woven with innumerable variations and
copied by other manufacturers, their designs
being made available to a wider public
through engravings. Using illustrations
taken from contemporary travel literature
and objects available in Paris, Boucher
embellished his scenes with numerous small
still lifes centred on Oriental objects
including pagodas, teapots and teacups.

Engraved after the death of the artist,
these prints demonstrate the continuing
admiration for Boucher's Chinese tapestries
in the eighteenth century.

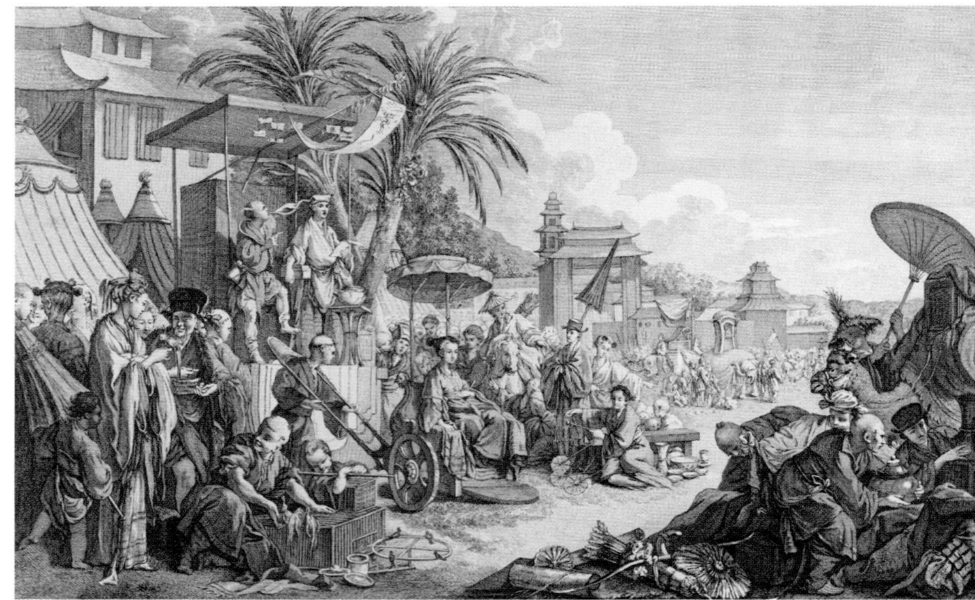

21

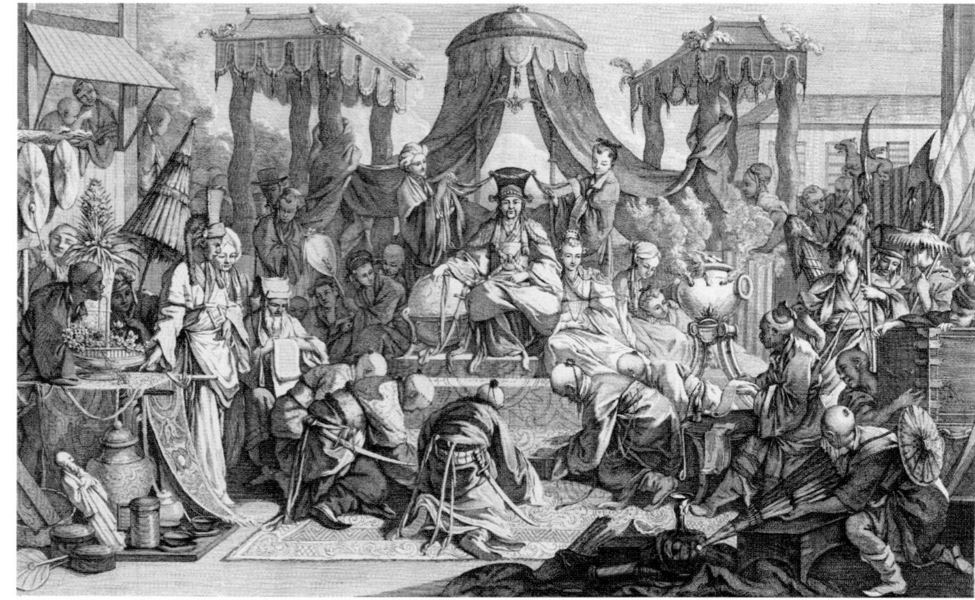

21

III

The pros and cons of drinking tea in the eighteenth century

Although at first considered a medicinal herb, tea was soon taken for pleasure. From the seventeenth century until well into the nineteenth debates raged among middle- and upper-class commentators about the properties of this new drink and the way it should be prepared – all documented in a large number of treatises. Physicians would warn against the negative effects of its unsupervised consumption whilst pharmacists, who supplied the tea, promoted its good qualities.

The three volumes presented here come from the collection of Dr Hunter, owner of *Lady taking Tea* from 1765, who gathered several editions of each publication. Fascinated by faraway lands and their fauna and flora, Hunter obtained a tea shrub and was instrumental in procuring for Queen Charlotte a specimen for her own collection of botanical curiosities.

22 Tea brick

Compressed tea leaves, 22.3 × 17.7 × 1.8 cm
Reproduced alongside
Hunterian Museum and Art Gallery, Glasgow,
inv. no. GLAHM E.1949.1

Tea bricks have been manufactured in China for more than two thousand years, the leaves being steamed and forced under hydraulic pressure into flat bricks to reduce exposure of the surface area. These bricks were ideal for transporting the tea and tea was largely traded in that form until about a century ago. From the tenth to the beginning of the twentieth centuries tea bricks were also widely used as a form of currency.

This tea brick is impressed with a Russian double eagle seal and may have been made in China as currency for trade with Russia.

23 Simon Paulli (1603–1680)

A Treatise on Tobacco, Tea, Coffee, and Chocolate, London, 1746
Open at Plate II, reproduced alongside
Special Collections, University of Glasgow Library
Sp Coll Hunterian Cl.3.2

The author of the first major European text on tea, Simon Paulli was a professor of botany, anatomy and surgery and physician to Christian IV, King of Denmark. His *Commentarius de Abusu Tabaci et Herbae Thee, etc.* was first published in 1635 at Rostock. The English translation of 1746 by one Dr James, *A Treatise on Tobacco, Tea, Coffee, and Chocolate,* ensured its widespread and enduring influence.

The plate illustrated describes such essentials as kettles, teapots and teaspoons.

Much of the text takes the format of a botanical discussion. A fierce critic of all four substances, Paulli marvelled at the way Europeans were "so infatuated and hood-winked" as to purchase plants that would encourage "Effeminacy and Impotence" and numerous other health problems. "As *Hippocrates* spared no Pains to remove and root out the *Athenian* Plague", he concluded, "so I have used the utmost of my Endeavours to destroy the raging epidemical Madness of importing Tea into Europe from China."

24 Philippe Sylvestre Dufour

Traitez nouveaux et curieux du café, du thé et du chocolat … [New treatises on coffee, tea and chocolate …], Lyons, 1685
Opened at plate 2; title page and plate 2 reproduced overleaf; frontispiece reproduced fig. 35
Special Collections, University of Glasgow Library,
Sp Coll. Hunterian BG59f-14

In 1671 Philippe Sylvestre Dufour, a Lyons pharmacist and the owner of a cabinet of curiosities, published the first popular and widely printed treatise on these new beverages, entitled *De l'usage du café, du thé, et du chocolat*. It was published again in 1685

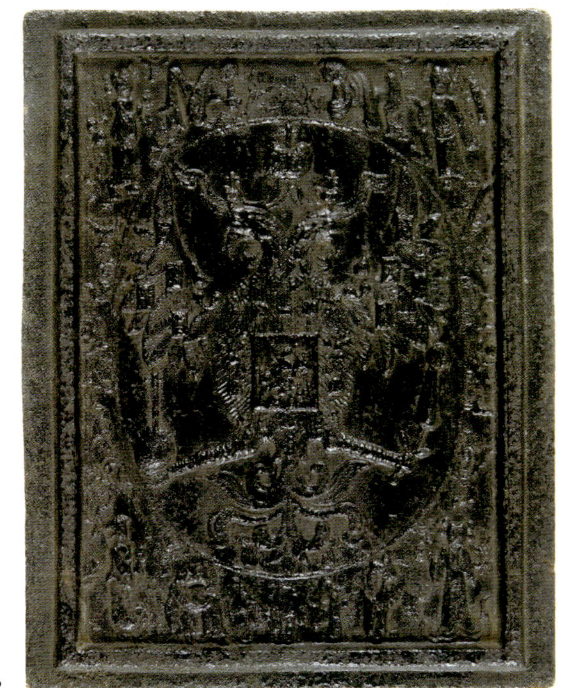

22

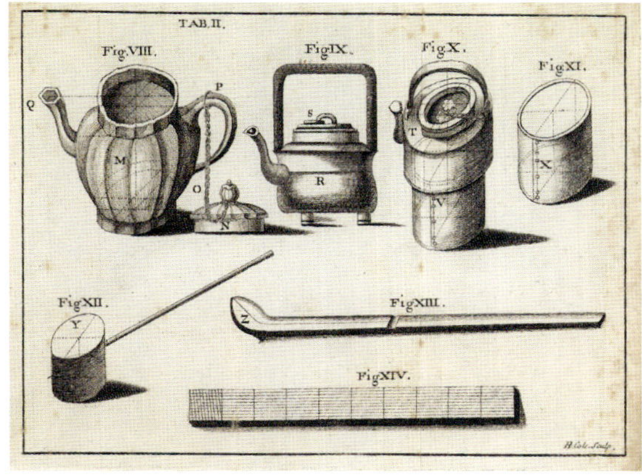

23

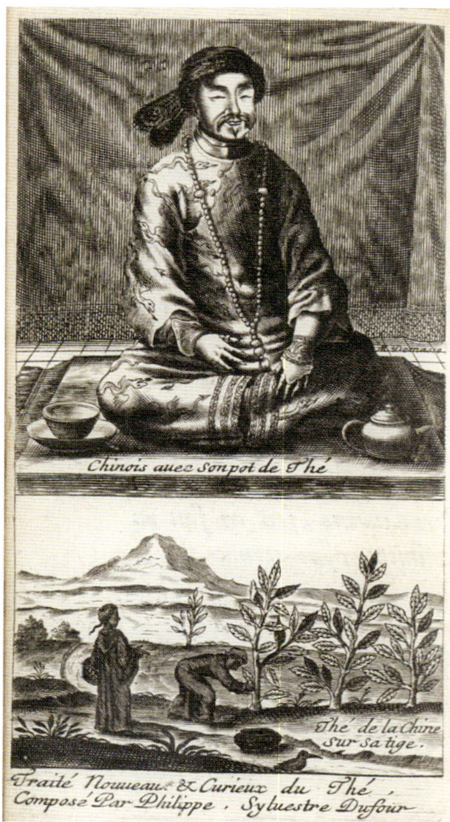

Chinois auec sonpot de Thé.

Thé de la Chine sur sa tige.

Traité Nouueaux & Curieux du Thé Composé Par Philippe . Syluestre Dufour

24

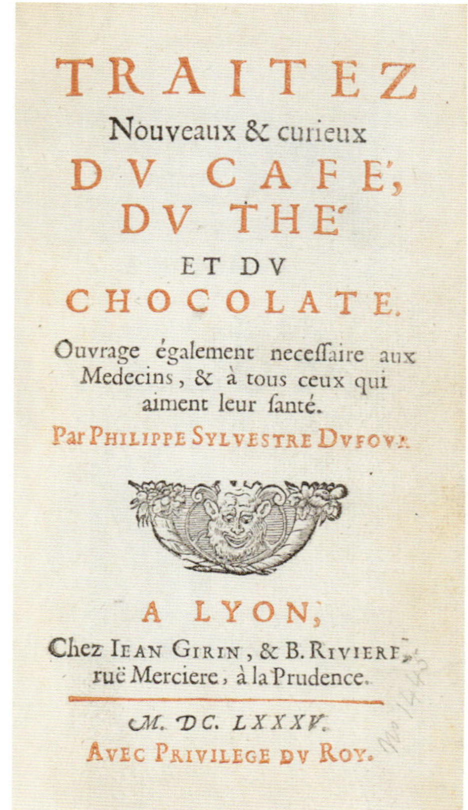

with additional information about the medicinal properties of coffee, tea and chocolate and translated into English the same year. Sources for Dufour's discussion of tea included letters from the Dutch East India Company's ambassador to the Emperor of China; an account of the Bishop of Beryte's journey to Cochin; an account of Father Alexandre de Rhodes's travels; and the medical observations of Nicholas Tulp, physician in Amsterdam. It was broadly in favour of the new drink. According to this treatise, tea could cure "all pains of the head, Rheums, and soreness of the eyes, of the breast, shortness of breath, weakness of the stomach, griping of the guts, weariness". The engraving on plate 2 features an imagined scene of a Chinaman with his pot of tea and a porcelain cup and saucer in which it is served. Below is a scene illustrating the picking of tea leaves.

25 An essay on the nature, use, and abuse, of tea in a Letter to a Lady; with an Account of its Mechanical Operation, **Dublin, 1725**
Open at title page; not reproduced
Special Collections, University of Glasgow Library,
Sp Coll. Hunterian BG.59.h.20

This slim, anonymous volume first published in London in 1722 illustrates the hyperbole surrounding eighteenth-century debate on the positive and negative qualities of tea. The relatively large number of surviving copies is a measure of its popularity. While affirming that tea has merits as a medicine, it warns of the negative effects of daily use, which, according to its nameless author, included risks of infertility in women, miscarriage and loss of good looks.

Boucher and Chardin in Britain in the 1760s

Of the two paintings at the heart of the exhibition this catalogue accompanies, *Lady taking Tea* was held in a British collection as early as 1765. At least twenty-five others by Chardin are known to have gone through the London salerooms by that year, but only ten by Boucher. Yet the visits of a number of British artists and collectors to Boucher's studio during that year, 1765, would crystallize his success in the latter years of the century (see cat. 27). From the 1770s onwards at least twenty works by Boucher passed through British salerooms every decade.

This section of the catalogue brings together a small group of works by Boucher and Chardin which illustrate the appeal of the two artists in Britain in the decade that saw the acquisition of *Lady taking Tea* by Dr William Hunter.

26 Jean-Siméon Chardin (1699–1779)
The House of Cards
Fig. 24
Oil on canvas, 81 × 101 cm
Bibliography: Carritt 1974
Rothschild Family Trust: Waddesdon Manor

Chardin's *House of Cards* first appeared on the British market as lot 37 in a sale of 1765 organized by Prestage, *Lady taking Tea* being lot 36; the two works were described as "pendants". Like most Chardin paintings imported into Britain, they were well-known compositions that had been engraved several times.[30] Their buyers were William Fauquier (*c.* 1700–1788) and William Hunter, members of the rising professional middle class. Fauquier was a successful financier who became a director of the South Sea Company and would succeed his father as Governor of the Bank of England. Hunter's mother was the daughter of a Glasgow magistrate and his father a member of the local gentry. Moving to London in 1740, Dr Hunter went on to become one of the most famous anatomists of his time and in 1768 first Professor of Anatomy at the newly created Royal Academy.

Fauquier and Hunter shared a passion for art and, involved with London cultural institutions (The Royal Society, Society of Antiquaries, Society for the Encouragement of the Arts), they cultivated friendships with artists, among them William Hogarth and the engraver and art dealer Robert Strange. Though hardly in the same league as a Walpole or a Mead, they both built art collections of around sixty works carefully selected to reflect their taste, sometimes enlisting the help of artist friends.[31] Sharing their contemporaries' preference for seventeenth-century Italian, Northern and, to a lesser degree, French pictures, they were typical of a group who also had an interest in modern artists, particularly Chardin, which arose out of their involvement with London art circles. In contrast to Hunter, Fauquier also developed a taste for Boucher and bought a landscape by him from the 1771 Strange sale. He is one of the very few British buyers known to have had both Boucher and Chardin represented in his collection (his other Chardin was *A Boy drawing* (*Le Jeune Dessinateur*), a painting which had been in England since 1741.[32]

27 Jean-Siméon Chardin (1699–1779)
The Scullery Maid and *The Cellar Boy*
Reproduced respectively fig. 25 and here top right
Oil on canvas, 45.7 × 36.9 cm
Bibliography: Rosenberg 1983, no. 96; Peter Black (ed.), *"My Highest Pleasures": William Hunter's Art Collection*, The Hunterian, University of Glasgow, in association with Paul Holberton publishing, London, 2007, nos. 15, 16, pp. 39, 41
Glasgow, Hunterian Museum and Art Gallery, inv. nos. GLAHA 43511, 43507

Besides *Lady taking Tea* William Hunter possessed two other Chardins, *The Scullery Maid* and *The Cellar Boy*, each of which is known in at least one other version. The first pair, exhibited at the 1738 Louvre Salon and engraved in 1740 by Charles Nicolas Cochin, was by 1740 in one of France's great eighteenth-century collections, that of the comte de Vence.[33] The second pair was acquired by Hunter, but at what date or from whom is unknown.

These were typical of the popular small genre scenes of the daily life of servants that Chardin was painting from the early 1730s, and probably what Hogarth in 1749 was recommending to British visitors to Paris as the "little pieces of common life" to be seen at Chardin's studio.[34] The presence of an oil sketch for *The Scullery Maid* in the Geminiani sale held in London in 1743 and the use of *The Cellar Boy* as an illustration in George Bickham's *The Museum of Arts – Universal Penmanship*, published in London in 1740–45, suggest that both compositions would have been well known in London when Hunter acquired them.

Although no information has survived of Hunter's acquisition of the two paintings, recent research has demonstrated how well-connected he was as a collector. A friend and patron of a great number of contemporary artists, he was particularly close to Hogarth, Strange and Ramsay, who were all personally acquainted with Chardin. He was also a close friend of Lady Hertford, wife of the British ambassador to France from 1763 to 1765, and had personal contacts with a number of personalities from the French art world such as the collector, art critic and art dealer Pierre-Jean Mariette, who knew Chardin well. Any of these contacts might have assisted Hunter to acquire the two paintings.

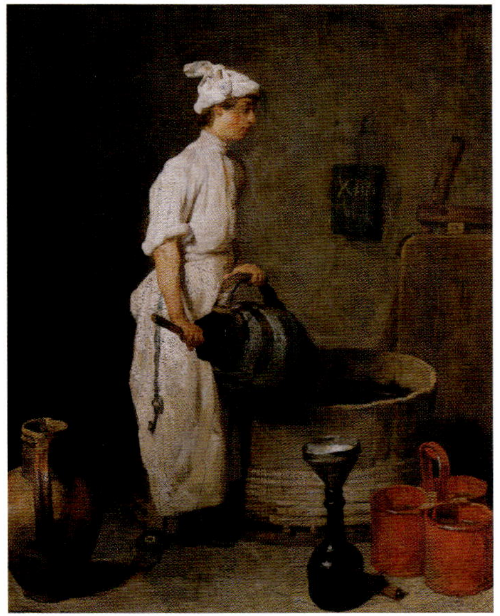

27

28 William Wynne Ryland (1732–1783) and William Watts (1752–1851) after François Boucher (1703–1770)
A Collection of Prints in Imitation of Drawings: *"Bath-sheba"*, 1764; study for *"Trinity"*, 1771
Reproduced overleaf
Published by Charles Rogers (1711–1784), London, 1778
Stipple engraving, 46.2 × 30.6 cm; mezzotint, 36.3 × 45.8 cm
Glasgow, Hunterian Museum and Art Gallery, inv. nos. GLAHA 9001, 9084

These prints by Ryland and Watts were commissioned and published by Charles Rogers after Boucher drawings in his collection. Rogers, senior officer of the Custom House in London, Fellow of the Society of Antiquaries and a passionate lover of art, had developed friendships with numerous artists and was of a background similar to Fauquier and Hunter. He was one of the few British collectors of his time to have met Boucher face to face and to have recorded the encounter in writing.

In the 1760s Rogers set to work on *A Collection of Prints in Imitation of Drawings*, a publication intended to reproduce Old Master drawings from famous British collections together with text explaining the

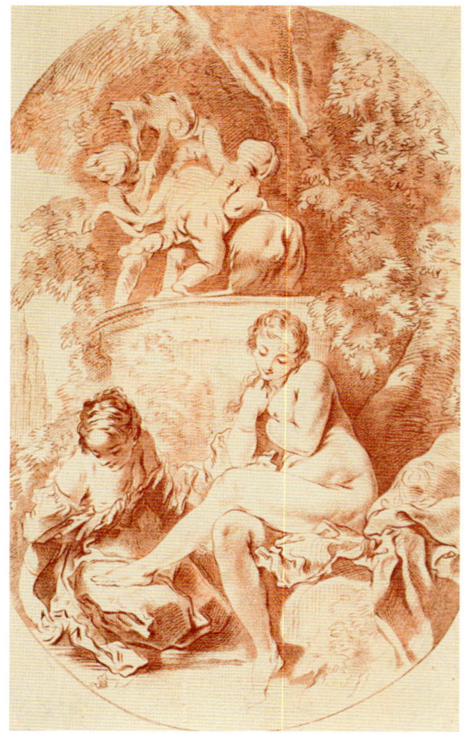

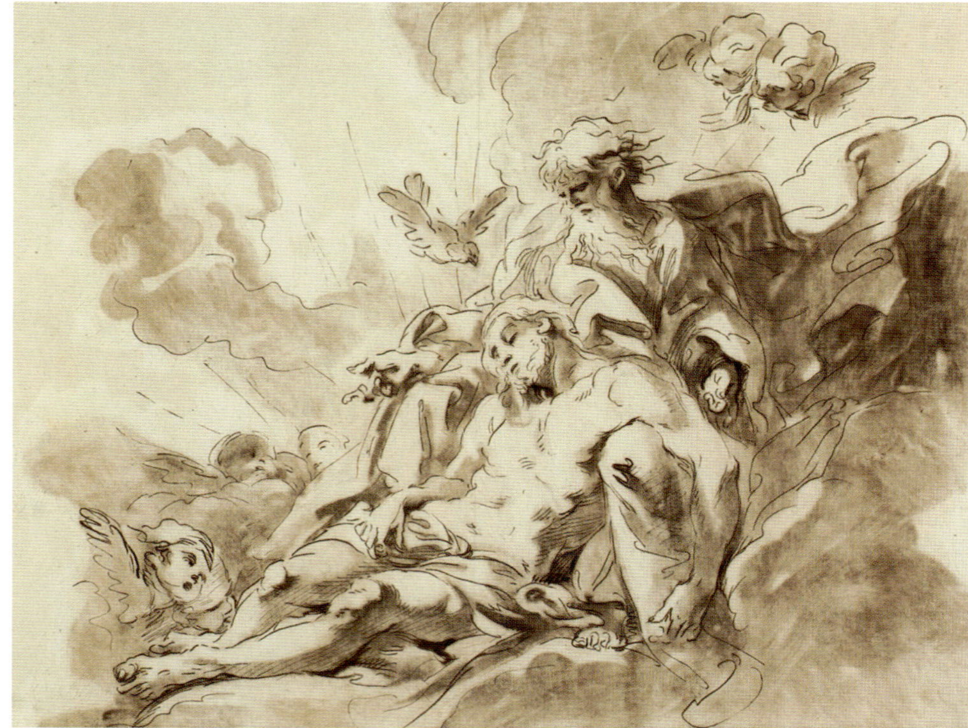

significance of the artists represented. The finished work consisted of 112 prints and 463 pages of text and had expanded to two volumes. It has been described as "one of the most impressive art historical writings of eighteenth-century England". Only two contemporary artists were included in the volume, the sculptor John Michael Rysbrack (1693–1770) and Boucher.

In his description of his Boucher drawings (pp. 197–200), Rogers points out that "*Bathsheba*", despite its biblical title, is a typical Boucher subject showing a nude lady bathing at a fountain.[35] Commenting on his "*Trinity*" (or *Ascension of Christ to Heaven*), he notes that "When M. Boucher was informed of this Work being intended, he complaisantly expressed great pleasure, saying that he himself would try whether he could make a Drawing for it; and in May 1765 very politely presented me with this noble design".

Other British visitors to Boucher's studio that year had included the future president of the Royal Academy Joshua Reynolds and the arbiter of taste and collector Horace Walpole. Until 1765, although a few of

Boucher's paintings would from time to time appear on the London market, British collectors tended to prefer his drawings. Immediately after his death the popularity of his pictures intensified and by the end of the 1770s his paintings were appearing more frequently in London salerooms, a success that may have been due in part to Rogers's inclusion of these two Boucher's drawings in his long awaited *Collection of Prints …*, finally published in 1778.

1 As noted by Ann Eatwell, images of solitary French ladies taking tea would become a common occurrence in the second part of the eighteenth century.

2 See p. 92 for a list of the few paintings of which the author is aware.

3 See Dufour 1685, p. 49.

4 Conisbee 1986, p. 168.

5 See New York, Detroit and Paris 1986, no. 38.

6 For a detailed description of the interior described by Boucher, see Whitehead 1992, p. 50.

7 For further details of the commission, and Boucher's ultimate failure to complete it, see New York, Detroit and Paris 1986, no. 51.

8 Juliet Carey, *Theatres of Life: Drawings from the Rothschild Collection at Waddesdon Manor*, exh. cat., Wallace Collection, London; Djanogly Art Gallery, Nottingham; Waddesdon Manor, 2007–09, no. 15, pp. 54–55.

9 Alastair Laing in New York, Detroit and Paris 1986, p. 181.

10 Chardin's paintings included *The Fast Day Meal*, 1731 (Louvre); *Lady taking Tea*, 1735 (Hunterian), *The Diligent Mother*, 1740 (Louvre); *La Garde Attentive*, c. 1747 (National Gallery of Art, Washington); two still lifes with a white teapot and grapes, c. 1756 (private collection and Algiers Museum); *The Jar of Apricots* (with a fuming cup of tea), 1758 (Art Gallery of Ontario); *White Teapot with White and Red Grapes, Apple,*

Chestnut Knife and Bottle, c. 1759 (private collection). Boucher's were *Le Déjeuner*, 1739 (Louvre); *The Element of Fire*, c. 1739–40 (original drawing in the Metropolitan Museum of Art; it was engraved by P.A. Aveline); engraved trade card by the comte de Caylus after Boucher, *At the sign of the Pagoda*, 1740 (Bibliothèque nationale de Paris); *Lady fastening her Garter*, 1742 (Museo Thyssen-Bornemiza, Madrid); sketch for *The Chinese Emperor holds Audience* tapestry, 1742 (Musée des Beaux-Arts de Besançon); *Le Thé à la Chinoise*, 1742 (Little Durnford Manor, Wiltshire; Trustees of the Count of Chichester); engraving by G. Huquier, *Le Thé*, from *Scènes de la vie chinoise*, and *Woman on a Daybed*, 1743 (Frick Collection, New York).

11　*Mme Crozat*, 1741 (Musée Fabre, Montpellier); *Mme Brion seated, taking Tea*, 1750 (Seattle Art Museum); and possibly a *Lady taking Tea* attributed to Aved in the Heywood-Lonsdare collection (on loan to the National Museums of Merseyside).

12　They were works by Joseph van Aken (c. 1699–1749); Richard Collins (d. 1732); Marcellus Laroon; Charles Philips (1708–1747); William Hogarth; Gawen Hamilton (c. 1697–1737); Robert West (18th century); Francis Hayman (1708–1776); William Verelst (active 1734, d. c. 1756); Enoch Seeman (1694–1744); Arthur Devis (1712–1787); and Joseph Highmore (1692–1780).

13　Surviving tea canisters dating to about 1730 are now in the Victoria and Albert Museum (for example, inv. no. M.314–1962); an impression of the coat of arms is in the British Museum.

14　In the official booklet accompanying the 1739 Salon Lancret's painting was wrongly described as "*Une Dame à sa Toilette, prenant du Caffé*", which indicates that for many in France, coffee, not tea, was the drink of choice.

15　G. Vertue, *Note Books*, ed. K. Esdaile, Count of Ilchester, and H.M. Hake, Walpole Society, vol. III, 1933–34.

16　Dufour 1685, p. 51.

17　Paris, London and Madrid 2006–07, cat. 55.

18　For further discussion of the porcelain teapot with its black handle, see Anne Eatwell's essay, pp. 67–69.

19　Further information on Hogarth's unusual silvered tea-tables can be found in Ralph Edwards, 'Hogarth's Tea-Tables', *The Burlington Magazine*, XCIII, no. 582, September 1951, p. 304. (I am grateful to Alison Yarrington for pointing out this article.)

20　Besides *Lady taking Tea*, works by Mercier depicting women drinking tea included *Girl with a Tea Tray*, published as a mezzotint in 1744 by J. Faber; *Bonjour*, dated 1745–50, showing a young woman stirring a cup of tea at a table with a tea set (private collection; pendant of *Bonsoir*); and *The Times of Day: Morning*, in which a young woman wearing a mob cap drinks tea, published as a mezzotint in 1758.

21　Remy 1771, lot 553: "*Le maître d'école de filles, celui de garçons, et 6 autres pièces gravées par Faber*".

22　For further information see Jan Daniël van Dam, 'European Redwares: Dutch, English and German Connections, 1680–1780', in Walford and Young 2003, p. 40. The author suggests that the Delft production of redware more or less ceased around 1730 because imported Chinese redware – which was no longer expensive – was sufficient for the European market.

23　Kilburn and Sheaf 1988, p. 147.

24　See, for example, Jan Josef Horemans the Elder (1682–1759), *Tea Party in a Netherlandish Garden: Springtime*, illustrated *ibid.*, p. 112.

25　I am grateful to Errol Manners and Nick Pearce for their advice.

26　See Perrin Stein, 'Les Chinoiseries de Boucher et leurs sources : l'art de l'appropriation', in Paris 2007, p. 91.

27　Quoted in D. Doran, *A Lady of the Last Century (Mrs Elizabeth Montagu)*, London, 1873, pp. 79–80: undated letter from Elizabeth Montagu to Elizabeth Carter.

28　Boucher had a number of soapstone figures of the eight Immortals in his collection: see Stein in Paris 2007.

29　*Ibid.*, p. 93.

30　The theme of the house of cards, popular among seventeenth- and eighteenth-century artists, inspired Chardin on a number of occasions. This painting is one of four known variations he painted on the theme between 1735 and 1741 (the others are in the Louvre and the National Galleries of London and Washington). He exhibited *House of Cards* paintings at the Salons of 1735, 1737 and 1741, all of which drew admiration from contemporary art critics. Three of these compositions were engraved in the eighteenth century, helping to diffuse knowledge of Chardin's compositions further afield. For *Lady taking Tea* see cat. 1.

31　Hunter and Fauquier bought heavily at the 1771 sale organized by Strange in London, for example.

32　Hunter's art collection is now in the Hunterian Museum and Art Gallery, Glasgow. Fauquier's "small but well-chosen collection" was sold at Christie's on 30 January 1789.

33　The *Scullery Maid* was destroyed in the twentieth century, and the *Cellar Boy* has recently re-appeared in a private collection.

34　See further below, 'Boucher and Chardin in Britain, 1730–1780', pp. 110–11.

35　Bathsheba was one of the favourite queens of David, King of Israel.

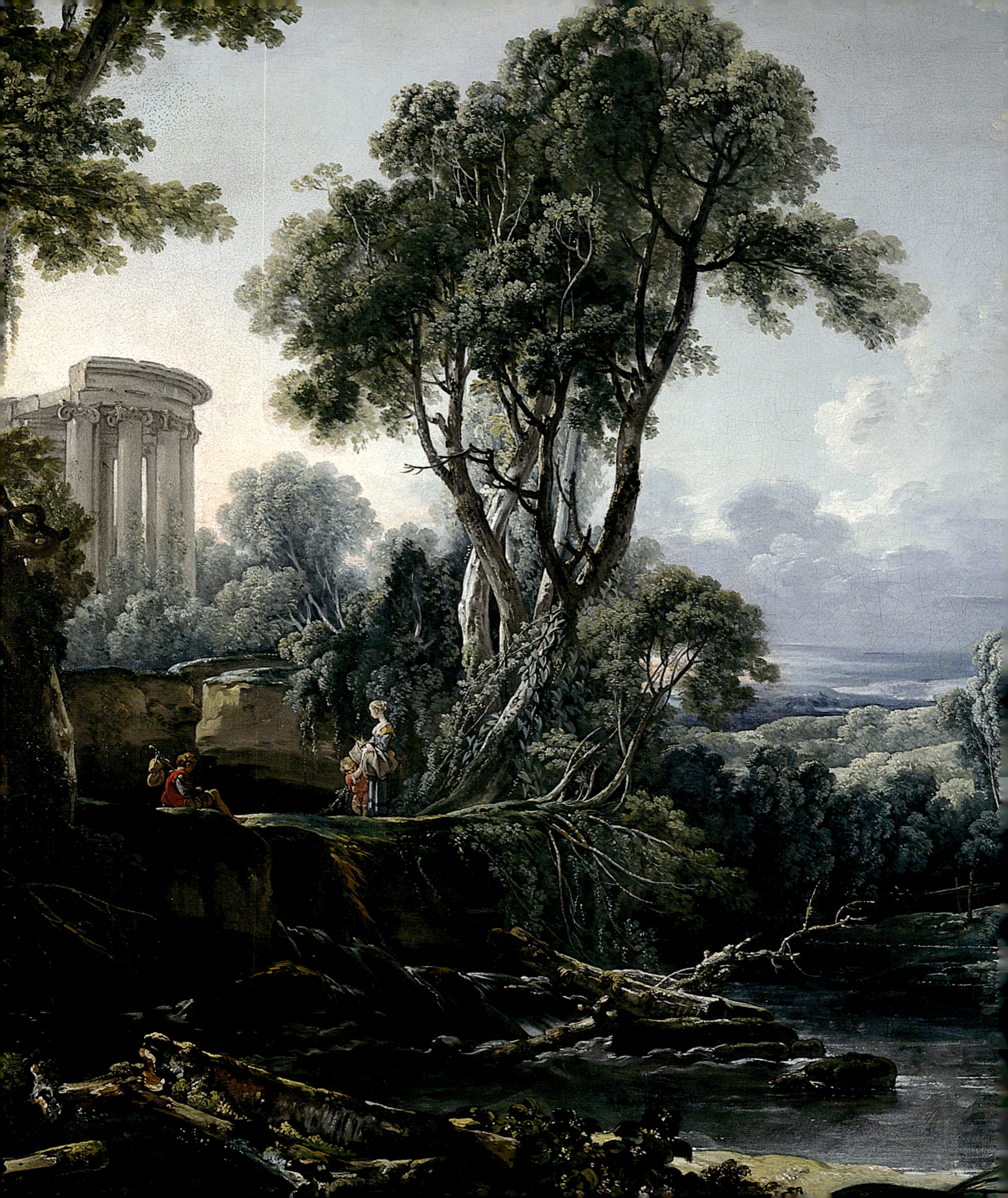

Boucher and Chardin in Britain 1730–1780

ANNE DULAU

The provenance of *Woman on a Daybed* is unknown before its appearance in the collection of Joseph Bardac in the early twentieth century; *Lady taking Tea*, however, can be traced to its purchase at a Covent Garden auction as early as 1765. That a Chardin painting was brought to a London auction room barely thirty years after it was painted brings us, in a fourth essay, to consider the popularity of Boucher and Chardin in Britain within the five-decade span of their careers.

When Boucher and Chardin started to exhibit regularly in Paris Salons in the 1730s,[1] the prevailing British view of French style as anti-patriotic and Jacobite was diminishing, prompting Pope's lines: "We conquer'd France, but felt our captive's charms;/ Her Arts victorious triumph'd over our Arms".[2] This interest in French contemporary art is confirmed by surviving English sale catalogues from the 1720s and 1730s, in which works by Watteau, Lancret and Pater started to appear around 1725.[3] From the 1740s Boucher and Chardin's work was critically acclaimed and attracting the attention of prestigious collectors all over Europe. Although neither ever visited Britain, evidence of their success has survived in contemporary British art and in collectors' inventories, sales catalogues and writings.[4] Here we are able to add new information, gathered from a number of primary sources, on direct contacts between Boucher, Chardin and the British art world, on those paintings by the two artists that passed through the London sale rooms, and on their collectors.[5]

BOUCHER, CHARDIN AND THE BRITISH ART WORLD

Recent literature has brought to light that British interest in eighteenth-century French art was more important than had previously been thought. Dr Mead's patronage of Watteau is well known, and also the presence in his collection of works by de Troy. It has been demonstrated that from the 1730s onwards a number of factors encouraged artistic interchanges

Fig. 73 (detail)
François Boucher
Landscape, 1743
Oil on canvas, 90.8 × 118.1 cm
Barnard Castle, Bowes Museum

between the two countries and resulted in awareness of the latest developments on both sides of the Channel.

From the beginning of the eighteenth century, an increasing number of French artists crossed the Channel to work in London. The first event relevant here was the move to London of two French artists with personal connections to Boucher and Chardin. They were the draughtsman, designer and engraver Hubert François Gravelot (1699–1773), who came in 1732, and the portrait painter and member of the French Academy Jean Baptiste Van Loo (1684–1746), who arrived in late 1737. The artistic circles to which Gravelot belonged in Paris included not only Boucher but Chardin and the engraver Jacques Philippe Le Bas (1707–1783), who, with his publication of prints after their paintings, would disseminate knowledge of both Boucher's and Chardin's work. Settling in the heart of the British artistic community in Covent Garden, Gravelot opened a drawing school in 1732 and instructed his English pupils in the latest developments in French art which he had learnt in Boucher's studio.

Gravelot is also likely to have been responsible for sending the London draughtsman Charles Grignion (1717–1810) to Paris to study under Le Bas about 1733. Perhaps it was he who suggested to the second Duke of Kingston and his tutor Dr Nathaniel Hickman that they visit Le Bas's studio when in Paris in 1732–35.[6] It is interesting to note that the first written record of a Boucher work in a British collection dates to April 1735, when the *Mercure de France* (a French periodical) announced that *La Belle Cuisinière* (*The Beautiful Kitchen-maid*; fig. 32, p. 46), which "*un seigneur Anglois a emporté à Londres*" (an English lord has carried off to London), had been engraved by Pierre Alexander Aveline (1702–1760) with verses by M. Lépicié (fig. 74).

J.B. Van Loo was among the first established French artists in the early 1730s to recognise Chardin's genius and did much to raise his profile in France. His London stay was a great success, and numerous English patrons of the arts passed through his studio in the following three years. Undoubtedly he would have shared his enthusiasm for Chardin's talents with those interested in French modern art.

Meanwhile British artists were being rallied by the engraver and painter William Hogarth, who was determined to develop an English school of painting capable of competing with its Continental counterparts. 1735 saw the opening of Britain's first academy of art, the St Martin's Lane Academy, where French artists like Gravelot and British artists like Hogarth and Grignion joined forces to support the endeavour. Such collaboration encouraged greater traffic between Paris and London, one example being the visit to Paris of the painter Joseph Highmore (1692–1780) in 1734.

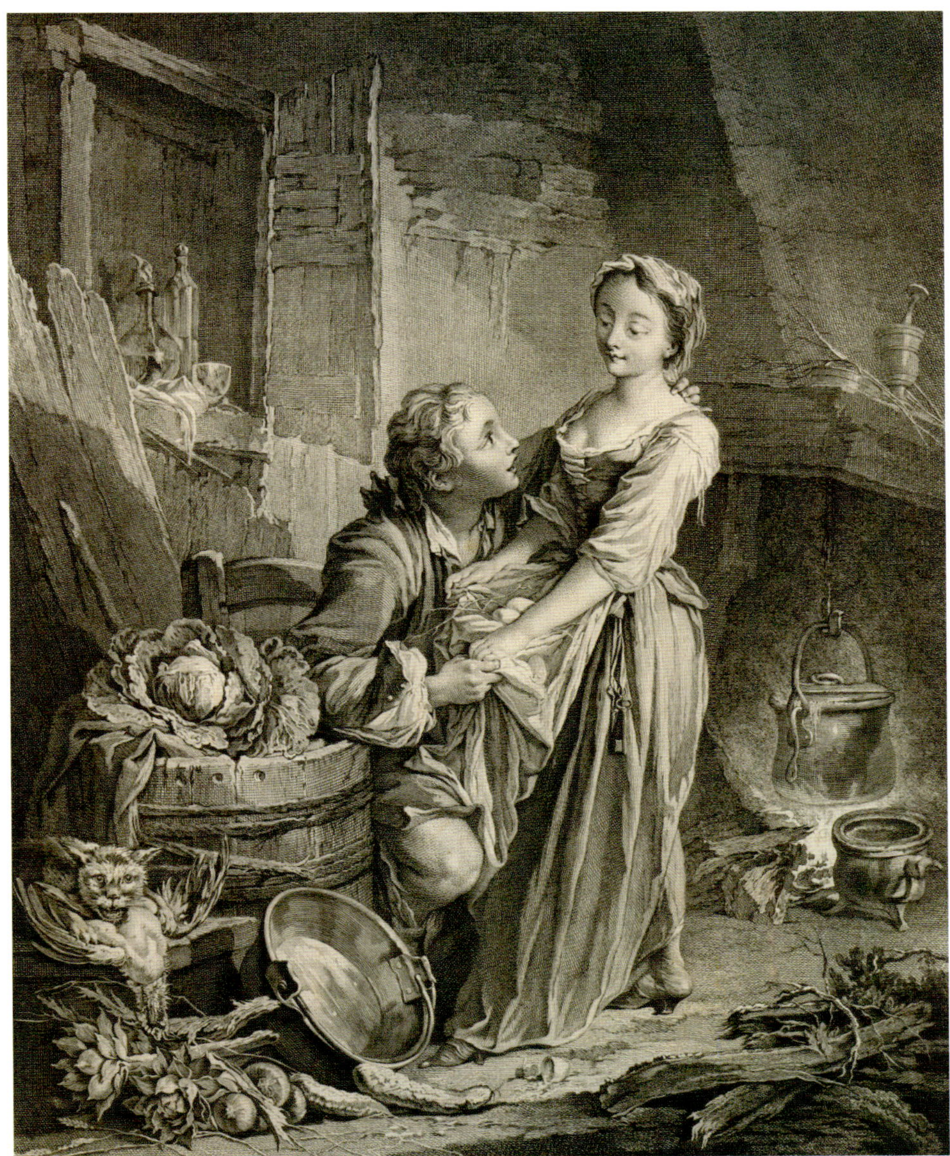

A pillar of the London artistic community from the 1720s and involved with the St Martin's Lane Academy, Highmore was a portrait painter with a strong interest in history and genre painting and took pride in keeping abreast of artistic developments on the Continent. Furnished with letters of introduction from Gravelot and others to French luminaries of the art world, Highmore spent several months in Paris in 1734, visiting the French Academy and consolidating existing contacts between French and British artists. However, although the diary of his journey has survived and mentions visits to many academicians, it specifies neither Chardin (an academician from 1728) nor Boucher (elected to the Academy that year).[7]

Other beneficiaries of these developing ties between the French and British art worlds included the portrait painter Allan Ramsay (in Paris in the summer of 1736), who had among his introductions a letter of recommendation to the celebrated art critic, collector and supporter of Chardin Pierre-Jean Mariette (1694–1774).[8] Ramsay then went on to study at the French Academy in Rome from 1737 to 1739. An important point of contact for young British and French painters, the Academy was under the direction of Boucher and Chardin's colleague Jean-François de Troy from 1738.

Despite resumption of hostilities between France and Britain in 1742, contact between the French and British art worlds increased throughout the following decade.[9] Hogarth twice travelled to Paris, in 1743 specifically to find the best available engravers to reproduce his *Marriage A-la-Mode* series (see cat. 19). As noted by Robin Simon, many of the engravers Hogarth visited in Paris that year were active in Chardin's circle and formed a tightly knit community.[10] There were François-Bernard Lépicié (1674–1749) and Nicolas-Henri Tardieu (1698–1755), who had both worked in London in the 1720s, Charles-Nicolas Cochin (1688–1754), the first to engrave Chardin's paintings, and Le Bas, who was a personal friend of Chardin. Among the English artists settled in Paris there were John Ingram (1721–1769?), who had arrived in 1741 and would engrave a number of sets after Boucher in 1744; and Andrew Laurent, known as André Laurent (1708–1747), who was a student of Le Bas, and had just published two engravings after Boucher.[11] As a result of this visit Hogarth entrusted the engraving of his paintings to Le Bas and his student Simon-François Ravenet (1706–1774) in Paris and to French fellow artists settled in London, Bernard Baron (1696–1762) and Louis-Gérard Scotin the Younger (b. 1698).

Interchange between the artistic communities of Hogarth and the St Martin's Lane Academy in London and Le Bas's studio in Paris reached a peak in the second half of the 1740s, with a visit *en masse* of the English contingent to Paris and a number of British students entering Le Bas's studio.[12] Among these was Robert Strange, who had taken part in the 1745 Jacobite Rebellion and had been forced to flee Britain after it was crushed that same year. First settling in Rouen, he entered the art academy recently set up by Jean-Baptiste Descamps (1714–1791) before moving to Le Bas's studio in 1748–49.[13] Although little information has survived of personal acquaintance between Britons and either Boucher or Chardin, Hogarth's recommendation to visit Chardin's studio, transmitted to the art connoisseur and collector Philip Yorke (1720–1790), later second Earl of Hardwicke, through Daniel Wray (1701–1783), indicates direct contact in these circles with the two French painters.[14]

This awareness also shines through the contemporary output of British artists. In the series of paintings produced for Vauxhall Gardens an understanding of French contemporary painting informs the composition and colouring of those painted by Hogarth, Hayman and Gravelot.[15] Hogarth's work from the 1740s also makes interesting comparison with Chardin's in particular but with Boucher's too, as shown by the position of the servant in *The Strode Family* (*c.* 1738; Tate Britain, London), reminiscent of Boucher's treatment of the human figure in *Le Déjeuner* (1739; Musée du Louvre, Paris).[16] An acquaintance with the French artist's work could also be gained, if not by direct contact, through engravings. Most of Chardin's genre paintings of the 1730s and 1740s were engraved within a year or two of their creation and many of Boucher's drawings were made available in printed form, as were some of his paintings.

Testaments to their popularity in Britain in the 1740s are the engraving made in London of *A Boy drawing* (*Le Jeune Dessinateur*; probably the version now in the Louvre, Paris) by John Faber (*c.* 1695–1756) in 1740 (fig. 75);[17] the publication by the engraver and printseller Paul Angiers (1723–1757) of *A New Book of Figures from Boucher* in 1750; and the reproduction in Bickham's *The Museum of Arts – Universal Penmanship*, London, 1740–45, of Chardin's *Le Garçon Cabaretier* (*The Cellar Boy*).[18]

The example of Faber is particularly telling. An associate of Hogarth in the 1730s, he became a leading mezzotint engraver. His engraving of two of Chardin's genre scenes coincides with the beginning of his collaboration with Philippe Mercier, a Berlin-born painter who moved to England in the early 1720s and contributed to the development of the English conversation piece. Although innovative in his approach to painting, Mercier was not skilled as an artist and found by the late 1730s that, with the rise of a new generation of portrait painters led by Allan Ramsay, it would be invidious to remain in that field. Aware of the success of Chardin's genre scenes, he turned his hand to paintings of everyday themes in the manner of Chardin, painted specifically to be reproduced in print form. Faber's mezzotints after Mercier, mostly published in the 1740s, played a significant part in popularizing the new genre introduced by Chardin in France.[19]

During the 1750s the bond between the French and British art worlds strengthened still further and, although the two nations were engaged in renewed war between 1756 and 1763, exchanges increased between St Martin's Lane Academy and Le Bas's studio. The engravers Robert Strange and Thomas Major, who had studied under Le Bas in the late 1740s, returned to London in 1750. Allan Ramsay and Joshua Reynolds, the two principal British portrait painters of that period, both spent time at the French Academy in Rome. Ramsay stayed there from 1752 to 1756 and Reynolds

Fig. 75
John Faber the Younger (*c.* 1695–1756)
after Jean-Siméor. Chardin,
A Boy drawing, 1740
Mezzotint, 32.7 × 22.4 cm
British Museum, London
inv. no. 1877,0811.755

from 1749 to 1752, stopping *en route* in Paris to visit artists' studios and almost certainly Boucher and Chardin, by then pillars of the French art world. Chardin's genre scenes had a particular impact on Ramsay, most visibly upon his return from Italy in 1756, and his contemporary output shows a profound understanding and intimate knowledge of the French artist's work.[20]

Boucher's influence could also be seen in British artists' interest in his pastorals, most notably Thomas Gainsborough's (1727–1788).[21] Later in the decade William Wynne Ryland (1733–1783), accompanied by Gabriel

Smith (1724–1783), printmaker and drawing master, was sent to Paris by his teacher to study engraving under Le Bas and figure drawing under Boucher. That teacher was Ravenet, who had himself studied under Le Bas before moving to London, where he often worked in collaboration with Hogarth. Ryland spent several years in the French capital, engraving a number of works by Boucher during his studies, and would later become another important point of contact between Boucher and British artists and collectors.

Other works by Boucher were engraved by British artists: Peter Paul Benazech (1730?–1798?), a student of the French engraver François Vivares (1709–1782), reproduced *The Beautiful Kitchen-maid*, in England since 1735, and two views of Charenton. The interest of the British public in Chardin's genre scenes is also confirmed by the *British Magazine*'s decision in 1762 to offer its readers impressions of François-Bernard Lépicié's 1743 engraving of *The House of Cards* (*Le Château de Cartes*; The National Gallery, London).

Contact was maintained between the French and British art circles throughout the 1760s. The French academicians Carle and Louis-Michel Van Loo were in London in 1764. Artists like Ramsay and Strange were regularly travelling to Paris, and several British visits to Boucher's studio are recorded. Boucher himself is known to have owned several works by British artists.[22] Two of these visits to Boucher's studio took place in 1765, the year of his appointments as Director of the Academy and First Painter to the King. They involved Charles Rogers (1711–1784), a senior officer of the Custom House in London, renowned drawing collector and Fellow of the Royal Society of Antiquaries, and the writer and politician, collector, art connoisseur and arbiter of taste Horace Walpole, fourth Earl of Orford (1717–1797), who had become friends over their passion for art.

Although Rogers is chiefly remembered for his drawing collection, an aspect of collecting which has deliberately been kept outside the scope of this study, the story of his involvement with Boucher is worth summarizing here as it gives an invaluable insight into the kind of contact that took place between British collectors and French artists, but has not perhaps been recorded. In 1765 Rogers visited Paris and paid a visit to Boucher's studio. He would no doubt have been encouraged to do so by the engraver Ryland, who had studied under Boucher in the late 1750s, and whom he was commissioning to reproduce in print form Old Master drawings in famous collections in England. These he intended to publish under the title 'Prints in Imitation of Drawings'. When Rogers mentioned his project to Boucher, the artist presented him there and then with a drawing to include in the publication (fig. 76). This anecdote hints at Boucher's awareness of the

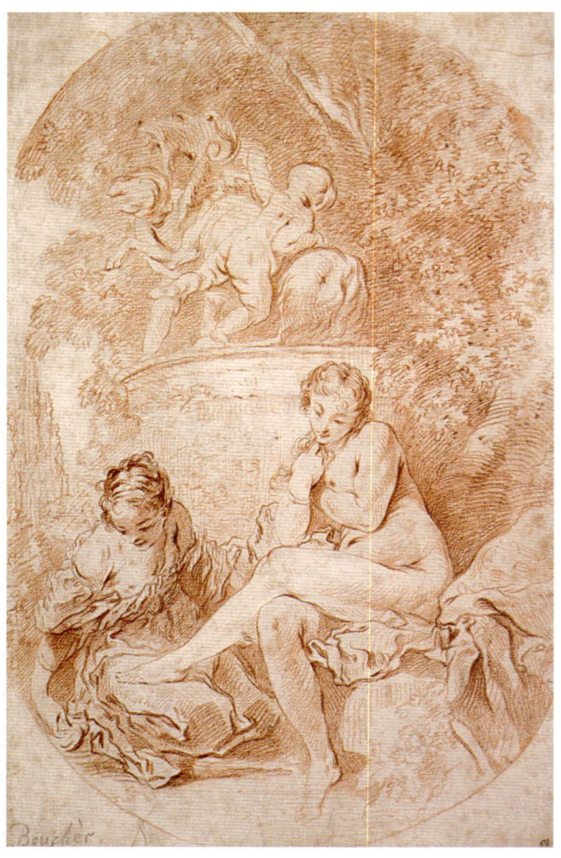

Fig. 76
François Boucher
Bathsheba, c. 1764
Drawing, 36.0 × 23.3 cm
British Museum, London
inv. no. 1908, 1014.1
From the collection of Charles Rogers

British market and reveals that the French artist was highly thought of in some British circles, for he was one of only two modern artists to be represented in Rogers's publication.[23] It also provides an insight into what contemporary British collectors thought of Boucher. Mentioning Boucher's "astonishing facility" and "gay and fertile imagination", Rogers stressed that "the amiable allusions of ancient Mythology, the Loves of the Gods … are the subjects he has represented with most satisfaction, and in which perhaps he has succeeded the best". His landscapes, "which are in general very beautiful", were also praised. Concerning colour, Rogers stated firmly that "the first pictures he painted at his return from Italy are in this respect far superior to those he has produced since" and that "In his last compositions, he has given a little into the Purple, and his Carnations seem to partake of reflections from a red curtain … on account of the weakness of his sight."[24]

Horace Walpole, Boucher's other well-known British visitor in 1765, was heralded the most important British collector of the century and considered the most Parisian of Englishmen. His first extended trip to Paris dated from that year and he swiftly became a favourite in fashionable salons and at the homes of French critics, collectors and connoisseurs such as Pierre-Jean Mariette and Ange-Laurent La Live de Jully.[25] They all knew Boucher and Chardin well and had helped to further their careers. At home Walpole was part of an important group of lovers of French culture and art which included the Lords Egremont, Brooke and Wemyss as well as the grandfather of the celebrated nineteenth-century collector of French eighteenth-century art, Lord Hertford.

It was as a guest of Lord Hertford (ambassador to the court of Louis XV from 1763 to 1765) that Walpole was introduced to Boucher in his studio. He may have paid further visits to the artist in his subsequent Parisian trips of 1766, 1767 and 1769 or met him at the salon of Mme Geoffrin, a well-known patron of the artist. Although Walpole is not known to have acquired works by Boucher and seems to have had little esteem for contemporary French painting,[26] he commissioned Jean-François Clermont (1717–1807) to make overdoor paintings for Strawberry Hill in the 1750s.[27] Clermont, a history and decorative painter, stayed in England during the 1740s and 1750s, where he worked for Walpole and other aristocrats wishing to include decorative paintings in the latest French style as dictated by Boucher in their interiors. Other patrons known to have used his services are Lord Radnor,[28] Sir James Dashwood,[29] Lord Stafford and the Prince of Wales.

A further direct link between Boucher and British collectors can be traced via the Gobelins tapestry factory through the Scot James Neilson (1714–1788). Head of one of the weaving departments by the 1750s, he was responsible for the ordering of a number of sets of tapestries after Boucher to be included in interior designs by Robert Adam in the 1760s.[30]

The last recorded visit to Boucher's studio in the 1760s was that of Reynolds, who took with him William Burke (1728/30–1798).[31] He too owned a drawing given to him by Boucher.[32] Reynolds's opinion of Boucher was recorded in two of his *Discourses* and, though often quoted, is worth repeating. In the *Sixth Discourse* he speaks of a "modern affectation of grace" in his painting; in the *Twelfth* he discusses Boucher's studio practices: "… in the former part of his life, when he was in the habit of having recourse to nature, he was not without a considerable degree of merit, – enough to make half the painters of his country his imitators; he had often grace and beauty and good skill in composition; but I think, all under the influence of a bad taste: his imitators are indeed abominable."[33]

Boucher died in 1770. Chardin, by then in his seventies, was suffering from poor health.

PAINTINGS BY BOUCHER AND CHARDIN IN ENGLAND DURING THEIR LIFETIME

In the 1730s connoisseurs in England, as elsewhere, preferred Old Masters to the new generations of British and Continental art. Up sprang the modern art dealer, who would travel through Europe to gather Old Master paintings and carefully select pieces of modern art he thought would sell well in the auction rooms beginning to open their doors in Covent Garden from the 1720s. For almost the first time English collectors could buy foreign art without having to travel to the continent.[34] A glance through surviving sales catalogues for the period shows that although Old Masters dominated the salerooms a number of works by modern French artists were starting to appear. At first these were mostly by Watteau, Pater and Lancret, the foremost exponents of a new genre known as the *fête champêtre*, of which the English had had first-hand knowledge from Watteau's visit to London in 1719–20.[35]

The first painting by Boucher recorded in a British collection was *The Beautiful Kitchen-maid*, in London by 1735, and three years later Chardin's *La Petite Fille aux Cerises* (*A Girl with Cherries*, destroyed; fig. 77) was up for sale in Covent Garden. Although both works typified the new genres Boucher and Chardin were instrumental in creating, their affinity with the type of northern seventeenth-century genre painting of which English collectors were particularly fond must have contributed strongly to their appeal. Regrettably the names of their owners are not known. *A Girl with Cherries* attracted the attention of Hogarth and informed his 1742 portrait of *The Graham Children* (Tate Britain, London).[36]

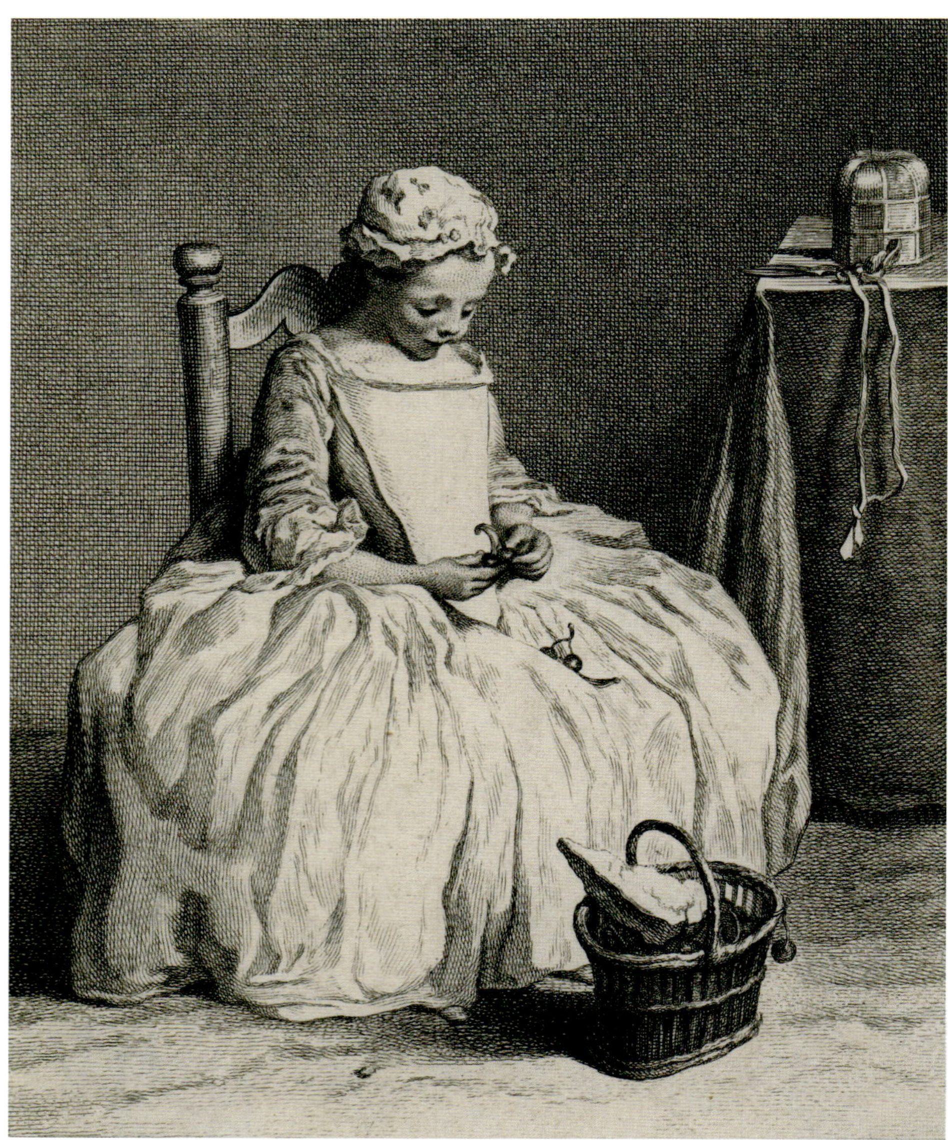

In the following four decades at least thirty-six paintings described as "by Chardin" went through the London salerooms, and thirty "by Boucher". Some were sold several times over the years: Chardin's *Boy drawing* was in sales in 1741, 1743, 1764 and 1789, and Boucher's *De trois choses en ferez-vous une?* (Of three things will you do one?) was in sales in 1744, possibly 1755, 1776 and 1796. Eighteen of the Chardin paintings can be identified with known compositions, all genre scenes from the 1730s apart from the copies or versions of *Le Bénédicté* (*Saying Grace*, 1740; Louvre, Paris) and *La Mère Diligente* (*The Diligent Mother*, fig. 83), which passed through the London salerooms in 1751. There were only three still lifes mentioned, and pictures of a cat and a dog (probably still lifes including those animals).

Whilst this confirms what previous writers have concluded, that British collectors were interested chiefly in Chardin's genre paintings of the 1730s, it also shows that there was a stronger interest in Boucher than had previously been thought.

The harmonious balance, simplicity of design and soft lighting characteristic of some of these genre scenes by Chardin had a visible impact on British artists. *A Boy drawing*, engraved in London by Faber shortly before its inclusion in a Covent Garden sale in 1741, would inform Ramsay's work, particularly his portrait of Philip, Viscount Mahon (1762).[37] *Boy playing with a Totum* (a version of *Le Toton* or *Child with a Top*, Louvre, Paris) was part of a 1743 sale and another in 1748–49. The muted colour scheme and concentrated expression on the older boy's face of *Two Boys of the Nollekens Family playing at Tops* (Yale Center for British Art, Paul Mellon Collection, New Haven), dated *c.* 1745, indicates that its author, Joseph Francis Nollekens (1702–1748), was aware of Chardin's painting, which he could have seen in London from 1743. Versions of *Le Singe Peintre* (*The Monkey as Painter*, Musée des Beaux-Arts, Chartres) and *Le Singe Antiquaire* (*The Monkey as Antiquarian*, Musée des Beaux-Arts, Chartres) were sold in 1760 and inspired a number of British artists. *The Monkey as Painter*, engraved by Surugue (fig. 78), whom Hogarth had met in Paris in 1743, informed the British artist's compositions for *Self-portrait painting the Comic Muse* (1758; fig. 79), *Time smoking a Picture* (1761; engraving) and the caricature by Paul Sandby (1730–1809) of Hogarth's *Self-portrait* of 1758, *Puggs Graces Etched from his Original Daubing* (1758; etching).[38] Although Hogarth might have taken his inspiration from the engraved composition more readily than from the painting itself, it is interesting that the two works inspired by Chardin's painting were made at about the time it is known to have arrived on the London market.

Lady taking Tea, which appeared in a 1765 London sale, may have influenced Philippe Mercier's painting of the same title and certainly informed Ramsay's portrait of Dr William Hunter.[39] Numerous other examples could be identified, though this is not the occasion, and it should be mentioned that not every Chardin or Boucher painting known to have been in Britain at the time was recorded through the salerooms: the route into the collection of William Hunter of *The Cellar Boy* and its companion, *The Scullery Maid*, is unknown.[40] Similarly, Ramsay may have had in his possession a portrait of Mme de Pompadour and *Le Déjeuner* attributed to Boucher.[41]

Boucher's paintings, whose titles were either vague (six *Venus and Cupids* are recorded in sales catalogues between 1751 and 1785) or matched no known compositions, are much harder to identify. At first a few only found their way to Britain and tended to be early genre scenes or pastorals

Fig. 78
Pierre Louis Surugue
after Jean-Siméon Chardin
The Monkey as Painter, 1743
Etching and engraving, 31.7 × 24.7 cm
British Museum, London
inv. no. 1983, 0127.7

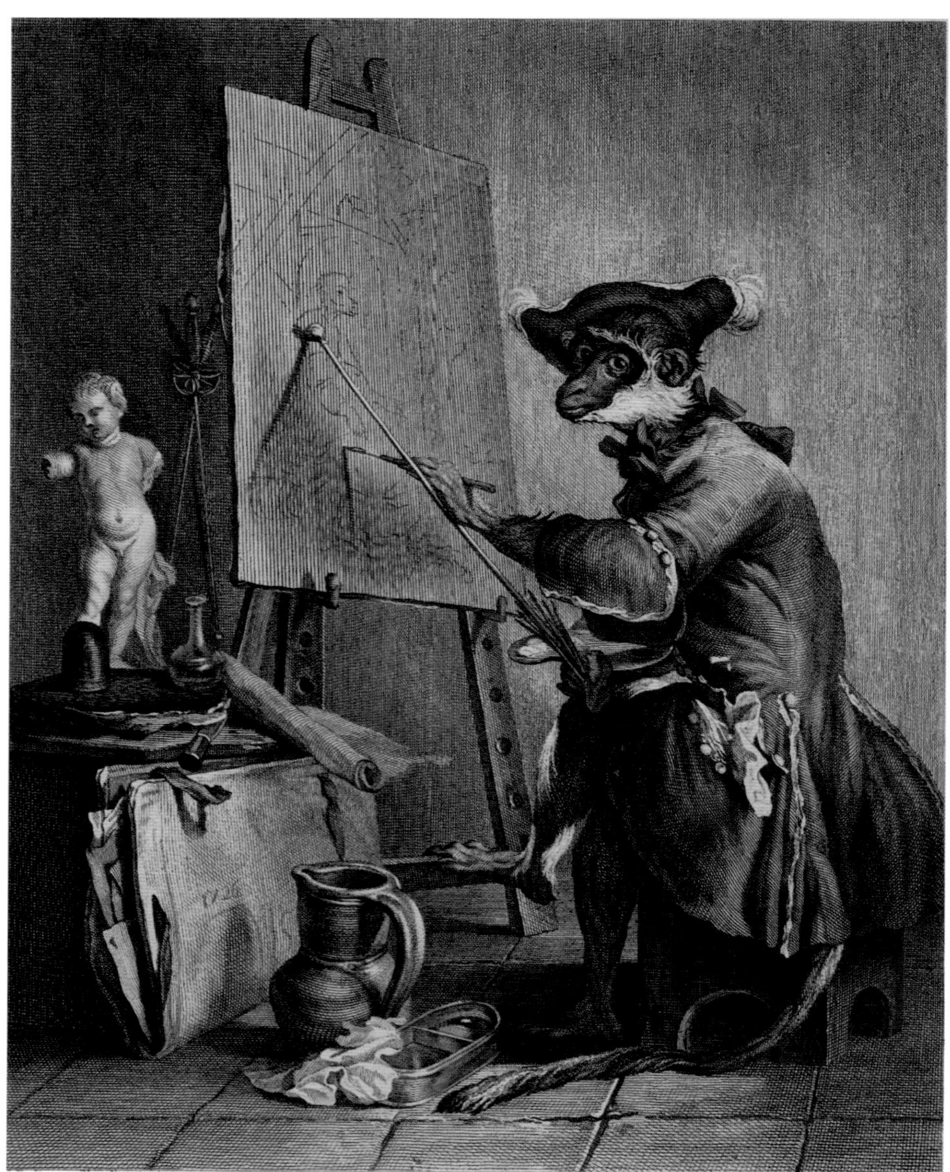

combining a distinctive northern feel with Italianate landscapes which
would have complemented the type of seventeenth-century Dutch works
of which British collectors were particularly fond.[42] They were *The Beautiful
Kitchen-maid* from the 1730s, *De trois choses en ferez-vous une?* (sold Sotheby's),
New York, 24 June 2002, lot 194; formerly collection of the Earl of Home)
and *Rural Life*. From the 1750s a few landscapes and gallant mythology
subjects started to appear, with generic titles such as *Venus and Cupid* and
A Watermill. Although the Rococo style Boucher helped to create found
an echo in contemporary British art, none of his identifiable paintings
known to have been in Britain at the time can be shown to have inspired

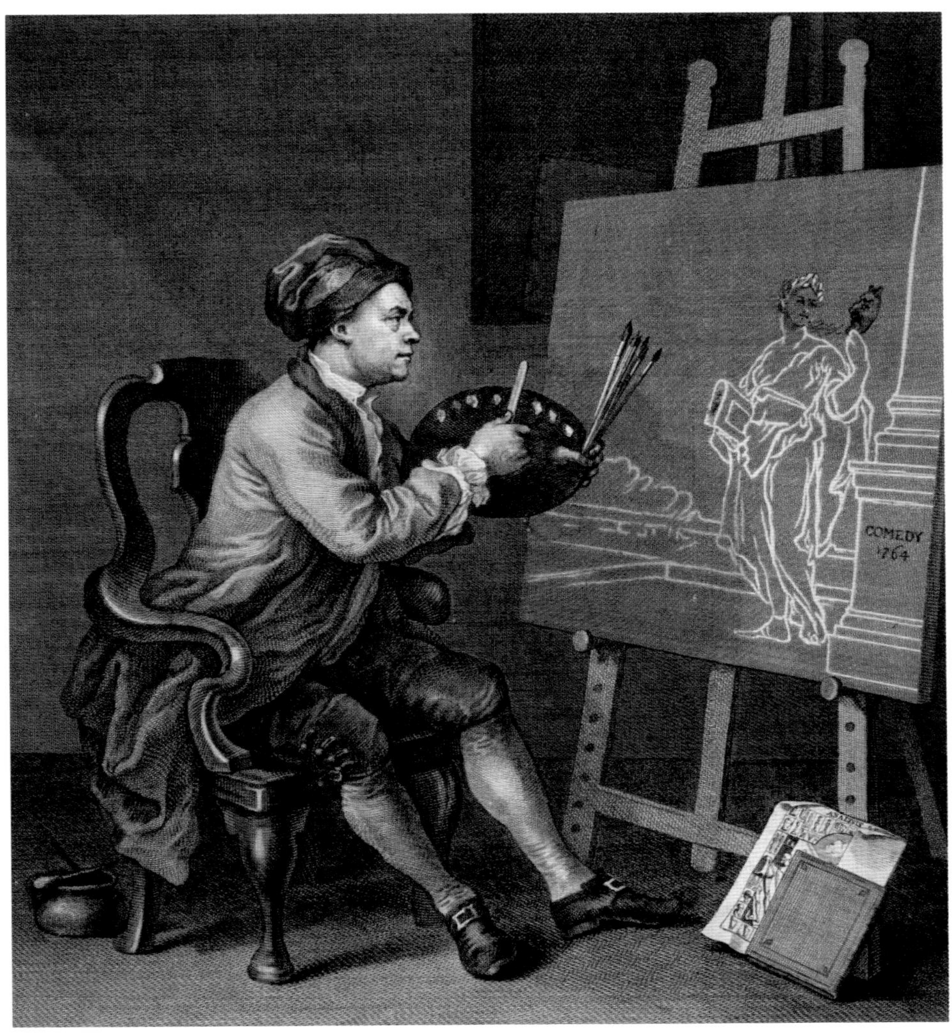

Fig. 79
William Hogarth
Self-portrait painting the Comic Muse, 1758
Etching and engraving, 40.0 × 35.4 cm
British Museum, London
inv. no. 1847, 0508.2

a specific response from British artists.

The detailed chronology (see appendix, pp. 136–39) demonstrates an absence in the 1760s of works by Boucher on the British market. British collectors in those days tended to prefer his drawings, or tapestries after his designs (Reynolds had several Boucher drawings in his collection and Rogers acquired thirteen over the years; of the twelve sets that were woven after Boucher's floral designs for the Gobelins tapestries in the 1760s, half were commissioned by English patrons). At the same time the development of English decorative pastorals in conjunction with the renewal of war with France has been thought responsible for diverting British patrons from anything with an obvious French Rococo flavour. Boucher's reputation in Britain seems to have grown after his death in 1770, as from then on his name would regularly appear in London sales,

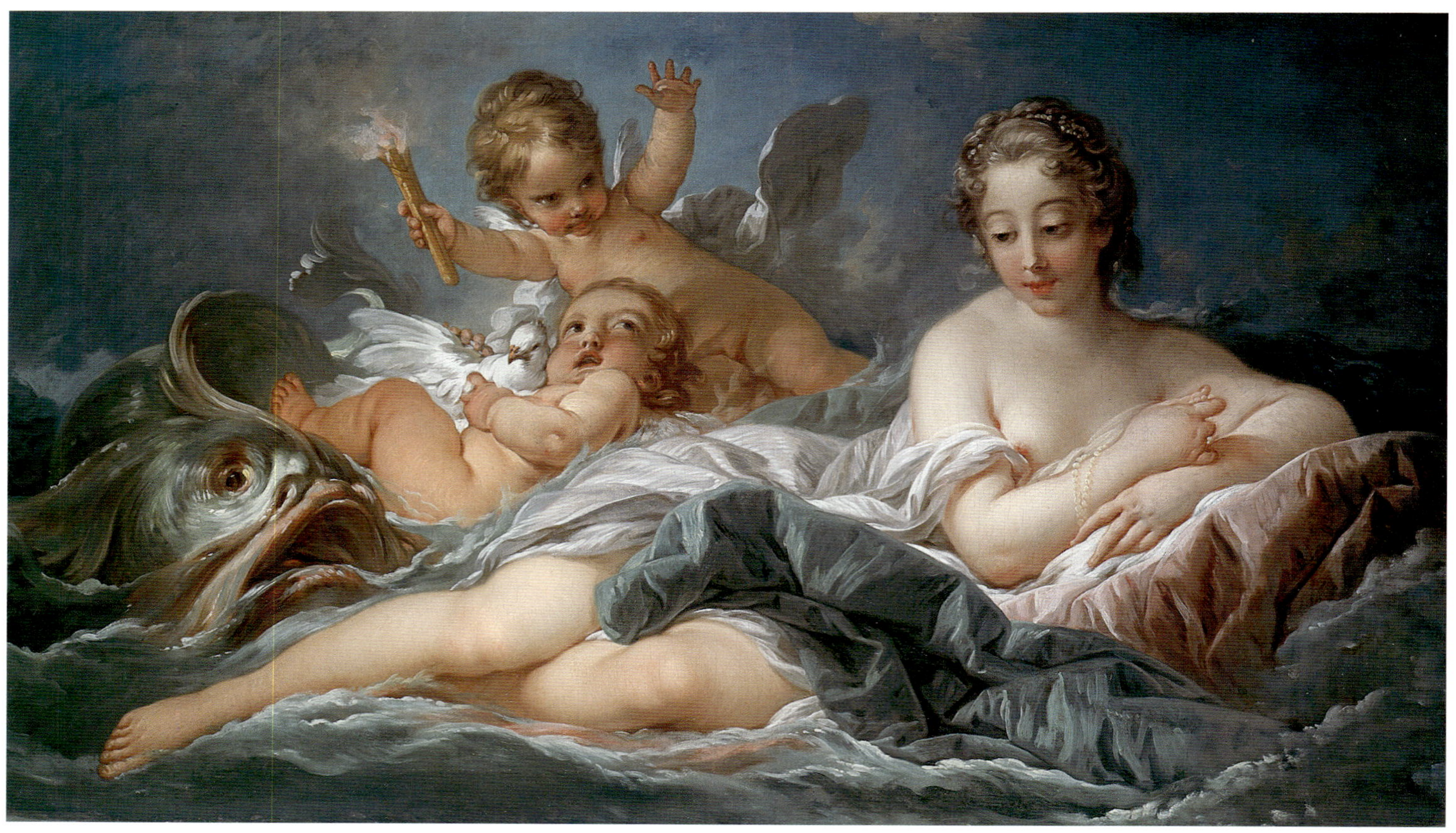

Fig. 80
François Boucher
Venus, 1754
Oil on canvas, 79.2 × 138.7 cm
The Wallace Collection, London
inv. no. P423

a fact that has not been previously noted. The detailed chronology reveals that nineteen paintings by Boucher are to be accounted for in the last decade of this study. They included a few early genre scenes but in the main were gallant mythology subjects, landscapes and heads of girls – beginning to be more representative of the varied output that characterizes Boucher's oeuvre. Among them were *A Lady sleeping* and a *Venus sleeping*, likely to be versions of a subject Boucher depicted repeatedly with variations. One of the best known is *Le Repos de Venus* (*Venus's Rest*; Staatliche Museen, Berlin), engraved by Duflos around 1742.

Another was *Jupiter and Europa*, probably a version of a favourite Boucher subject, *The Rape of Europa* (*L'Enlèvement d'Europe*).[43] Boucher started painting such subjects, usually illustrating amorous episodes from Ovid's *Metamorphoses*, in the 1730s, and they soon became a favourite with collectors of his work on the Continent. Among the other works associated with known paintings are *Summer* and its companion, *Autumn*, which probably presented putti and nymphs in landscapes alluding to the four seasons, another Boucher speciality from the 1730s (see examples in figs. 80, 81).[44]

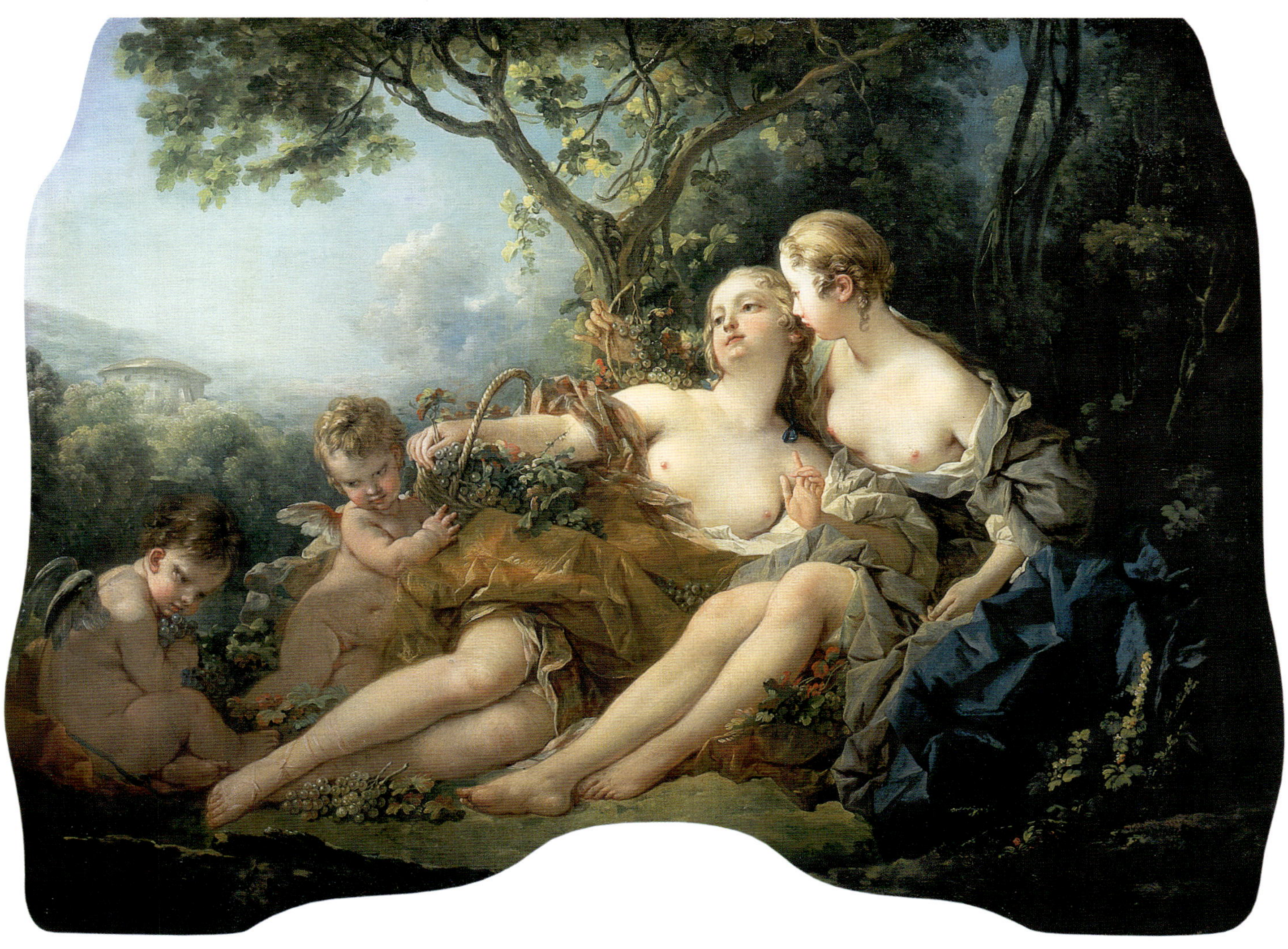

Chardin on the other hand disappears from the saleroom until 1786, and only a handful of his paintings are recorded in the last fifteen years of the century. This is curious, since interest in Chardin seems not to have waned. His influence continued to be felt in British art, for example in the work of Henry Walton (1746–1813), an artist and picture dealer who met Chardin in Paris in 1773 or 1774 and whose few genre pictures owe to Chardin their feeling for tone.[45] Similarly, collectors still had an interest in his work, for the third Duke of Dorset arranged through Reynolds to have *A Boy drawing*, then in a British collection, copied in pastel before 1779.

THE IMPACT OF DEALERS ON THE IMPORT OF WORKS BY BOUCHER AND CHARDIN

Besides the rapid growth of artistic exchange between London and Paris, the five decades of this study also witnessed the establishment of the sale-rooms and auction houses from which the modern art market would spring. This went hand in hand with the rise of the professional art dealer, who played a vital role in the initial importation to London of works by Boucher and Chardin as in the first three decades of our study the majority were sold through a handful of dealers.

Andrew Hay (d. *c.* 1754)

It was Hay who in 1738 sold the first known Chardin to appear in the London salerooms (*A Girl with Cherries*, exhibited at the 1737 Salon, engraved in 1738 by Charles-Nicolas Cochin shortly before it left Paris). Among the earliest art dealers in Britain, the Scots-born Hay held his first recorded specialized sale at Covent Garden in 1725 and spent the next twenty years travelling to France and Italy gathering paintings for sale in London, moving easily in artists' and connoisseurs' circles and taking membership of the artistic and antiquarian Rose and Crown Club. Although selling principally Old Masters, Hay had included the occasional Watteau and Lancret in his sales, and his interest in Chardin is no surprise in view of his contact with the French and British art worlds. In France he was well acquainted, for example, with Le Bas, who drew a portrait of his Scottish acquaintance in chalk (J. McGouan 1804 sale).[46] Considering that Le Bas was both engraver and dealer and acted as an agent for Chardin, he may have helped or perhaps advised Hay to acquire *A Girl with Cherries*. In London the dealer was familiar with the group of artists associated with the St Martin's Lane Academy and must have benefited from Gravelot's contacts in the French art world. What is particularly interesting is that Hay seems to have been the first to sell a painting by Chardin at a public auction and that it had been painted only a year or so before, thus giving London auction-goers a unique opportunity to see with their own eyes one of Chardin's latest works in the new genre he was then developing.

The Scottish dealer was also the first to sell paintings by Boucher in London, including some in one of the last sales he organized in 1744. They were *De trois choses en ferez-vous une?* (described in the 1744 sale as *A Young Man and his Mistress*) and *La Vie champêtre* (*Rural Life*; described in the 1744 sale as *A Harvest with Figures*; fig. 82), both Italianate landscapes with Dutch-inspired figures characteristic of Boucher's style at his return from Italy in the mid 1730s. Alastair Laing believes it was the genre rather than the artist's reputation that attracted Hay, since it corresponded to what English contemporary collectors are known most to have admired.[47]

Whilst no further sales of Boucher paintings are listed for that decade, fourteen works by Chardin have so far been recorded. They appeared in four sales dated from both the beginning and end of the 1740s, suggesting that the war raging between France and Britain between 1743 and 1748 must have affected the importation of foreign pictures to London. The majority were again brought in by dealers – amateurs like Francesco Saverio Geminiani and professionals like Dr Bragge.

Francesco Saverio Geminiani (1687–1762)

A composer and music theorist, Geminiani moved to London in 1714, and there became one of the best-known musicians of his day, moving among the highest echelons of English society. By the 1730s the musician was sharing his time between Paris, Dublin and London and had become known as a dedicated lover of art. A familiar figure in Paris and London artistic circles, Geminiani supplemented his income by organizing three London sales of pictures he had picked up on his Continental trips in 1741, 1742 and 1743.

All eleven Chardins sold by Geminiani in his 1741 and 1743 sales were versions of paintings included in the 1738 Salon, where the artist had exhibited small pictures inspired by the daily life of juveniles and kitchen staff.[48] Geminiani lived in Dublin from 1737 to 1740 and in Paris that year, returning to London in 1741. Did he buy his paintings directly from Chardin's studio? This bulk purchase coincides with Chardin's presenting two of his works to Louis XV and receiving commissions from Count Tessin in 1740. By then the artist's success in France was well established, as noted by the *Mercure de France* for September 1743: "His pictures continue to be in great demand. They delight all who have eyes to see and feeling enough to be moved by this naïve and faithful imitation of nature. He has the gift of bringing the canvas to life."[49] The first and last to import Chardin paintings in such quantity, Geminiani clearly thought highly of the artist and believed his style would attract English collectors.

The arrival of so large a group of works representative of Chardin's latest manner and specialization in those "little pieces of common-life" that would ensure his success abroad, the engraving of one (*A Boy drawing*) the same year by Faber and the presence in Covent Garden of at least two French artists with strong connections to Chardin's artistic circles (Gravelot and van Loo) must all have made England among the first outside France to appreciate him.

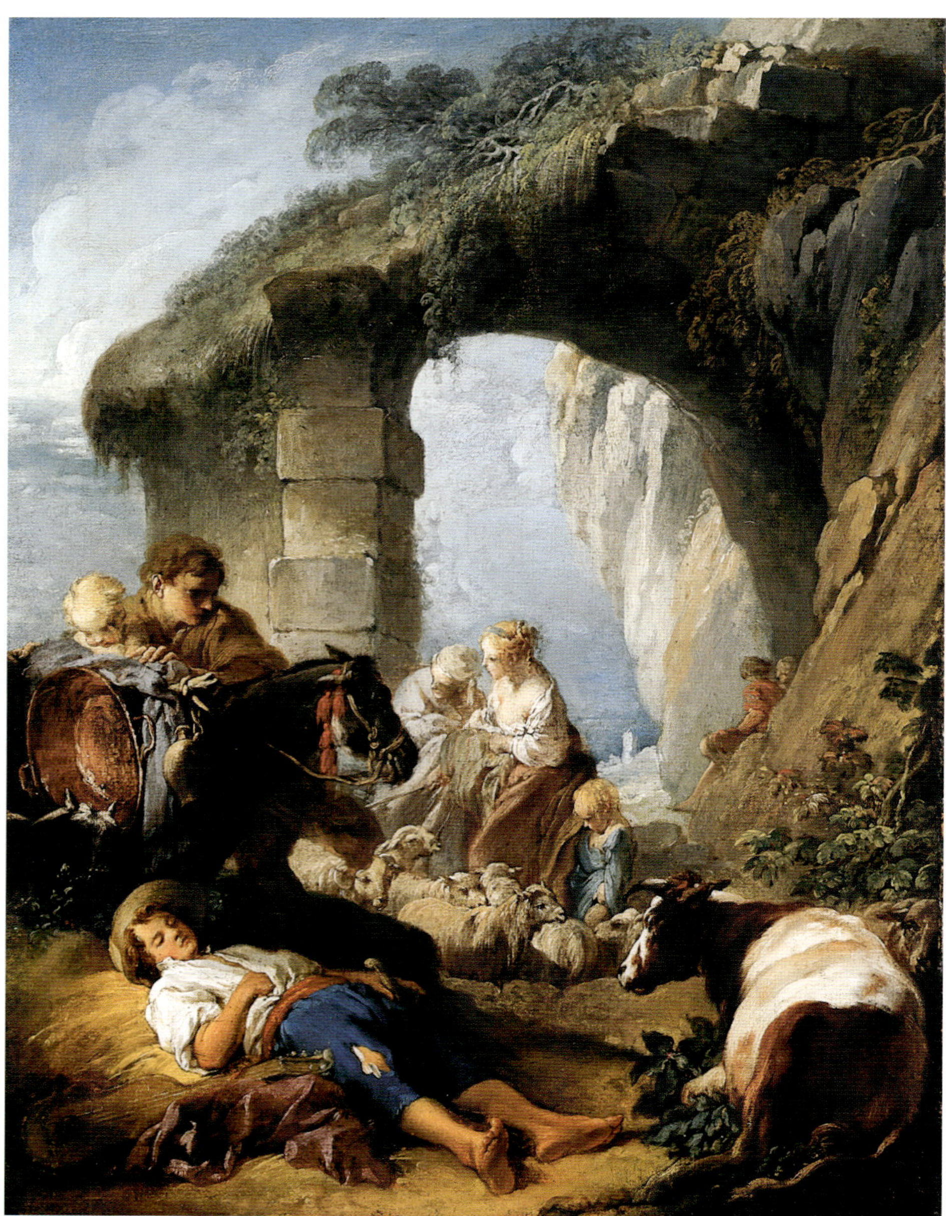

Fig. 82
François Boucher
Rural Life, c. 1730
Oil on canvas, 61 × 48 cm
The Brownlow Collection, Belton House
The National Trust

Dr Bragge (dates unknown)

Dr Bragge was the only dealer besides Andrew Hay to import paintings by both Boucher and Chardin. One of the first gentleman connoisseurs and art dealers, he had abandoned his studies in medicine for art and was one of the most important figures of the London art market.[50] Like Hay and Geminiani he had made numerous contacts abroad and would travel to the Continent to gather works of art to sell in London. More cautious than Geminiani, Bragge included only one Chardin in his sales, *La Gouvernante* (*A Young Gentleman and his Governess*; possibly the painting now in the

Egerton Collection, Tatton Park, National Trust), in 1749–50. A version of the painting given by Chardin to Louis XV in 1740 and copied for Count Tessin in 1741, it was well known through its engraving by F.B. Lépicié in 1739. The buyer of the painting is not recorded.

In 1751, despite having stated in the introduction of his 1749–50 sale catalogue that he intended to retire from business, Bragge decided to resume his activities as a dealer "at the particular desire of his friends" and was presenting a "collection of Dutch, Flemish, French, and Italian pictures of Dr Bragge, collected by himself abroad".[51] This time he included a Boucher "*Venus and Cupid*", the first gallant mythology subject to pass through an English auction room. In the seven other sales Bragge is known to have organized for that decade two more Bouchers appeared, one entitled "*A Watermill*" – so Bragge may also be credited with the import of the first Boucher landscape – and the other *Rural Life*, already in Britain from the 1740s. Information on Dr Bragge and his contact with the French art world is slender, nor is it possible specifically to identify those Boucher paintings he imported to London.[52] We can, however, conclude from these sales that he played a role in introducing to the London market the kinds of paintings – gallant mythology and picturesque landscape – for which Boucher had gained renown in the rest of Europe.

Stephen Rongent (d. 1764)

Little is known of Rongent except that he organized a number of sales in the 1750s. It is unlikely that he imported new works to the market, as the two Boucher paintings he sold, "*Venus and Cupid*" and "*Girl and Boy*", might have been respectively the "*Venus and Cupid*" sold by Bragge four years earlier and the *De trois choses en ferez-vous une?* by Hay in 1744.

Thomas Major (1720–1799)

The engraver, publisher and art dealer Thomas Major sold in 1751 versions of two of the best-known Chardin compositions. He had studied engraving from 1747–50 in Paris at the studio of Le Bas, with whom, after his return, he kept in touch, sometimes acting as his agent. This 1751 sale consisted of the painting collection he had pulled together when living in Paris, which included versions of *The Diligent Mother* (fig. 83) and *Saying Grace* (fig. 84). The first of these were executed as a pair, exhibited at the 1740 Salon and presented by Chardin to Louis XV. Another version of *The Diligent Mother* was exhibited at the 1746 Salon, and several more of each have been recorded in eighteenth-century sales. Engraved in 1740, the first versions greatly enhanced the artist's reputation abroad, and with the success of Chardin in 1740s London it is unsurprising that Major believed

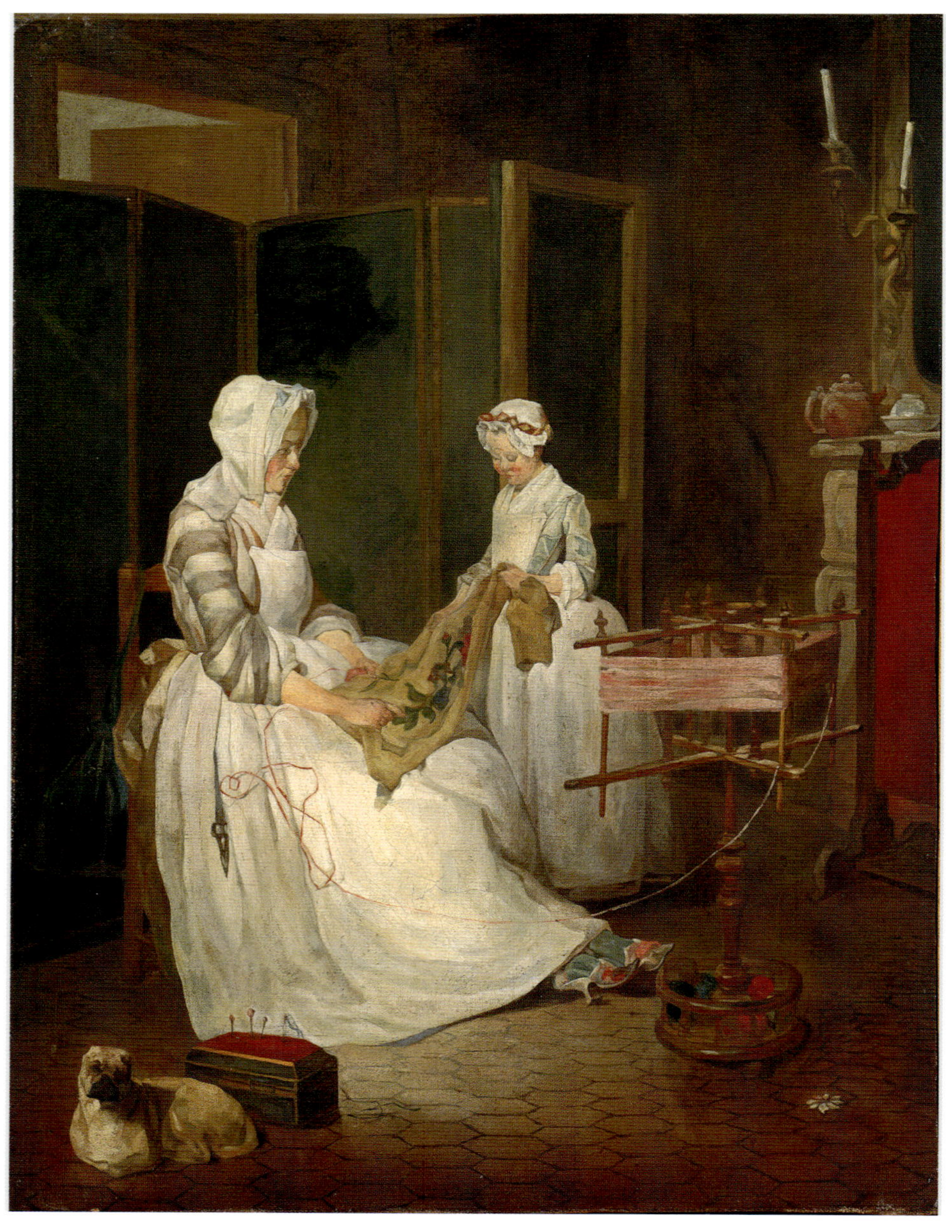

Fig. 83
Jean-Siméon Chardin
The Diligent Mother, 1740
Oil on canvas; 50 × 39.5 cm
Nationalmuseum, Stockholm
inv. no. NM 784

versions of the two compositions would sell well there. Major also had an interest in Boucher, and published his *Livre chinois* in London (included in his inventory for 1754).[53]

The arrival on the English art market scene of the dealer Robert Strange and the auctioneer James Christie in the late 1760s and early 1770s revived the dealing of Boucher paintings at auction which had ended with Rongent's 1755 sale. This is paradoxical, as numerous contacts between Boucher and Britain have been recorded for that period. The disappearance of the dealers responsible for the early importation of his works to

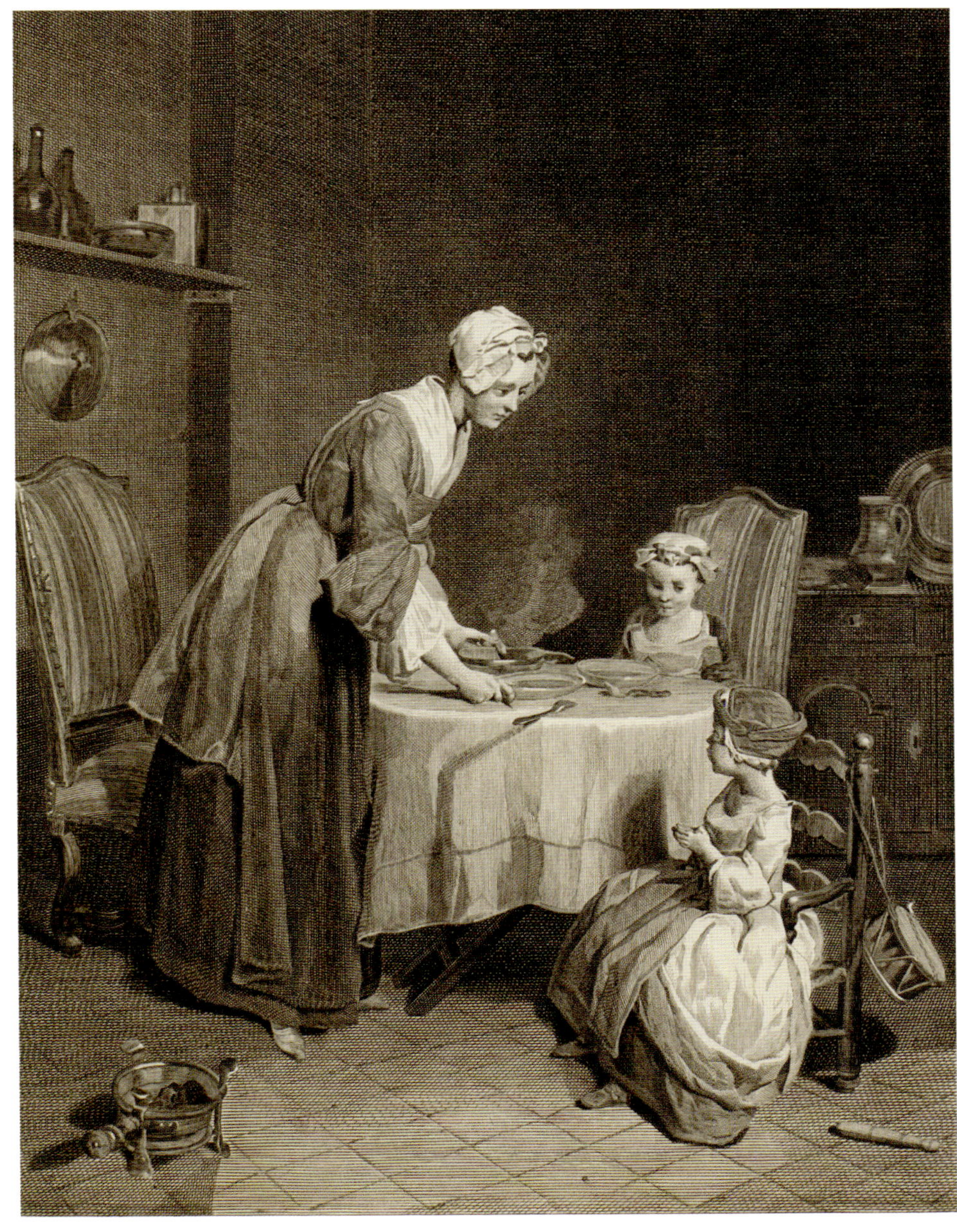

London may partly explain the absence of works by Boucher in the sale-rooms between 1755 and 1771.[54]

Robert Strange (1725–1792) and James Christie (1730–1803)

Of the nineteen Boucher paintings sold in the 1770s barely a third were imported into London by dealers or auctioneers. These were Robert Strange, who had studied in Le Bas's studio in the late 1740s, and James Christie, the first auctioneer known to have use agents abroad. Paris

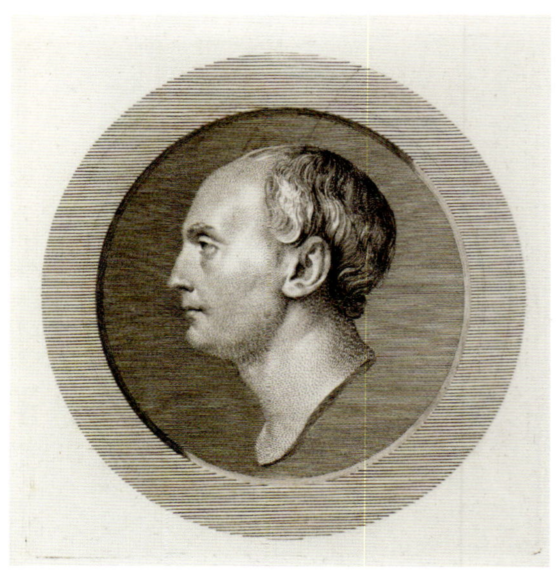

Fig. 85
Robert Strange after Jean-Baptiste Greuze
Portrait of Sir Robert Strange, 1791
Engraving, 15.2 × 15.2 cm
Hunterian Museum and Art Gallery
University of Glasgow
inv. no. GLAHA 23964

remained an important base for Strange, where he was well acquainted with both dealers and artists – Jean-Baptiste Greuze (1725–1805) drew his portrait about 1760 (on loan to the Scottish National Portrait Gallery in Edinburgh), which Strange himself later engraved (fig. 85). He had spent part of the 1760s visiting prestigious collections on the Continent with a view to engraving their most famous works, taking the opportunity to gather pictures to sell on his return to London.[55]

James Christie had entered the expanding London auction world in the early 1760s, first in household sales and then going on to specialize in paintings towards the end of that decade. By the early 1770s he was employing several Continental agents to search for pictures to send to London to facilitate a couple of sales a year with pictures "consigned from abroad".[56]

Strange and Christie chose mostly landscapes and "amiable allusions of ancient Mythology, the Loves of the Gods", both subjects Rogers would describe in his *Prints in Imitation of Drawings* as Boucher's speciality. They were a landscape, a *Lady sleeping*, a *Venus sleeping*, two landscapes with figures, and pictures entitled *Summer* and *Autumn* – probably pastorals or scenes with putti and nymphs depicting the Four Seasons. Although the often imprecise generic titles make it difficult to identify them with certitude, they were undoubtedly gallant mythology subjects, pastorals or landscapes. This indicates a definitive change in Anglo-Saxon attitudes towards Boucher's work, which had previously been characterized by a preference for his early genre scenes. Strange may have helped to raise the profile of Boucher's later style in London: his series of sales between 1771 and 1775, heavily marketed from 1769 with an unveiling, accompanied by a descriptive catalogue of the collection he was proposing to sell in 1769 and 1770, had been the talk of London.

BOUCHER AND CHARDIN'S COLLECTORS

During the first two decades of our study paintings by Boucher and Chardin in the London salerooms were imported mainly by dealers who had direct contact with the Parisian art world. As the names of the buyers were at first omitted from surviving sales catalogues, it has not been possible to identify the earliest collectors of the two French artists' works. In the late 1740s pieces by Chardin started to turn up in private collectors' sales, offering the first clues as to who his British admirers were. Though from the 1750s sales catalogues remain concise, the names of buyers begin to appear. These names are not always possible to identify with known persons, but it does become feasible to build up a profile of Boucher and Chardin's collectors.

The first collectors' names to be associated with the French artists go back to the 1740s. Amateurs of Chardin included the well-known architect, painter and garden designer William Kent (1684–1748), who owned Chardin's *Boy playing with a Totum,* and a Mr Glover, probably Richard Glover (1712–1785), who bought *A Courtesan* in 1742 at auction.[57] Connected to the circle of art lovers patronizing the artist and art dealer Arthur Pond in the 1740s, Glover was a collector, politician, playwright and poet friend of Frederick, Prince of Wales. Boucher's collectors were the eighth Earl of Home (d. 1761), a connoisseur who had travelled the Continent as an army officer and bought *De trois choses ferez-vous une?,* and a Mr Peters, who bought *Rural Life.* He was probably the Dr Peters mentioned by Ian Pears as belonging to that breed of medical men with a taste for art emerging in the eighteenth century.[58] Other well-known physicians with an interest in contemporary art included Dr Mead, who had purchased two *fêtes galantes* direct from Watteau in 1720.

Both Glover and Kent had collections representative of the works favoured by their contemporaries, with a majority of Italian, Dutch and Flemish seventeenth-century paintings. Little is known of the exact content of Lord Home's or Peters's collections. This combination of collectors from the aristocracy with art lovers of the emerging professional middle classes (lawyers, civil servants, doctors and the artists themselves) would persist over the next three decades of our study.

Aristocratic collectors

These tended to be scions of the great families of collectors and arts patrons mentioned in Walpole's lists of the top British collections of the time, members of exclusive clubs and fellows of the Royal Society or the Society of Antiquaries. Moving in the same circles as Walpole, the Yorke family or others known for their appreciation of French arts and culture and their direct connection with Boucher or Chardin's circles, they also patronized artists such as Ramsay, Reynolds and Hogarth, whose knowledge of Boucher and Chardin's work has been described. Such aristocratic collections tended to be dominated by art of the seventeenth century, Italian, Northern and, to a lesser degree, French, and included only one work by Boucher or Chardin. This suggests their acquisition would have been made to complete the representation of every major school in collections that were being built over generations.

Only two aristocrats have so far been found among Chardin's collectors. Charles Wyndham, second Earl of Egremont (1710–1763), bought *The Diligent Mother* (Petworth House until 1927) at the 1751 Major sale whilst Francis Wemyss, seventh Earl, also known as Hon. Francis Charteris (1723–1808), bought *Saying Grace* (Gosford House). They would no doubt have exulted in owning versions of paintings by Chardin in the collection of Louis XV. Egremont was on a Grand Tour in 1729–30 following two years at a French academy, and a member of the Society of Dilettanti from 1742. Wemyss was a patron of Allan Ramsay, who painted portraits of Wemyss, his wife Lady Katherine Gordon and his sisters Helen Dalrymple and Lady Walpole Wemyss. The whole family was very much interested in French contemporary culture, as is shown not least by the gowns of his wife and sisters in Ramsay's portraits painted between 1748 and 1754. It was of his portrait of Lady Helen that Ramsay said: "*Les joues de My Lady Nelly Wemyss parlent François*" (the cheeks of My Lady Nelly speak French)[59].

Among the aristocratic collectors with an early interest in Boucher was Francis Greville (1719–1773), known as Lord Brooke, first Earl of Warwick, and John Campbell (1693–1770), fourth Duke of Argyll. Warwick belonged to London Francophile circles surrounding Lord Walpole and Lord Hertford. In Paris in 1741 he had his likeness painted by the renowned French portraitist Nattier, to whom his wife, a daughter of the Duke of Hamilton, also sat in 1754. A year later he purchased a Boucher work entitled *A Girl and a Boy* (possibly *De trois choses ferez-vous une?*) at the 1755 Rongent sale.

Argyll was a patron of Allan Ramsay and Robert Strange, who both had first-hand knowledge of the latest developments in French painting and acted when required as advisors to their patrons. His son, married to the celebrated beauty Elizabeth Gunning, admired French taste (it was he who would redecorate Inverary Castle in the French manner in the 1770s, hiring French artists and craftsmen to create a late Rococo interior in the heart of the Highlands). When in Paris in 1763 he commissioned portraits of himself and his wife from Drouais. The sale of the fourth Duke of Argyll's collection at Langford on 23 March 1771 was an important event for the British art world and included lot 18, "Boucher *Jupiter and Europa*".

Sales from the 1770s (see Chronology) point in the direction of two further aristocratic collectors connected with Boucher – Thomas Bromley, second Lord Montford (1733–1799), and Rachel Russell, Duchess of Bridgewater (*c.* 1698–1777). Montfort's father, Henry Bromley (1705–1755) was a politician, a friend of the Yorke family, and belonged to the Pope's Heard Club, the Royal Society Club and other learned societies. As a patron of Arthur Pond in the 1740s Montfort's father also had ties with the 'Customs House Group' collectors, whose interest in Boucher will shortly be explored in further detail.[60] The Duchess of Bridgewater took as her second husband Sir Richard Lyttelton (1718–70), a well-known art collector. In Italy in 1760–62 they purchased a number of pictures, using the services of, among others, Thomas Jenkins (1722–1798) and Strange. A collector in her own right, the Duchess was known for her taste for Dutch paintings.

Part of the new breed of middle-class collectors emerging in the mid eighteenth century, these were professional men in medicine, banking and law. Art was their passion as well as a means to express their social elevation. Feeling their way into the market, they would commandeer the assistance of artists and dealers while they gained confidence. The City collectors were such a group – City merchants, government office-holders and financiers who met each other in the 1740s during regular visits to the print shop of Arthur Pond (1701–1758) and began collecting Old Master paintings and drawings under the guidance of the artist. A painter, printseller and art dealer, Pond was an important pivot of the British art world who met many of his clients through clubs, the Royal Society or the Society of Antiquarians. A collector in his own right, he had contact with the French market and dealers like Gersaint, and was well connected to London Francophile circles (Lady Hertford and her friends were among his clients).[61] A posthumous sale of 1760 included a number of prints after Boucher and Chardin, evidence that Pond had an interest in their work and stocked prints by them in his shop.[62]

The City collectors soon became known as the 'Customs House Group', their most influential members including Charles Rogers, Nathaniel Hillier and John Barnard (d. 1784), whose connoisseurship and taste were particularly admired. Even a lesser-known member such as William Fauquener was able to bequeath 39 volumes of prints and drawings to the British Museum. Together they shared information about auctions and works available, sometimes even acting as agents for each other, and all became members of the Society of Antiquaries. Interestingly, they all seem to have shared an interest in Boucher and Chardin. The most notable were Dr Charles Chauncey (1709–1797), an avid collector listed among Walpole's forty-seven most important British collectors for 1757; Sir Henry Bankes, an Alderman of the City of London; Jones Raymond, a Director of the East India Company who was among the few British collectors to have an interest in both Boucher and Chardin, as shown by his purchase of a work by each in the mid 1750s;[63] and Christopher Batt (d. 1756). Chauncey, Batt, Bankes and Raymond owned works attributed to Chardin called "*A Sketch of Women and Children*" and "*A Cook's maid sleeping*" and to Boucher called "*A Water Mill*" and "*Rural Life*" (Belton House until 1929; fig. 82).[64]

The collector Roger Harenc, though little known, is nevertheless among the most important early collectors of Chardin's work in Britain.[65] According to Ian Pears, Harenc was a man of modest fortune but an enthusiastic buyer at auctions, purchasing pictures at 32 sales between 1734 and 1760. One of them, a *Mary Magdalen* by Guido Reni, was engraved by Robert

Strange in 1753. Harenc belonged to that first generation of middle-class collectors and had three Chardins in his collection at the time of his death.[66] Two, *A Boy drawing* and *A Girl musing* (identified by David Carritt as *Le Jeune Dessinateur* and *Jeune Ouvrière en Tapisserie* from the 1743 Geminiani sale) had been on the British market from the 1740s. The third is more difficult to identify: described as "*A Boy's head in a round*", it may have been a version of *Le Château de Carte*, dated 1737.[67]

The most important collectors to emerge from the 1760s and 1770s were William Fauquier, Dr Hunter and Dr Morgan. Following men like Roger Harenc, Hunter and Fauquier belonged to the second generation of British middle-class collectors. As their interest in Boucher and Chardin is considered in detail in the catalogue (no. 27), suffice it to say here that between them they owned five Chardins and one Boucher. Morgan acquired four paintings by Boucher – a pair of landscapes and figures in 1771 and another pair in 1780, this time showing girls with herbage. This makes him one of the most important collectors of Boucher in eighteenth-century England. Although it has proved difficult to find out much about him, his name appears regularly in sale catalogues of the period and his taste seems to have matched the usual profile of the eighteenth-century British collector of seventeenth-century northern genre, Italian and French pictures.

To conclude, it seems fair to suggest that, outside France, Britain was among the first to appreciate the modern manner adopted by Boucher and Chardin. This was owing partly to the personal acquaintance of a number of British artists with the two Frenchmen, and partly to the rise of dealers with a taste for modern art who ensured that London's salerooms were early in including examples of Boucher and Chardin's paintings.[68]

Chardin's "little pieces of common life" encountered immediate success with collectors across the Channel and informed the work of a whole generation of British artists in genres from portraiture to conversation pieces and 'fancy' pictures. Boucher's specialities of gallant mythology, pastorals and landscapes had less impact on the developing British school of painting, and found scant favour among collectors until the latter part of the century.

Their collectors were often from London's Francophile circles, where aristocratic families mixed with artists and members of the rising middle class. The most assiduous belonged to the latter, and by the 1770s collectors such as Morgan started to appear, ahead of the renowned nineteenth-century avid British Boucher collectors like the fourth Marquess of Hertford (1800–1870) and various members of the Rothschild family. Chardin's paintings, on the other hand, would never be as present in the London salerooms as they had been between 1740 and 1765, a position dependent on the crucially important role played by British artists and dealers in promoting his fame in Britain.

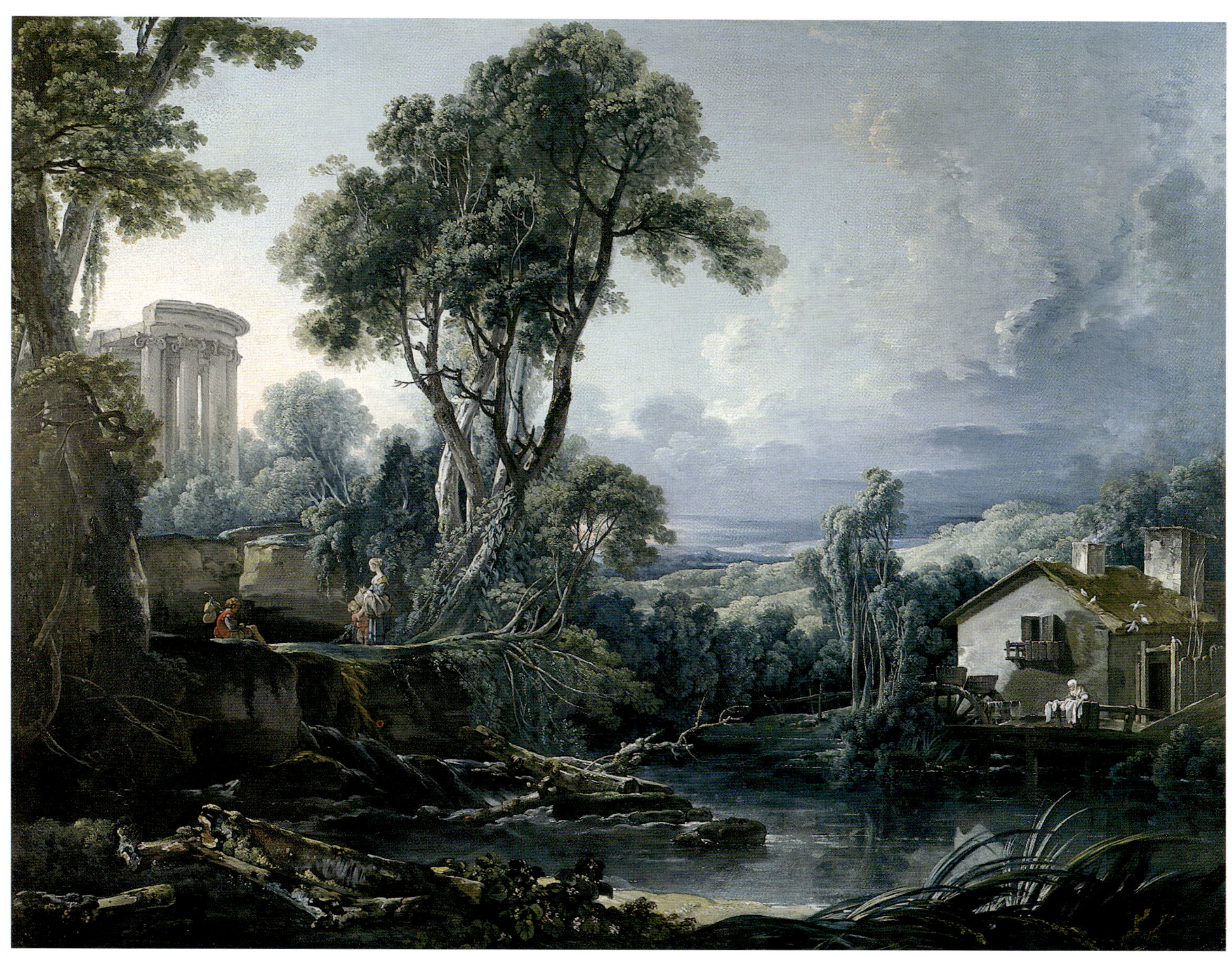

Fig. 86
François Boucher
Landscape, 1743
Oil on canvas, 90.8 × 118.1 cm
Barnard Castle, Bowes Museum

1 Until 1737, the date at which the Louvre Salon was reinstated (it had been suspended since 1704, apart from the Salon held in 1725), French artists could share their work with the public on an annual basis at the Exposition de la Jeunesse in Place Dauphine. Chardin started exhibiting at the Exposition de la Jeunesse in 1728, sending sixteen paintings in 1734. When the Louvre Salon first reopened its doors in 1737 he sent seven paintings, nine the following year and six in 1739. Boucher exhibited several small paintings in the placeDauphine in 1725. He contributed six works to the 1737 Louvre Salon and three each to the 1738 and 1739 Salons.

2 Alexander Pope, *The First Epistle of the Second Book of Horace Imitated*, London, 1737, pp. 263–64.

3 See Raines 1977.

4 Primary sources consulted were found in the online Getty provenance database; Christie's archives; the National Art Library, National Galleries of Scotland and National Gallery archives for eighteenth-century sales catalogues; Eighteenth Century Collections online. It is hoped that this essay will inspire researchers to seek out additional primary sources and conduct a more systematic study of the subject.

5 The main writings on the subject are: Waterhouse 1952; Haynes 1968; Carritt 1974; Raines 1977; Pierre Rosenberg in Paris, Cleveland and Boston 1979; Sutton 1984; Conisbee 1985; Brunel 1986; Laing 1986; Alastair Laing in New York, Detroit and Paris 1986–87; Roland-Michel 1994; 'Boucher, Britain and the first three Marquesses of Hertford', in Hedley 2004, pp. 161–64; Simon 2007. For the importance of Huguenots in the London art world, see Tessa Murdoch, *The Quiet Conquest: The Huguenots 1685 to 1985*, Museum of London in association with A.H. Jelly, London, 1985.

6 In 1735, Le Bas dedicated a large engraving after David Teniers to Dr Hickman, strongly suggesting that he would have met Highmore, who records spending time with Hickman. See Simon 2007, p. 31 for further details.

7 Johnston 1976–78, pp. 61–104.

8 Smart 1992, p. 27.

9 The Peace of 1716, which had encouraged visitors to both sides of the Channel, ended in 1742. Hostilities reached a climax in 1745 with the Jacobite rebellion, partly supported by the French, and created an uneasy political context for the rest of the decade. It is believed, for example, that Gravelot's return to France in 1745 was due mainly to the hostility towards the French in the British capital in the aftermath of the rebellion.

10 Simon 2007, pp. 29–33.

11 *Le Pasteur Galant* and *Le Pasteur Complaisant* after Boucher, advertised in the *Mercure de France* and *Gazette de France* of December 1742.

12 In 1748 William Hogarth, Francis Hayman, Henry Cheere, Thomas Hudson, Joseph Van Aken and his brother all went to Paris together; British students in Le Bas's studio included Luke Sullivan (1705–1771), Robert Strange, and other Scots sent to him by Richard Cooper and Thomas Major (1720–1799).

13 This raises the question of the connection between a taste for French art and Jacobite sympathies, which would merit some study.

14 See Simon 2007, p. 26.

15 For further information see Waterhouse 1952; Gowing 1953.

16 See Simon 2007, pp. 27–35, for Hogarth's knowledge of Chardin's work.

17 *A Boy drawing* went through the London market in 1740, 1743 and 1764.

18 George Bickham (*c.* 1704–1771) was an engraver and printseller with an enormously varied output, from engraved songsheets to printed guides, printed *chinoiserie*, books of ornaments and political prints. A successful operator, he seems to have had his finger on the nation's pulse and aimed to supply its every whim.

19 Faber was not the only engraver to work with Mercier. For further information see Ingamells and Raines 1976–78, cat. 11.

20 See Smart 1992.

21 See Denys Sutton in Manchester 1984, pp. 7–9.

22 Remy 1771, p. 75, lot 530: "*trois estampes gravées par Robert Strange, d'après le Titien*"; lot 531: "*Romulus et Remus; César qui répudie Pompée; Joseph avec Putiphar, d'après le Guide, aussi par R. Strange*"; p. 76, lot 533: "*Une estampe de Philippe Laure par W. Wollet*"; lot 539: "*Rubens, sa femme et son fils, gravée par Ardell*"; p. 78, lot 550: "*La mère de Rembrandt par Ardell*"; lot 551: "*Trois estampes d'après Van Dyck par Ardell*"; lot 552: "*huit portraits gravés par Ardell d'après différents maitres*"; lot 553: "*Le maitre d'école de filles, celui de garçons, et 6 autres pièces gravées par Faber*"; p. 79, lot 560: "*Quatre grands paysages avec figures, gravés par Wollett & Elliott*"; p. 82, added lot between 598 and 599: "Fables d'Esope *de Barlow en Anglois*"; p. 82, lot 611: "*Desseins des édifices, meubles, habits, machines et ustensiles des Chinois, par M. Chambers, Architecte. London. 1767*".

23 The story is told in more detail in cat. 28.

24 Charles Rogers, *A Collection of Prints in Imitation of Drawings*, London, 1778, pp. 195–97.

25 Mariette was particularly interested in Walpole, translating his *Anecdotes* on painting and learning English in his old age for that purpose. See Clark 1914.

26 He dismissed La Live de Jully's collection of contemporary French paintings, describing them as "a few good, many indifferent". See W.S. Lewis (ed.), *The Yale Edition of Horace Walpole Correspondence*, London, 1937–71, V, p. 295.

27 Hyde 2006, p. 48.

28 Hilda F. Finberg, 'Radnor House, Twickenham: A Drawing by Samuel

29 Preston Remington, 'A Mid-Georgian Interior from Kirtlington Park', *The Metropolitan Museum of Art Bulletin*, vol. 14, no. 7, March 1956, p. 158.

30 See Hedley 2004, pp. 163–64; Fiske Kimball, 'The Moor Park Tapestry Suite of Furniture by Robert Adam: Bequest of Alma V. Lorimer', *The Philadelphia Museum Bulletin*, vol. 36, no. 189, pp. 2–11.

31 William Burke, a political writer, was a close friend of the well-known Edmund Burke, author of *A Philosophical Enquiry into the Origin of our Ideas of the Sublime and Beautiful* (1757) and may have been related to him.

32 *Young Woman with two Amorini*. This was one of several Boucher drawings Reynolds owned. For further information on Boucher drawings in Reynolds's collection see Shoolman Slatkin 1973, pp. 676–77.

33 For fuller quotations and further information on these visits see Denys Sutton in Manchester 1984, pp. 7–9.

34 For further information on the development of the British art market, see Lippincott 1983, pp. 98–125; Pears 1988, pp. 67–105.

35 For further information on contemporary sales of works by Watteau, Lancret and Pater in English collections see Raines 1977; for British interest in Watteau see Martin Eidelberg, 'Watteau Paintings in England in the Early Eighteenth Century', *The Burlington Magazine*, CXVII, no. 870, September 1975, pp. 576–83.

36 Simon 2007, pp. 29–30.

37 Smart 1992, p. 154.

38 Simon 2007, p. 33.

39 See *My Highest Pleasures, William Hunter's Art Collection*, University of Glasgow and Paul Holberton publishing, London, 2007, pp. 41–42.

40 *Ibid.*

41 As noted by Alastair Laing, works fitting that description were included in the sale of Ramsay's son's collection, Christie's, 19 June 1855, as lot 278 ("Boucher, portrait of Mme de Pompadour") and lot 279 ("Boucher, 1739, 'Interior, with a family party'").

42 Alastair Laing had already reached this conclusion in his contribution to New York, Detroit and Paris 1986–87, pp. 110–12.

43 This work was in the collection of the Duke of Argyll, being sold at Longford in 1771.

44 New York, Detroit and Paris 1986–87, p. 129.

45 Waterhouse 1952, p. 135.

46 This was lot 5, day 8, of the John McGouan drawing sale organized by T. Philipe in London, 26 January 1804 and seven following days. McGouan also had drawings by Boucher in his collection (lot 80–81, day 1).

47 Laing 1986, pp. 166–68.

48 See the Chronology for details of the paintings, and Carritt 1974 for their identification within Chardin's oeuvre.

49 Quoted in Wildenstein 1969, p. 59.

50 See Pears 1988, pp. 92–96.

51 See his sale catalogue, dated 19–21 March 1751, preserved in the National Gallery Library.

52 Ian Pears has noted that Bragge seems to have worked with the French dealer Pierre Rémy (Pears 1988, p. 92).

53 For further information see Stein 2007, p. 87. For information on French prints on the British market see Clayton 1997.

54 Hay died in 1754 and Rongent in 1762; there were no sales reported for Dr Bragge in the 1760s.

55 For further information on the important role of Robert Strange, see Dennistoun 1855.

56 For further information on the transformation of the art market and dealer James Christie, see Pears 1988, pp. 89–90.

57 For futher information on Glover see Lippincott 1983, p. 40; and the online Oxford Dictionary of National Biography (http://www.oxforddnb.com).

58 See Pears 1988, p. 110.

59 Smart 1992, p. 110.

60 Lippincott 1983, p. 47.

61 The main reference for Arthur Pond is Lippincott 1983.

62 They were nine prints after Lancret and Chardin (1760; lot 7, 21 April); 12 prints by Boucher (lot 34, 28 March); 23 prints by Boucher (lot 14, 29 March); 14 prints by Boucher (lot 60, 3 April); *Cries of Paris* after Boucher (lot 12, 14 April); 10 prints by Boucher (lot 51, 18 April).

63 For details on him see Lippincott 1983, pp. 61–63.

64 Raymond bought his sketch of a woman and children at the sale of the collection of his deceased friend Batt in 1756.

65 Harenc's daughter married into a leading Scottish Jacobite family. Some of the British collectors with an interest in French contemporary art may well have had Jacobite sympathies. I am grateful to Martin Hopkinson for this suggestion, which deserves to be further considered.

66 Pears 1988, pp. 104–05.

67 See nos. 162 and 163 in Wildenstein 1969, p. 176.

68 As noted by Pierre Rosenberg in Paris, Düsseldorf, London and New York 1999–2000, p. 21. Hay was the first to present a painting by Chardin in a public sale.

Sources

National Art Library, Victoria and Albert Museum, sale catalogues of
the principal collections of pictures sold by auction in England
within the years 1711–1759, 2 vols.

Christie's archives

Online Getty provenance database

National Gallery archives for eighteenth-century sales catalogues

The British Library

Publications

Alexander Ananoff, *François Boucher*, 2 vols., Lausanne and Paris, 1976

Alastair Laing, *François Boucher 1703–1770*, New York, Detroit, Paris,
1986–87

Pierre Rosenberg (ed.), *Chardin 1699–1779*, Paris, Cleveland, Boston,
1979

D. Carritt, 'Mr Fauquier's Chardins', *The Burlington Magazine*, CXVI, no.
858, September 1974, pp. 502–09

1725   Boucher was among the artists commissioned by Nicolas
Dorigny (1657–1748), who had been asked by "*les anglais*" to
have drawn by French painters a series of allegorical
compositions in honour of great Englishmen. An engraver and
draughtsman, Dorigny was working in England from 1711 to
1724, where he was responsible for the engraving of the
Raphael cartoons then kept at Hampton Court. The series was
commissioned by Owen McSweeney and became known as
*Tombeaux des Princes des grands Capitaines et autres hommes illustres
qui ont fleuri dans la Grande Bretagne vers la fin du XVII.& le
commencement du XVIII. siècle, gravés par les plus habiles maitres de
Paris d'aprés les tableaux et desseins originaux des plus célèbres
peintres d'Italie.* First published in Paris by Basan (1737), it was
also published in London in 1741. The French painters
selected for the task were led by Boucher. They produced nine
drawings which were engraved by the best French engravers
available, such as Cochin *père*, Le Bas and Larmessin.

1735   April. Boucher's *The Beautiful Kitchen-maid* is in London. It was
engraved by Pierre Alexander Aveline (1702–1760).

1738   Andrew Hay sale, London

Lot 31 Chardin, *Girl with Cherries* (destroyed in London,
1939/40), exhibited at the 1737 Salon, and engraved
in 1738 by Charles Nicolas Cochin (1688–1754)
before being taken to London. No buyer's name; sold
for £2.15.0. This was the first public sale with catalogue
to include a Chardin.

1741   London edition of the *Tombeaux des Princes, des Grands
Capitaines* … which included designs by Boucher.

1741   Francesco Saverio Geminiani sale, London

Lot 19 Chardin, *A Boy at his drawing (Le Jeune Dessinateur,*
National Gallery, London), exhibited at the 1738 Salon
and engraved by John Faber (1684–1756) in 1740. No
buyer's name. It went through the London salerooms
several times, and through the collections of Mr
Harenc and Mr Fauquier.

Lot 20 Chardin, *A Girl at needle work*, its companion (*Jeune
Ouvrière en tapisserie,* lost), exhibited at the 1738 Salon.
No buyer's name. It went through the London
salerooms several times, and through the collection of
Mr Harenc. Both were sold for £24.3.0.

1741 Anonymous sale

Manner of Boucher, *Diana and Endymion* (unidentified; Ananoff records a *Diane et Endymion* as his cat. no. 36; dated *1729*). No buyer's name.

1742 Outbreak of war between France and England

1743 Geminiani sale, London

I, Lot 21 Chardin, *A girl at her needle, a sketch* (a version of *Une jeune ouvrière qui choisit de la laine dans son panier*, exhibited at the 1738 Salon). No buyer's name.

I, Lot 22 Chardin, *its companion* (a version of *Un Jeune Dessinateur*, exhibited at the 1738 Salon). No buyer's name. Sold with its companion for £0.12.0.

I, Lot 47 Chardin, *Dead Game* (unidentified). No buyer's name. Sold for £1.14.0.

II, Lot 67 Chardin, *A Woman, with a Frying Pan, a sketch* (a sketch for *L'Ecureuse*, exhibited at the 1738 Salon?). No buyer's name. Sold for £0.12.0.

II, Lot 84 Chardin, *Dead Game* (unidentified). No buyer's name.

II, Lot 104 Chardin, *A girl with needlework*. Possibly the same as lot 20 in the 1741 Geminiani sale. No buyer's name. Sold for £12.12.0.

II, Lot 105 Chardin, *its companion*. Possibly the same as lot 19 in the 1741 Geminiani sale. No buyer's name. Sold for £7.1.6.

II, Lot 136 *Savoyars Dancing* (unidentified). No buyer's name. Sold for £2.15.0

II, Lot 151 *A Boy playing with a Totum* (a version of *Le Toton or Child with a Top*, Musée du Louvre, Paris, exhibited at the 1738 Salon and engraved by François-Bernard Lépicié (1698–1755) in 1742 as *Le Toton*). Sold for £6.6.0. No buyer's name. It re-appears in Mr Kent's sale, 1748/49.

1744 15 February. Andrew Hay sale, Mr Cock

I, Lot 30 Boucher, *A Young Man & his Mistress (De trois choses en ferez-vous une?)*. Bought by Lord Hume (8th Earl of Home) for £16.5.6.

II, Lot 33 Boucher, *A harvest with figures and a man sleeping*, painted at Rome (*La Vie Champêtre*, engraved in 1741 by Elizabeth Lépicié [1714–1773]). It was sold for £15 to Dr Peters.

1745 Jacobite Rebellion

1746 End of war between France and Britain

1746 Mr Glover sale

I, Lot 33 Chardin, *A Courtesan* (unidentified). No buyer's name.

1748–49 William Kent (1684–1748) sale

Lot 151 Chardin, *A Boy playing with a Totum*; as Geminiani 1743 sale, III, lot 153. No buyer's name.

1749/50 15–16 February. Dr Bragge sale

I, Lot 35 Chardin, *A Young Gentleman and his Governess* (four versions of *The Governess* were listed in 18th-century sales before 1750; the original version was exhibited at the 1739 Salon and engraved that year by François-Bernard Lépicié). It was sold for £18.18.0. No buyer's name.

1751 April. Major sale

Lot 38 Chardin, *The Industrious Mother* (two versions are known). The original version, offered to Louis XV, was exhibited at the 1740 Salon and engraved by François-Bernard Lépicié that year; it is now in the Louvre, Paris. The present version, bought by Lord Egremont for £24.3.0, was formerly in the Rockefeller collection, New York.

Lot 39 Chardin, *Figures saying Grace, its companion* (at least four versions are known). The original version, offered to Louis XV, was exhibited at the 1740 Salon and engraved by François-Bernard Lépicié in 1744; another version was exhibited at the Salon of 1746. The present version, bought by Lord Charteris (Lord Wemyss) for £24.3.0, is still with the family of the Earl of Wemyss.

1751 19–21 March. Dr Bragge sale, Prestage

II, Lot 39 Boucher, *Venus and Cupid*. Sold for £5.7.0. No buyer's name. Such subject-matter had become a speciality of Boucher by the 1750s. Ananoff records more than fifteen works with this subject. Paintings of this title re-appear in the Stephen Rongent 1755 sale, and in a collection sold at Christie's 26–27 May 1780.

1755 22–23 January. Dr Bragge sale, Prestage

II, Lot 39 Boucher, *A Water Mill, Fig.* (unidentified). It was sold for £7.10.0 to Raymond. This could be *Landscape with Watermill and Temple*, 1743, now in the Bowes Museum, Barnard Castle, never exhibited nor engraved. Such landscapes were a popular subject with Boucher. A *"Paisage ou l'on voit un Moulin"* was exhibited at the 1740 Salon; A *"Paisage ou paroit un Moulin à eau"* was exhibited in the 1743 Salon and engraved by Le Bas; another at the 1765 Salon.

20 February. Peter Le Mastre or Maistre of Broxburn, near Hoddesdon Herts, sale, Langford

Lot 17 Chardin, *A Cook-Maid sleeping* (unidentified). Sold to Dr Chauncey for £7.2.6.

Lot 57 Chardin, *A woman paring turnips* (*La Ratisseuse*; several versions of the work, exhibited at the 1739 Salon and engraved by François-Bernard Lépicié in 1742, have been recorded). Sold for £9.0.0. No buyer's name.

1755   January. Stephen Rongent sale (probably a dealer)

II, Lot 3ç Boucher, *Venus and Cupid.* Sold for £3.5.0 to Mr Lane. A painting of that title was in the Bragge 1751 sale.

II, Lot 58 Boucher, *A Girl and a Boy* (unidentified). Sold for £1.13.0 to Lord Brooke. This could be *De trois choses en ferez-vous une?* or a version of *Kitchen-maid and Young Boy* (private collection). Others of that title appear in the 1776 sale of Lord Montfort's collection and in the 1796 sale of Mr Jones.

1756   France and Britain at war

14–15 April. Christopher Batt sale, Langford

II, lot 55 Chardin, *A Sketch of Women and Children* (unidentified). Sold for £2.19.0 to Raymond.

Dr Bragge sale

II, Lot 32 Boucher, *A Harvest (Rural Life,* possibly the painting sold by Hay in his 1744 sale*)*. Purchased by Henry Bankes (d. 1774) of Wimbledon House, Alderman, for £13.2.0.

1759   25–26 April. Thomas Hart and additional pictures consigned from abroad, Prestage

I, Lot 12 Chardin, Two pieces, *a Cat* and *a Dog* (unidentified). No buyer's name. Chardin exhibited a painting representing a dog, a monkey and a cat painted after nature at the 1753 Salon (no. 62). They belonged to Mr de Bombarde (present whereabouts unknown). Another *tableau d'animaux* is listed at the 1755 Salon (no. 47).

1760   27–28 February. Sir J. Eyles sale

Lot 40 Chardin, *Two Pieces of Monkeys* (versions of *Le Singe Peintre* [The Monkey as painter] and *Le Singe Antiquaire* [The Monkey as antiquarian] were exhibited at the 1740 Salon and engraved in 1743 by Pierre-Louis Surugue). No buyer's name. Paintings of that title reappear in 1800 in the Bullok sale at Christie's and in the 1818 Hamilton sale. At least three versions have been recorded in 18th-century sales. The theme of monkeys was very popular then, both in France and in England.

1761   Boucher appointed Rector of the Academy; Chardin in charge of hanging the paintings at the annual Salon

1762   28–29 April. Charles Leviez sale, including "several valuable paintings lately purchased by him abroad".

Lot 14 Chardin, *Figures and Still Life* (unidentified). No buyer's name.

1763   End of war between France and Britain.

1763   The 6th Earl of Coventry commissions a set of tapestries after Boucher for Croome Court, Worcestershire. Others who commissioned tapestries from the Gobelins are William Weddel (Newby Hall); Sir Henry Bridgeman, 1st Baron Bradford (Weston Park), Sir Lawrence Dundas (Moor Park), Robert Child (Osterley Park), the Duke of Portland (Welbeck Abbey).

1764   21 January. M. Deuet of Paris sale

Lot 10 Chardin, *A Kitchen* (unidentified). No buyer's name.

1764   1–3 March. Roger Harenc sale, Langford & Sons

II, lot 3 Chardin, *A Boy's head in a round.* This could be a version of *The House of Cards* (the Louvre version was originally round; the version formerly in the Henry de Rothschild collection was set within a circular stone bull's eye opening; see Rosenberg 1979, cat. 65). No buyer's name. A version of *The House of Cards* went through London sale rooms the following year, where it was bought by Mr Fauquier.

II, lot 57 Chardin, *A Boy drawing* (as lot 20, Geminiani 1741 sale; II, lot 104, Geminiani 1743 sale). No buyer's name.

II, lot 58 Chardin, *Its companion, A Girl musing* (as lot 19 Geminiani 1741 sale; II, lot 105 Geminiani 1743 sale). No buyer's name.

1764   19–21 April. Anonymous sale

II, lot 37, *A Lady writing a letter* (the original version, now in Postdam, was exhibited at the 1734 *Exposition de la Jeunesse* and the 1738 Salon; it was engraved by Etienne Fessard *c.* 1738. There are three smaller versions known. Possibly the painting used by John Faber for his 1740 engraving, of which no copies are known?). No buyer's name.

1765   Boucher appointed Director of the Academy and First Painter to the King.

1765   Charles Rogers visits Boucher's studio. Boucher presents Rogers with a drawing of *The Trinity* for his *Prints in Imitation of Drawings*, published in 1778. Rogers had 13 drawings by the artist at his death.

1765   26–27 February. Prince de Carignan and others sale, Langford

I, lot 36 Chardin, *A Lady Drinking Tea (Lady taking Tea,* Hunterian Museum and Art Gallery, University of Glasgow, exhibited at the 1739 Salon and engraved twice). It was bought by Hunter for £8.0.0.

I, Lot 37 Chardin, *A Boy building a House with Cards. Its Companion (The House of Cards,* a subject Chardin treated four times, and exhibited in 1735, 1737 and 1741). Carritt (1974) believed that this version, now in the Rothschild Family Trust collection, was the earliest, engraved by Pierre Fillœul. It was purchased by Robinson, possibly acting as an agent for Fauquier, for £6.0.0.

1765   25–26 March. Samuel Newton sale

I, lot 9 Chardin, *A piece of still life with a still* (unidentifiable). No buyer's name.

1768   Boucher resigns as Director of the Academy.

1770   Death of Boucher

1771   7–9 February. Strange sale, Christie's
       I, lot 1 Boucher, "*a landscape – painted with that spirit which we
           generally find in the works of this master – 8 ¹/₂ inches high
           by 6 inches wide* (unidentified). It was sold for £3.3.0 to
           Mr Fauquier.
       I, lot 18 Boucher, "*A Lady Sleeping – The character of this head is
           agreeable, and expresses that freedom so peculiar to the
           generality of this painter's works. 1 foot 6 ¹/₂ high by 1 foot
           2 wide*" (unidentified; probably an odalisque or a
           Venus, such as *Le Sommeil de Vénus* [Venus sleeping],
           1739, Ananoff cat. 173). It was sold for £11.0.6 to
           Mr Hart. Strange was the first to offer Boucher
           paintings of that subject-matter (a favourite subject
           among Continental contemporary collectors) in the
           London salerooms.

1771   23 March. Duke of Argyll sale, Langford
       Lot 18 Boucher, *Jupiter and Europa* (probably a *Rape of Europa*,
           a subject often treated by Boucher). Unsold.

1772   27–29 February. Sale of pictures consigned from abroad,
       Christie's
       II, lot 39 Boucher, *Two landscapes and figures* (unidentified; the
           1750 Salon included a pair of landscapes, "*ornés de
           Figures sur le devant*", belonging to Mr. Langlois, now
           lost. There are numerous other landscapes by Boucher
           that could correspond to that description). It was sold
           for £11.0.6 to Dr Morgan.

1773   3–4 March. Mr Willison sale, Christie's
       II, lot 2 Boucher, *A small picture and a landscape* (unidentified).
           Sold for £31.6.0. No buyer's name.
       5–6 March. Strange sale, Christie's
       I, lot 20 Boucher, *Venus Sleeping* (unidentified). Sold for £4.0.0
           to Mr Boudon.

1773   27–29 January. Joseph Salvador sale, Christie's
       III, lot 26 Boucher, *Two landscapes, winter and summer*
           (unidentified). Sold for £6.6.0 to Mr Godfrey. Boucher
           painted numerous representations of this age-old
           subject over the years, in which he broke with the
           tradition of depicting the labours performed at
           various times of the year to replace them with
           pleasant pastimes. They often represented pastoral
           subjects for spring and summer and sledging for
           winter.

1774   24–26 January. Brandenburgh sale, Christie's
       III, lot 15 Boucher, *Nymphs bathing* (unidentified) and *A
           drawing of a head*. No buyer's name.

1776   16–17 February. Lord Montfort sale, Christie's
       I, lot 40 Boucher, *A Boy and a Girl* (possibly *De trois choses en
           ferez-vous une?*). No buyer's name.

1777   4–5 February. Sale of pictures consigned from abroad, Christie
       and Ansell
       I, lot 41 Boucher, *Summer, and Autumn its companion*. Might this
           be *Putti playing with Birds (Summer)* and *Putti playing with
           a Goat (Autumn)*, Laing 1986–87, cat. 15? They appear
           in the sale of M. Fortier of 2 April 1770 as
           lot 42, *L'Eté … et l'Automne*, and re-appear in the 19th
           century on the London market. Boucher's first
           compositions of this kind showing putti or children at
           play date from the early 1730s, and were to become a
           speciality of Boucher's, together with his depictions of
           nymphs and shepherdesses. Boucher went on to
           produce many more scenes with putti depicting the
           Four Seasons and, as noted by Laing (p. 129), "One of
           the ways in which he became the darling of collectors
           was by his prolific output of putti pictures in these
           years". Bought by Mr Fetz (?).

1778   1–2 June. The Duchess of Bridgewater and an anonymous
       collection sale, Christie's
       II, lot 10 Boucher *Narcissus* (unidentified). Bought by Mr
           Doughty for £3.10.0.

1779   Death of Chardin
       4–5 February. Anonymous sale, Christie and Ansell
       I, lot 70 Boucher, *Pan and Syrinx* (Ananoff records two
           paintings under that name, cat. 519, dated 1759, and
           cat. 548). Sold to Mr Brice for £3.18.0.
       9–12 March. Peters sale
       Boucher (?), *Femme couchée sur son canapé* (Woman lying on her
       sofa; several compositions could correspond to this
       description; see Ananoff, cat. 285). Sold to Mr Dubois.
       23–24 April 1779. Anonymous sale, Christie and Ansell
       II, lot 12 Boucher, *Two fancy heads of girls – oval* (unidentified).
           Sold to Mr Alves for £1.1.0.

1780   10–11 March. Anonymous sale, Christie's
       I, lot 7 Boucher, *A pair of girls with herbage* (unidentified; likely
           to be pastorals). Bought for £1.4.0 by Dr Morgan.

1780   26–27 May. Anonymous sale of a collection brought from
       Brampton Place, county of Kent, Christie's
       I, lot 92 Boucher, *A Venus with Cupid* & [sic??] (unidentified).
           Sold for £2.10.0 to Mr Kend[?]ll.

SELECTED BIBLIOGRAPHY

PUBLICATIONS

Bailey 2005
Colin B. Bailey, 'Marie-Jeanne Buzeau, Madame Boucher (1716–1796), *The Burlington Magazine*, CXLVII, April 2005, pp. 224–34

Bailey 2006
Colin B. Bailey, '"Details that surreptitiously explain": Boucher as a Genre Painter', in Melissa Hyde and Mark Ledbury (eds.), *Rethinking Boucher* (Issues and Debates 15), Los Angeles, 2006, pp. 39–60

Baxandall 1987
Michael Baxandall, *Patterns of Intention: On the Historical Explanation of Pictures*, Yale University Press, New Haven and London, 1987

Brown 1995
Peter Brown, *In Praise of Hot Liquors*, Fairfax House, York, 1995

Brunel 1986
George Brunel, *Boucher*, Trefoil Books, London, 1986

Bruyant 2000
Florence Bruyant, 'À propos de Chardin et de Marguerite Saintard : éléments biographiques', *Bulletin de la Société de l'Histoire de l'Art Français*, 2000, pp. 85–104

Butel 1989
Paul Butel, *Histoire de thé*, Paris, 1989

Cailleux 1966
Jean Cailleux, 'Who was Boucher's best beloved?', *The Burlington Magazine*, vol. CVIII, no. 755, February 1966

Carritt 1974
David Carritt, 'Mr Fauquier's Chardins', *The Burlington Magazine*, CXVI, no. 858, September 1974, pp. 502–09

Clark 1914
Ruth Clark, 'Horace Walpole and Mariette', *The Modern Language Review*, vol. 9, no 4, October 1914, pp. 520–23

Clayton 1997
Timothy Clayton, *The English Print, 1688–1802*, Yale University Press, New Haven and London, 1997

Cochin 1780
Nicolas Cochin, 'Essai sur la vie de Chardin', Ms published in *Précis analytique des travaux de l'Académie des Sciences, Belles-Lettres et Arts de Rouen*, no. 78, 1875–76, pp. 417–41; also in Roland-Michel 1994

Conisbee 1986
Philip Conisbee, *Chardin*, Phaidon Press, Oxford, 1986

Conisbee (ed.) 2007
Philip Conisbee (ed.), *French Genre Painting in the Eighteenth Century* (Studies in the History of Art 72 [Studies in the History of Art, Symposium Papers 46]), Washington D. C., 2007

Dennistoun 1855
James Dennistoun, *Memoirs of Sir Robert Strange … and … Andrew Lumisden*, 2 vols., London, 1855

Earle 1989
Peter Earle, *The Making of the English Middle Class: Business, Society and Family Life in London, 1660–1730*, London, 1989

Ellis 2005
Markman Ellis, *The Coffee House, A Cultural History*, London, 2005

Emmerson 1992
Robin Emmerson, *British Teapots and Tea Drinking 1700–1850*, London, 1992

Faulkner (ed.) 2003
Rupert Faulkner (ed.), *Tea East and West*, V&A Publications, London, 2003

Gaehtgens (ed.) 2002
Barbara Gaehtgens (ed.), *Genremalerei* (Geschichte der klassischen Bildgattungen in Quellentexten und Kommentaren, 4), Berlin, 2002

Goncourt 1948
Edmond and Jules de Goncourt, *French XVIII Century painters*, Phaidon Press, London, 1948

Gowing 1953
Lawrence Gowing, 'Hogarth, Hayman and the Vauxhall Decorations', *The Burlington Magazine*, XCV, no. 598, January 1953, pp. 4–17

Haynes 1968
John Haynes, 'The French Taste in English Painting: Kenwood', *The Burlington Magazine*, CX, no. 785, August 1968, pp. 479–81

Hedley 2004
Joe Hedley, *François Boucher: Seductive Visions*, The Wallace Collection, London, 2004

Hyde 2006
Melissa Hyde, *Making up the Rococo: François Boucher and his Critics*, The Getty Research Institute, Los Angeles, 2006

Ingamells and Raines 1976–78
John Ingamells and Robert Raines, 'A Catalogue of the Paintings, Drawings and Etchings of Philip Mercier', *The Walpole Society*, LVI, 1976–78

Ingamells 1989
John Ingamells, *The Wallace Collection Catalogue of Pictures, III: French before 1815*, London 1989

Ingamells 1992
John Ingamells, *The Wallace Collection Catalogue of Pictures, IV: Dutch and Flemish*, London 1992

Johnston 1976–78
Elizabeth Johnston, 'Joseph Highmore's Paris journal, 1734', *The Walpole Society*, XLII, 1976–78, pp. 61–104

Jörg 1982
Christiaan J.A. Jörg, *Porcelain and the Dutch China Trade*, The Hague, 1982

Kemp 1976
Martin Kemp, 'The Hunterian Chardin's X-rayed', *The Burlington Magazine*, CXVIII, 1976, pp. 228–31

Kemp 1978
Martin Kemp, 'A Date for Chardin's "Lady Taking Tea"', *The Burlington Magazine*, CXXX, January 1978, pp. 22–25

Kilburn and Sheaf 1988
Richard Kilburn and Colin Sheaf, *The Hatcher Porcelain Cargoes: The Complete Record*, Christie's, London, 1988

Kowalski-Wallace 1994
Beth Kowalski-Wallace, 'Tea, Gender and Domesticity in Eighteenth-Century England', *Studies in Eighteenth Century Culture*, XXII, 1994, pp. 131–45

Laing 1986
Alastair Laing, 'Playful Perfection: Boucher in Britain', *Country Life*, 5 June 1986

Lefrançois 1994
Thierry Lefrançois, *Charles Coypel. Peintre du roi (1694–1752)*, Paris, 1994

Leribault 2002
Christophe Leribault, *Jean-François de Troy (1679–1752)*, Paris, 2002

Lippincott 1983
Louise Lippincott, *Selling Art in Georgian London: The Rise of Arthur Pond*, Yale University Press, New Haven and London, 1983

Mintz 1931
Sidney W. Mintz, *The Changing Roles of Food in the Study of Consumption*, in John Brewer and Roy Porter (eds.), *Consumption and the World of Goods*, London 1993

Parmentier 1996
Jan Parmentier, *Tea Time in Flanders*, Hong Kong, 1996

Pascal and Gaucheron 1931
André Pascal and Roger Gaucheron, *Documents sur la vie et l'œuvre de Chardin*, Paris, 1931

Pears 1988
Ian Pears, *The Discovery of Painting: The Growth of Interest in the Arts in England, 1680–1768*, Yale University Press, New Haven and London, 1988

Posner 1973
Donald Posner, *Watteau: A Lady at her Toilet* (Art in Context), London, 1973

Raines 1977
Robert Raines, 'Répertoire des tableaux de Lancret, Pater et Chardin dans les ventes anglaises avant 1760', *Archives de l'art français: receuil de documents inédits …*, XXV, 1977, pp. 177–83

Remy 1771
Pierre Remy, *Catalogue Raisonné des Tableaux, Desseins, Estampes, Bronzes, Terres cuites, Laques, Porcelaines de différentes sortes, montées et non montées; Meubles curieux, Bijoux, Minéraux, Cristallisations, Madrépores, Coquilles & autres Curiosités qui composent le Cabinet DE FEU M. BOUCHER, Premier Peintre du Roi*, Paris, 1771

Ribeiro 2002
Aileen Ribeiro, *Dress in Eighteenth-century Europe 1715–1789*, Yale University Press, New Haven and London, 2002

Roche 1998
Daniel Roche, *France in the Enlightenment*, London, 1998

Roland-Michel 1994
Marianne Roland-Michel, *Chardin*, Editions Hazan, Paris, 1994

Rosenberg 1983
Pierre Rosenberg, *Tout l'œuvre peint de Chardin*, Paris, 1983

Ruggiu 1997
François-Joseph Ruggiu, *Les Elites et les villes moyennes en France et en Angleterre (XVII–XVIII siècles)*, Paris, 1997

Sargentson 1996
Carolyn Sargentson, *Merchants and Luxury Markets: The Marchants Merciers of Eighteenth-Century Paris*, London, 1996

Savill 1982
Rosalind Savill, 'François Boucher and the Porcelains of Vincennes and Sèvres', *Apollo*, March 1982, pp. 162–70

Savill 1988
Rosalind Savill, *The Wallace Collection Catalogue of Sèvres Porcelain: II*, London, 1988

Simon 2007
Robin Simon, *Hogarth, France and British Art: The Rise of the Arts in 18th century Britain*, Hogarth Arts, London, 2007

Smart 1992
Alastair Smart, *Allan Ramsay, Painter, Essayist and Man of the Enlightenment*, Yale University Press, New Haven and London, 1992

Shoolman Slatkin 1973
Regina Shoolman Slatkin, 'A Note on a Boucher Drawing', *The Burlington Magazine*, CXV, no. 847, October 1973, pp. 676–77

Snodin 1984
Michael Snodin (ed.), *Rococo*, V&A Publications, London, 1984

Tavener Holmes 1991
Mary Tavener Holmes, *Nicolas Lancret 1690–1743*, Harry N. Abrams, Inc., New York, 1991

Ukers 1935
William Ukers, *All about Tea*, 2 vols., New York, 1935

Verlet 1967
Pierre Verlet, *French Furniture and Interior Decoration of the 18th Century*, Barrie & Rockliff, London, 1967

Walford and Young 2003
Tom Walford and Hilary Young (eds.), *British Ceramic Design 1600–2002*, English Ceramic Circle, Beckenham, 2003

Waterhouse 1952
Ellis K. Waterhouse, 'English Painting and France in the Eighteenth Century', *Journal of the Warburg and Courtauld Institutes*, XV, 1952, pp. 122–35

Weatherill 1988
Lorna Weatherill, *Consumer Behaviour and Material Culture in Britain, 1660–1760*, London, 1988

Whitehead 1992
John Whitehead, The *French Interior in the Eighteenth Century*, Dutton Studio Books, London, 1992

Wildenstein 1959
George Wildenstein, 'Le décor de la vie de Chardin d'après ses tableaux', *Gazette des Beaux-Arts*, LIII, February 1959, pp. 98–106

Wildenstein 1969
George Wildenstein, *Chardin: Catalogue raisonné*, Oxford, 1969

Young 1999
Hilary Young, *English Porcelain, 1745–95: Its Makers, Design, Marketing and Consumption*, London, 1999

EXHIBITION CATALOGUES

Berlin 2003–04
Christoph Vogtherr (ed.), *Die "Briefsieglerin" von Jean-Siméon Chardin. Neue Einsichten in ein restauriertes Meisterwerk*, Schloss Charlottenburg, Berlin, 2003–04

Brussels 1999
Tea for 2: Les rituals du thé dans le monde, Galerie du Crédit Communal, Brussels, 1999

Dijon and London 2004–05
Françoise Joulie, *Boucher et les peintres du nord*, Musée Magnin, Dijon, and The Wallace Collection, London, 2004–05

Dublin and Greenwich 2003
Love Letters. Dutch Genre paintings in the Age of Vermeer, National Gallery of Ireland, Dublin, and Bruce Museum, Greenwich, 2003

Karlsruhe 1999
*Jean Siméon Chardin 1699–1779.
Werk Herkunft Wirkung*, Staatliche
Kunsthalle, Karlsruhe, 1999

Manchester 1984
Denys Sutton (ed.), *François
Boucher*, Manchester City Art
Gallery, 1984

New York, Detroit and Paris
1986–87
Alastair Laing (ed.), *François
Boucher 1703–1770*, Metropolitan
Museum of Art, New York; Detroit
Institute of Arts; Grand Palais,
Paris, 1986–87

New York 1999
Bertrand Rondot (ed.), *Discovering
the Secrets of Soft
Paste Porcelain at the St. Cloud
Manufactory, ca. 1690–1776*,
Bard Graduate Center, New York,
1999

Ottawa, Washington
and Berlin 2003–04
Colin Bailey (ed.), *The Age of
Watteau, Chardin, and Fragonard:
Masterpieces of French Genre Painting*,
National Gallery of Canada,
Ottawa; National Gallery of Art,
Washington, D.C.; Staatliche
Museen zu Berlin, Gemäldegalerie,
Berlin, 2003–04

Paris, Cleveland and Boston 1979
Pierre Rosenberg (ed.), *Chardin
1699–1779*, Grand Palais, Paris;
Cleveland Museum of Art,
Cleveland; Museum of Fine Arts,
Boston, 1979

Paris, Düsseldorf, London and
New York 1999–2000
Pierre Rosenberg (ed.), *Chardin*,
Galeries Nationales du Grand
Palais, Paris; Kunstmuseum im
Ehrenhof, Düsseldorf; Royal
Academy of Arts, London;
Metropolitan Museum of Art, New
York, 1999–2000

Paris, London and Madrid 2006–07
Mark Hallett and Christine Riding,
Hogarth, Musée du Louvre, Paris;
Tate Britain, London; La Caixa,
Madrid, 2006–07

Paris 2007
George Brunel (ed.), *Pagodes et
Dragons : Exotisme et fantaisie dans
l'Europe Rococo, 1720–1770*, Musée
Cernuschi, Paris, 2007

Valenciennes 2004
Martin Eidelberg, *Watteau et la fête
galante*, Musée des Beaux-Arts,
Valenciennes, 2004

PHOTOGRAPHIC CREDITS

The Photographic Department of Glasgow University made the photographs for cats. 9, 11, 16, 19, 20, 21, 22, 23, 24, 25, 28; figs. 25, 50. 84, 85
Thanks to Stephen McCann, Neill Miller and Stuart J. Campbell.
The Hunterian Museum and Art Gallery Multimedia Department supplied images for cat. 1 (figs. 4, 7, 9, 12, 16), 27 (fig. 25).
Thanks to Graham Nisbet.

For permission to reproduce works in their collections, we would like to thank the following institutions:

Bibliothèque Nationale, Paris, figs. 36, 39
Bowes Museum, figs. 73, 86
Burrell Collection, Glasgow Museums © Culture and Sport Glasgow (Museums) cat. 16
Christie's, London © Christie's Images Limited, fig. 69
Musée Cognacq-Jay, Paris, fig. 32
National Gallery of Art, Washington, fig. 23
National Gallery of Scotland, Edinburgh, cat. 8
National Portrait Gallery, London, fig. 46
Nationalmuseum, Stockholm cats. 3 (figs. 63, 71), 5 (figs. 59, 62, 65); figs. 18, 57b, 83
National Trust © The National Trust Photo Library, figs. 49 Photo: Andreas von Einsiedel, 61 Photo: Brenda Norrish, 82 Photo: John Hammond
Musée des arts décoratifs, Paris © Les Arts Décoratifs, Musée des Arts Décoratifs, Paris, fig. 64 photo: Jean Tholance
Museo Thyssen-Bornemisza, Madrid © Colección Carmen Thyssen-Bornemisza care of Museo Thyssen-Bornemisza. Madrid, cat. 4 (fig. 15, 57a; 58, 70), fig. 51

Réunion des Musées Nationaux, figs. 5 © Hervé Lewandowski, 19 and 20 © Christian Jean, 38 © Martine Beck-Coppola, 52 © René-Gabriel Ojéda, 53 © Gérard Blot
Staatliche Museen zu Berlin, figs. 21, 29

A particular thanks to the following institutions for generously waiving reproduction fees:

British Museum, London, cats. 17, 18; figs. 48, 74, 75, 76, 77, 78, 79
Day & Faber, London, cat. 7, fig. 30
The Frick Collection, New York, cat. 2 (figs. 2, 8, 10, 13, 14, 17)
The Goldsmith Company, London, fig. 42
Musée International de la Chaussure, Romans-sur-Isère, fig. 72
Collection Guillen © Christophe Villard
National Gallery of Ireland, cat. 10
National Gallery, London, cat. 6, fig. 27
The National Trust, Waddesdon Manor, fig. 55 Photo: Mike Fear, 56 Photo: John Freeman, 60 Photo: Mike Fear, 68 Photo: Eost & MacDonald
Neues Schloß, Bayreuth, fig. 6
Philadelphia Museum of Art, figs. 43; 44
Private Collections:, cats. 12a, 12b, 12c, 13a, 14, figs. 47; 66
Special Collections, University of Glasgow Library, cats. 23, 24, 25; fig. 35
Stiftung Preußische Schlösser und Gärten Berlin-Brandenburg, figs. 3, 22, 28
Victoria & Albert Museum, figs. 34, 37, 40, 41, 67
Waddesdon Manor, Rothchild Family Trust, cat. 26 (fig. 24)
Wallace Collection, London, figs. 11, 26, 31, 33, 45, 54, 80, 81